THE WORLD'S BEST HORSE

Steve Donoghue, the world's greatest Derby specialist

BY LADY WENTWORTH

AUTHENTIC ARABIAN HORSE
THOROUGHBRED RACING STOCK
HORSES IN THE MAKING
THE SWIFT RUNNER
DRIFT OF THE STORM
ARAB HORSE NONSENSE (Cartoons)

PONY CARRIAGE IN COUNTRY LANE

LADY WENTWORTH

THE WORLD'S BEST HORSE

GEORGE ALLEN AND UNWIN LTD

RUSKIN HOUSE · MUSEUM STREET · LONDON

FIRST PUBLISHED IN 1958

PRINTED IN GREAT BRITAIN
in 12 pt Perpetua type
BY UNWIN BROTHERS LTD.
WOKING AND LONDON

CONTENTS

CONTENTS

CONTENTS

The Author judging at the London Show, July 29, 1954

ILLUSTRATIONS

LIST OF ILLUSTRATIONS

COLOUR PLATES

INTRODUCTION

THE title of this book is, I confess, somewhat of a deliberate trap for the unwary. I can hear them exclaim: "World's Best Horse, indeed! There is no such thing!" Or, indignantly, "The Arab again, of course!" On the contrary, I am setting out to show the merits of all breeds, each of which is specialized for its own purpose and is probably the best for its purpose.

The odium of comparisons is not my fault but that of those who cannot learn to admire one breed without disparaging another, and the object of my researches has been to show how breeds originated, progressed and improved without prejudice.

Everyone has his own preferences as to what he likes best and I am no exception, but it may surprise some people to know that my favourite breeds are Thoroughbreds first and Arabs, Percherons, and Welsh Starlight ponies next in that order, but I also delight in good Hackneys, Hunters, Palominos, Shetlands, Agricultural breeds, in fact, any good specimen on four legs. So here's to "The World's Best Horse" from the biggest to the smallest inclusive.

"We salute them both"

13

Cold-blooded Head

Hot-blooded Head

PREFACE

WHEN people talk of the world's best horse they probably differ as to what is the best according to whether they are hunting, polo, or racing men, harness, agricultural, or saddle enthusiasts.

There is, however, one very safe general test of merit—there can hardly be any argument that the outstanding horse is the one which is steadily worth the biggest price. Money talks—indeed, money shouts here so loudly that there can be no question that the Thoroughbred racehorse is supreme, with his Arab progenitor second in value, while his relatives, either directly or indirectly through the Arab ancestor, make up our best hunters, remounts, hack, and pony stock.

When a classic Thoroughbred colt not eighteen months old may fetch anything up to 28,000 guineas at auction, and stallions anything up to a quarter of a million sterling, there is no gainsaying that they are the world's leading breed.

Supreme in price the classic Thoroughbred is also supreme in speed and conformation. The general public never sees him at his best, for during his racing career he is an undeveloped and often overstrained youngster, just at the worst age of teething and growing. It is only after he has gone to stud that his full glory is seen.

This classic beauty comes from the original Arab blood, whose exquisite lines have been developed and enlarged by centuries of selection, and though this selected type has long outstripped the Arab model in speed, power, and stride, the Arabian is still the speediest natural undeveloped breed, and still unrivalled in long-distance racing by any breed.

There is a coarse slower element in the Thoroughbred, but the finest specimens of Derby winners generally show increasing quality as the blood concentrates more and more back to the Arabian foundation.

Next to the Thoroughbred, the Arab is the most financially valuable; in fact, the record price given by any one man for a horse of any breed, £67,200, was paid for the El Karta racing filly by Sultan el Naseri, in A.D. 1290.

The world's best hunters seem to have been bred in Ireland, and Irishmen have contributed not a little to racing fame. They have a natural tact and personal magnetism, and that invaluable gift of blarney in a soft Irish brogue, which is quite as irresistible to horses as to girls, and incites the most refractory colts to try and live up to the standard of being "A terrible foine horse entoirely."

One of the best men with horses I ever knew, was, however, a Cockney. He began his career in a racing stable by being put barebacked on an unbroken two-year-old and being

15

thrown off till he could stop on. Thirty-seven times in one morning was he pitched off only to be mercilessly put back.

"Black and blue?" said he, "I should say I was! Purple and green more like, and sick as a cat! Couldn't sit down for a blinkin' week I couldn't, nor turn me neck. And the 'orse near as bad for 'e took a turn or two on 'is own 'ead gettin' me orf on mine." He lived, ate and slept alone in the saddle room and kept an iron pot full of tea always stewing on the hob, adding tea to it till it was pitch black and the spoon stood up in it. He had a horror of wasting anything and used to finish up all the horses' medicines himself rather than throw them away, so the wonder is that he did not die sooner. Asked why he did not marry he said, "Not me Sir, none of them nasty long black 'airs in me grub—not if I knows it."

He had one common weakness—drink—and periodically went fighting mad, knocking out everyone from peers to policemen when the fancy took him. His nose was like a flash of forked lightning. He did not have D.T. or see any snakes or any of the things doctors prophesied as his inevitable doom, or live to be hanged as the magistrates foretold, but ended his career one night standing on the back of a chair and overbalancing while trying to wind up the saddle-room clock with a corkscrew!

The best horse in the world collects round him some of the best people and others who are . . . well, *not* perhaps the best in the world. But whoever they may be, they are generally "characters."

CHAPTER I

GENERAL HISTORY

IT is unfortunate that almost all, if not all, the learned scholars who have classified fossils and other equine remains have had so little first-hand experience of horses in the flesh or of the laws which govern breeding. In classifying each slightly divergent skull as a distinct variety of horse with a new Latin name they have created a bewildering confusion of alleged breeds which do not really exist, as they do not know what constitutes a recognizable breed and appear unaware or regardless of the possibility that some of the skulls, presumed to be horses, might equally well have belonged to mules or asses which, taken without corroborative evidence, are in no way distinguishable from those of crossbred horses and ponies. We ask ourselves why no allowance seems to have been made for this, and what has become of them all. There were domesticated and wild onagers, and countless donkeys and mules which must have existed under the same conditions of fossilization as horses and it is rather disturbing to realize that some of them may be masquerading as horses in our scientific nomenclature just as some of the prehistoric rock drawings have been labelled horses which are certainly mules. It is much the same as if we were to classify all the mongrel dogs and street curs each as a separate sub-species dignified with Latin names. Whether the names are Latin, Greek or Esperanto would be immaterial except that the classic languages are generally reserved to imply an important scientific status, and in this way I have used a Latin classification myself.

If numbers of the same shape of skull are unearthed a collective name would be justified for the type represented, but it is astonishing to find that the classification of more than one alleged breed does not even depend on a skull but on nothing more solid than the discovery of isolated teeth, as in the case of Equus Caballus Plicidens, for instance. Equus Caballus Spelæus is equally hastily christened on the evidence of a few more teeth and fragmentary bones. Even if the single example is complete in itself it would be unsafe to generalize on it, and when it is only a fragment I maintain that its classification as a breed amounts to "species mongering," i.e. making distinctions for distinction's sake without regard to wider biological relations.

Most of this fanciful classification of comparatively modern types can therefore be disregarded as, even granting that all the excavated specimens were really horses, much of it is probably based on nothing more than individual variation arising from the mingling of types originating from the same double source of foundation, "Hot" and "Cold" blood. These countless modifications do not constitute separate breeds but are sporadic and as such confusing to the simpler issues.

There is undoubtedly a tendency among research workers in this sphere to supplement meagre positive evidence with theoretical padding where "daring speculation" takes the place of proof and the theory of prehistoric equine evolution from a rabbit-sized, four-toed ancestor for instance is apt to be treated by average writers as a proved fact. It is necessary to point out that far from being a proved fact it is actually a highly controversial question about which equally eminent scientists on both sides hold diametrically opposed beliefs.

PREHISTORIC THEORIES

I am not dealing here with the pros and cons of the theory of evolution as a general principle but I cannot help distrusting the shifting sands which seem to be considered sufficiently solid ground as building sites for theorists as regards the horse in particular. All of us are familiar with the four or five skeletons exhibited as a graduated series representing the alleged progress of the horse over some fifty million years, but not many of us know that some of the links which form at first sight such a plausible progression have been reconstructed in plaster of Paris from the merest fragments to fit a preconceived idea of what they *ought* to have been. A partly imaginary plaster of Paris creature is frankly more a fake than a fact and where the original fragment is only a tooth it becomes something of a scientific romance. "Intelligent anticipation" has even given the name of Hippops to a creature with no existence at all, but to which five toes have already been assigned!

Owing to what the American scientist Lyddeker called "the misleading American habit of applying the word 'horse' to certain queer four-toed and three-toed miniature prehistoric creatures," there is great confusion in the public mind as to what "Equus" actually means, and even a quite recent educational book by Geddes and Thomson quotes Lull in support of the "modern horse" having existed in America and treats Equus Scotti as a modern horse. Perhaps it is not surprising as Lull wrote, "the modern horse 'Equus' first appears in the Upper Pliocene beds of Eurasia and N. America." Most people would I think conclude, as I did also, that the words "modern horse" meant the modern horse of to-day, but on referring the phrase to an eminent authority he explained to me that the word "modern," used geologically, is merely comparative to still older forms and that Lull meant the later forms of fossil *Genus* Equus, not the modern *species* Equus *Caballus*. There were no horses (Caballus) either above or below ground in America till the Spaniards brought them about four hundred years ago. It is difficult to reduce these differing views as to what should or should not be included in the genus into comprehensible form but it may be useful to make the attempt.

THE COLOSSAL PILTDOWN HOAX

I have not yet accused the reconstructionists of deliberate falsification (no doubt they are mostly an earnest body of honest geologists), but in view of the colossal hoax of the plaster of Paris fake of the Piltdown skull, deliberately planned to supply the Monkey-to-Man missing link, and which has successfully duped the whole galaxy of the world's most brilliant scientific stars for over forty years and is described in the British Museum report as so entirely unscrupulous and inexplicable yet executed with such supreme skill as to have no parallel in the history of science, it seems high time to put a stop to these masterpieces of the faker's art, assembled out of the merest fragments of miscellaneous bones, from being foisted on the public in future as genuine proofs of an evolutionary process so convincing as to undermine the foundations of Christian belief in the myth of a Creator altogether!

This impudent fraud—not the first of its kind, but transcending the bounds of all patience—is a serious warning of the temptations which beset our glue and plaster of Paris confraternity of art workers, and a further warning to historians not to take the evolutionary reconstructed series of the genus equus too seriously.

It should give the habit of dogmatism a severe shock to its complacency when we find ourselves faced with the undeniable truth that scientific investigation may become an obsession and create such an overmasteringly passionate desire to fill the gaps in the chain of "Intelligent anticipation" that the Wish becomes Father to the Fact without due regard to proof of its parentage and may be considered justification for faking the gaps.

The Piltdown imposture has been at last exposed, but how about the faked equine fossils with sets of imaginary legs—a solitary tooth furnished with complete skeletons and credited with striped hides? Will these continue to appear in educational pamphlets till some inconveniently honest research worker destroys the phantom of an ancestral Past?

My argument does not concern the rather unflattering claim of *Homo Sapiens* to cousinship, still less with affiliation involving consanguinity with the Apes, but registers a protest against what I consider the unsound methods by which *equus caballus* has been made the foundation of and indeed established on and foisted on the public as the supreme example of proved evolution.

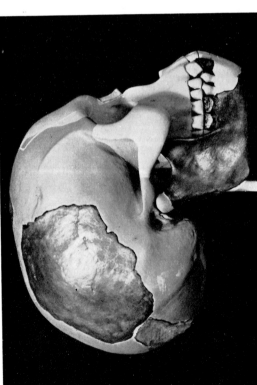

The Piltdown Forgery (See page 19)

The world's most famous evolutionary hoax, which imposed on scientific credulity for 40 years, is a lamentable example of the dangers of over-enthusiastic evolutionary enthusiasm. It stands as a serious warning against blindly accepting other evidence of reconstructed evolutionary art, as seen below.

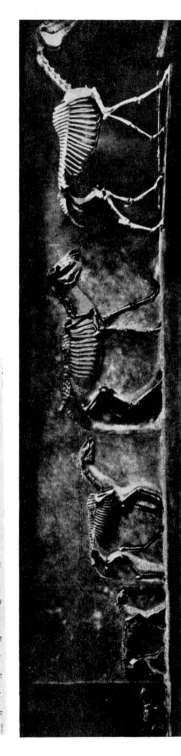

The so-called natural hereditary progressive evolution of the horse is shown here, based on linking the merest fossil fragments, a handful of powdered bone or a single tooth, yet assembled with complete sets of multiple imaginary toes—notably the specimen whose remains are only a small rabbit-sized skull—but forming the foundation of the evolutionary tree.

We admire the incredible ingenuity but are unable to endorse the vast conclusions drawn.

The brains and wits of man are in constant struggle against Nature's obstinate tendency to reversion, not to speak of passive resistance by mulish sterility, or the inhibitions of blood allergy barring departures from hereditary laws, or similar changes by amalgamation of species which Nature forbids.

As this is the usually accepted series it is well to remember that most of it is imaginary.   (See page 19)

Briefly it would seem that the fossils of *Genus* Equus belong to and are a branch of the Ungulates or hoofed mammals (a term comprehensive of sheep, cattle, rhinoceri, deer, pigs, etc.), but they are quite different species to the present-day horse, E. Caballus. The hoofed mammals included other extinct species and the whole series ceased abruptly leaving a gap of some million and more years between the last of the fossils at the close of the Pleistocene period and the arrival of the living horse of A.D. 1490 in America. There was also a similar gap (plus the Atlantic Ocean) between the last fossil of America and the first horse of Europe. The European chain was completely broken during the Oligocene period. Lyddeker tells us both chains were not only broken but became finally extinct millions of years ago, and if so could not possibly be *ancestral* to the horse of to-day. Theoretical reconstruction begins in America (latest estimated date fifty million years ago) with Eohippus, a ferret-like carnivore type, and in Europe with a midget fossil herbivorous creature, "the Antediluvian rabbit" called Hyracotherium, the sole remains of which are one tiny imperfect skull no bigger than that of a rabbit, with "teeth like a pig or monkey" and of which even Professor Pycraft (an enthusiastic evolutionist) says "anything less like a horse it would be impossible to imagine." It was, he says, originally classed among the rodents as its name indicates. Yet in spite of the fact that the rest of the creature was missing, Professor Ridgeway confidently asserts that it had four toes in front and three behind, and Pycraft says it was striped! It sometimes appears pictorially as a reconstructed skeleton at the head of the Equus series with all its missing toes complete. A four-toed skeleton foot at the head of Lyddeker's series (see *The Horse and its Relatives*) is entitled Hyracotherium *or* Eohippus. It cannot be both if Eohippus belongs to the extinct American series and Hyracotherium to the European series; and accepting Lyddeker's own statement that "the Hyracotheridae family died out at the close of the Eocene period *leaving no descendants*," its connection with the modern horse is nil. The British Museum Guide possibly realizing it could not be both, uses the same plate but drops Eohippus in favour of Hyracotherium. But here we are faced with the *non-sequitur* that Hyracotherium had no feet, being only an imperfect skull, so whatever the photograph represents it could not be Hyracotherium's foot! The series on this plate moreover ends with Hipparion which is now admittedly not a horse at all and is even credited with having possessed a proboscis! We are therefore left stranded and as if both became extinct millions of years ago they could neither of them be ancestral to anything now living. The next creatures each take millions of years to develop—there are no links to bridge the gaps, all the series seem to have an arbitrary number of ribs which show a disorderly increase and decrease entirely at variance with the theory of steady progression.

It will be seen too how extremely conjectural osteology must be in deciding what living animals, now extinct, were like when it is remembered that skeletons of hares and rabbits are indistinguishable. So, we are told, are the skeletons of lions and tigers and of countless birds and animals which cannot and do not interbreed, being different species. Yet osteologists with nothing but *the bones to guide them* would almost inevitably class the said animals as identical. If different species (often inimical to each other) and differing greatly in life yet are indistinguishable as skeletons, how much more may the skeletons which have so great a divergence from each other have differed in breed when alive? I have been familiar from a child with these evolutionary arguments owing to my father's correspondence with Huxley, Ridgeway and others, while Professor Pycraft talked to me by the hour of nothing else, so I have full knowledge and appreciation of the fascination exercised on the scientific mind by its excursions into those remote regions of ancient fossilization embracing such vast periods of time that a million or more years of disconnected intervals cease to be regarded as a vacuum worth mentioning. Being myself in daily touch with the laws of breeding and nature I (like Nature) abhor a vacuum! I also hesitate to accept a theory which entails admitting a wholesale principle of universal natural upward progression independent of environment, climate and conditions proceeding at the same pace in different parts of the world without human assistance or intercommunication and reaching the same final stage at the same moment. Now every breeder knows that natural "evolution" might more properly be called devolution, as the brains and wits of man are in constant conflict with the natural tendency to *degenerate* and *revert*, not to improve and progress, and the moment human selective aid is withheld retrogression sets in both in size and quality. As a practical breeder in constant conflict against the laws of retrogression by which the garden rose persistently returns to the briar when human control ceases, I am completely sceptical. Even the theory of the survival of the fittest is unsound applied to wild herds as the best specimens are often exposed to far more risks as defenders of the herd, and in regard to many animals hunted for food or for their skin and horns, man is their worst enemy. They also inbreed and degenerate. There are other reasons which cause hesitation. I have explained them at length in *Thoroughbred Racing Stock*. The student can draw his own conclusions.

NON PROVEN

These will no doubt vary according to the degree of logic our minds are prepared to apply to the evidence and the amount of evidence we are prepared to do without, and if anyone finds the "Antediluvian Rabbit" theory too far-fetched he will at any rate be in good company for many eminent scientists who have gone into every detail of the evidence still consider the matter "non-proven." In fact the latest scientific research as summed up by George Gaylord Simpson (Columbia University Press, *Biological Series*, No. 15, 1947) rejects the principles as vague, unsatisfactory and contradictory, founded on mere supposition and guesswork, and he says no time need be wasted on the idea of continuous progression which is on the contrary divergent and even reversionary. In any case it has no bearing on the horse of to-day as it gets no further than the genus, not the species, and the present species has walked on single hoofs and shown the same structure as far back as history can trace him. We might indeed ignore the prehistoric side were it not for the increasing modern tendency to treat its theories as Holy Writ.[1]

FALSE PREMISES

In recent times we again come up against the tiresome tendency to jump to conclusions and argue therefrom on false premises. The late "Mankato" J. B. Robertson based a whole house of cards on the number of *ribs and lumbar* vertebrae of certain racehorses, one of which was Stockwell, whose sole remains were *a skull and two legs*! Further investigation revealed that not only had Robertson never seen any of the horses on whose bones he founded dogmatic conclusions but that none of them had ever been examined by anybody at all! Bearing all this in mind we are forced to take some of the classified specimens and the multitudinous conclusions drawn from them with a grain of salt. The whole question can be treated much more simply, and stripped of its complications the modern horse resolves itself into two main lines of ancestry which can be broadly divided into two definite foundation types. (1) Cold Northern (or more correctly North-Western) blood and (2) Hot Southern or Eastern blood, the intermixture of which produces the intermediary types of (3) Cool or warm blood. These roughly follow the human types of their respective spheres each varying only with the limits of its own main characteristics. Geographically the dividing line between (1) and (2) seems to have originally been an irregular curve bounded by the Caucasus and Himalayan ranges and the Caspian sea. On and around this borderland we find as might be expected that the types have met and mingled, resulting in a large variety of mixed types favouring whichever blood may predominate in their ancestry, for the blend of hot and cold blood produces intermediary types just as the mixing of blue and yellow produces varying shades of green—but these are unstable in hue according to the predominance of blue or excess of yellow, and in horses can only become stabilized by systematic inbreeding and specialization, sometimes natural, but usually artificial.

There are two historical grandstands from which fine views of early mixed stock can be obtained; one overlooks the wide lands of central Europe and Asia, and the other overlooks the Mediterranean borderlands. From both these viewpoints the vicissitudes of many early mixed breeds can be watched in great variety for in these regions the primary horse stock, Northern and Southern, fundamental types have met and interbred from the earliest times and from these centres have spread over the Eurasian Continent. They may be studied in the rock scratchings of the ancient world and in pictorial art, sculptures and coins of historic times.

With the aid of these figures and certain contemporary skeletal remains it is possible

[1] The rare appearance in horses of a sort of double leg or extra foot has been taken as positive proof of a many-toed ancestor, but when the same thing occurs in chickens and dogs nobody ascribes it to anything but a freak and when calves or cats or puppies are born with two heads or occasionally three, it is not advanced as a proof of reversion to an ancestral hydra but is attributed to a misdirected attempt at twins or triplets, and the supernumerary abortive legs of horses and cattle are most likely due to a similar cause.

to trace the story of the original wild stock of the world, and to study the development of the Northern (cold-blooded) type, the Southern (hot-blooded) type, and the mixed (warm-blooded and luke-warm) types which have been produced from the fusion of Northern and Southern root stocks. I have for convenience labelled them as follows:

No. 1. THE NORTHERN COLD-BLOODED TYPE (*Equus Caballus Frigidus*)

This ram-headed coarse type with all its descendants and derivatives may be said to represent power and weight and tolerance of cold climates. To this foundation belong the Great Horses of Europe and in a varying degree our cart-horse breeds (since mixed with oriental blood), the large horse of Ancient China and Persia, the Mongolian and Germanic breeds of smaller type and some of the coarse European ponies.

This type is distinguished by a convex skull, heavy bones of a porous texture, convex shallow lower jaw, small undefined jowl, a short mouth, thick throat, and semi-closed stiff nostrils, formless chin, angular narrow eyes set high in the skull near the ears which are rather coarse and blunt, coarse hair, thick skins, short straight neck, drooping hind quarters and low-set tail with trailing tail carriage, large teeth, short bars to the mouth and more ribs and lumbar vertebrae. The outlines of these animals are angular and might be termed "gothic," architecturally, and they belong to the phlegmatic slow temperament found in their present descendants.

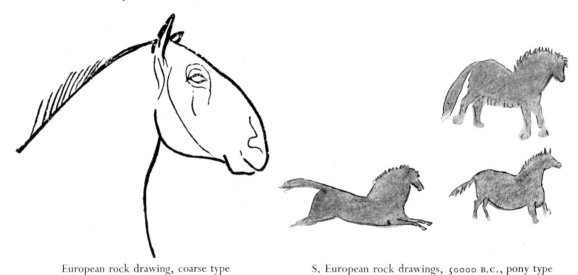

European rock drawing, coarse type   S. European rock drawings, 50000 B.C., pony type

COLD-BLOODED STOCK

In the prehistoric cave drawings of Europe, possibly dating back some 50,000 years, we see a large and a couple of smaller varieties of this Northern stock which all have

24

erect manes like donkeys. There is also a better bred pony of modern Celtic type with concave skull in the Spanish caves, and a speckled pony, which suggests oriental origin and is evidently the same breed as the modern Appaloosa, and there is also a parti-coloured pony of Shetland type with flowing mane and crested neck.

A distinction must be drawn between certain of the cold-blooded types belonging to China and those of Europe, notably in the case of the Mongolian Tarpan, of which there

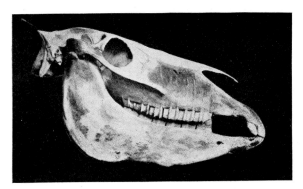

Mongolian skull

are several varieties, which represent cold blood below zero! The latter is a native of Mongolia, the borders of China and the Russian steppes and exists on the northern borderlands in a feral condition, modified by domestic crosses.

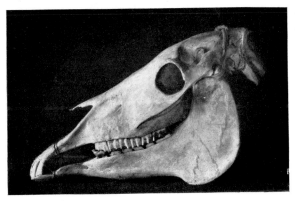

Arab skull

Mongolian Tarpans are of the lowest and ugliest type, so nearly asses that controversies have raged as to whether they could be classed as horses at all. At one time they were, in fact, classified as asses, yet Polish writers claim that the Tarpan was ancestral to the Arab, whereas nothing could be farther from the truth. The measurements based on a Tarpan skull and connecting it with the Arab are fantastically inaccurate. Also the Tarpan has

25

nineteen ribs and six lumbar vertebrae, which dissociates it completely from the Arab which has seventeen to eighteen pairs of ribs and five to six lumbar vertebrae. Photographs of Arabs and Tarpans, if compared, will show immediately how great was the gulf between them, and a study of the small refined Arab skull with its undulating outlines, its ivory delicacy of bone, and its enormous eye sockets and very small teeth, will reveal the enormous difference which exists between the Arab and the Mongolian with its prodigious head, huge teeth and convex underjaw. It is not ancestral to any of our pony breeds.

CHINA

The more massive types of horse stock in China were originally also of Mongolian extraction, introduced into China by Fo Hi, *circa* third century B.C., and some of the

Chinese or Japanese horseman

ancient representations of these Great Horses show a skull *slanting back* from the eyes to the ears in a manner which seems to have been peculiar to China. At any rate up to now I have not been able to trace this point elsewhere except in the *Spanish Ass* and the Nerbada or Siwalik skull. There seems to be a confusion about the Nerbada skull as this is the one said by Ewart to have been "bent back" whereas the one in the British Museum labelled Siwalik is the bent one. Another interesting point about Chinese horse stock is that in 126 B.C., in the district of Ferghana, horses were said to exist which *sweated blood*. This seems to suggest some connection with the Spanish Andalusian horses which showed the same peculiarity, and I have known an Arab mare whose neck sweated blood. Another

THE GODOLPHIN ARABIAN

An authentic oil painting from life, signed J. Wootton and dated 1731. This is the best picture existing of the horse at the age of 7 years, and shows an unmistakable high-class Arabian

possible link with Spain is the appearance of high-stepping horses in early China, of a type which closely resembles the modern Hackney. These may also have been of Spanish ancestry as they are represented as arriving from some foreign land and recall Spanish horses more closely than any others. See Hackney, p. 173.

Apart from these isolated instances we find that the bulk of Chinese horse and pony stock is descended from the main Northern, cold-blooded root but exhibits certain special characteristics developed owing to the influence of Chinese methods of horse breeding. Japan had the usual crossbred stock and never used harness horses till the end of the nineteenth century. It is a remarkable fact that Chang Tang, 1766 B.C., was proverbial as a preventer of cruelty to animals.

No. 2. THE SOUTHERN, HOT-BLOODED ROOT STOCK
(Equus Caballus Arabicus)

HOT BLOOD

The original hot-blooded root stock is Arabian. The pure type only appears historically in the rock pictures of Arabia and Egypt (2000 B.C.) and in Arabia it is often depicted galloping with a rider carrying a spear. The first hieroglyph of a horse is a perfect Arabian on the tomb of Pihiri, 2000 B.C. The Arab horse owing to its type and skeletal peculiarities should be classified as a separate species, and from it all the Southern varieties and fast racing stocks are derived. It represents fire and beauty, and is distinguished by a concave, gazelle-like head, with prominent forehead, large full circular eyes set low in the head, sharply-cut small ears, tapering face, large flexible nostrils, rather long mouth, and very large jowl, a long arched neck, a tail set high and carried high, small teeth and long bars to the mouth and less ribs, lumbar and tail vertebrae (see p. 245).

Only one example of a derivation from this type appears on the rock paintings of Southern Europe, in the form of a speckled pony type.

ANCIENT ARABIA

In ancient Arabia the pedigree of the Arab horse can be traced back for 5,000 years to the wild horses Hoshaba and Baz which were captured by and belonged to Baz the great-great-grandson of Noah and the memory of this wild stock belonging to times when Arabia was "a land of trees and rivers" is firmly fixed in the nomad oral traditions, the nomad children still playing a game of "wild horses."

The ancient Arabs worshipped the Sun, Moon and Stars and the horse idol called Ya'uk and in Southern Arabia the idol was Ya'bub (a swift horse).

The pure Arab type appears on the temple walls of Egypt brought by Arab invaders and the wars of Seti and Rameses against Syria and Northern Arabia, 2500–1500 B.C. Sometimes these horses are driven, sometimes ridden. Egypt conquered the coasts of Phœnicia, c. 1600 B.C., thus mingling their respective horse stock.

Further particulars of the history of Arab root stock will be found in the Arab Horse section, the details above only appearing here in order to point out the ancient lineage of the breed and to emphasize the fact that the source of all hot blood was Arabian B.C. and not Libyan A.D. as Sir William Ridgeway surmised. He was right in his recognition of a

Ancient Arabian horse idol, B.C.

super breed of hot racing blood distributed all over the globe and revolutionizing the world, but he planted his genealogical tree upside down, as this super breed did not come from Libya in the first place, from Arabia, nor was it invariably bay with a star and what he called "bracelets."

The much mixed horse of North Africa crossed with cold blood was only one of the many branches of Equus Caballus Ardens derived from the age-old root stock of Arabia, and indeed a later development compared with those of many other countries. Ridgeway admits, without realizing what the admission entails, that "it is most unlikely that the nomad Libyan, who never kept any account of strains, could have produced artificially in a comparatively short time, the most wonderful breed of horses the world has ever known with characteristics so indelibly fixed that they can permanently modify the form and colour of all other breeds." It is not only unlikely but impossible.

Coarse-headed Libyan horse, 300 B.C.

EWE-NECKED, BARB HORSES

Owing to the prominence given to the Barb horse by Ridgeway's bay breed of Phantom Libyan with the star and "bracelets," it is necessary to give special attention to the fact that as I have already shown there were no horses prehistorically in Libya or the Barbary States. The narrow strip of North to North-West African coast bounded by the Sahara, including Tunisia and Algeria, has from time immemorial been a corridor for foreign invasions from north and east and the horses have consequently been a completely mixed lot varying only with the amount of Arabian blood introduced via Egypt, beginning with the Arabian tribes of Beni Helal which migrated traditionally about 2000 B.C., and settled eventually with their horses in the lands beyond Egypt to the west. But this must have

29

been after 1500 B.C. or else they must have gone beyond Libya as there is no record of horses in the booty taken during the western wars of the Pharaohs in Libya at the very time when Seti was sweeping up thousands of mares in his wars with the Syrian and North Arabians in the east. The northern invasions of Spain brought cold-blooded types into Barbary from the other end and the Spanish convex-headed horses were a most dominating influence in more modern times. The next flood of hot blood came with Saracen invasions of Islam and whole tribes settled in the States, Morocco being the site of the best of the migrated Arabian horses till about 100 years ago, their pedigrees being carefully kept on Arab traditional lines. It must be remembered that the North African corridor was the main trade route by land from Syria to Europe, Spain, France and Italy.

Head of modern Barb

Vandals invaded the whole of Barbary in the fifth century A.D. and in A.D. 814 the Caliphate of Bagdad extended from Morocco to North of the Tigris. The Huns brought horses into Southern Europe and the types mixed. Horse breeding in the Barbary States has been a perpetual struggle between hot and cold blood. Latterly hot blood is again getting the upper hand.

The causes of this universal distribution from Arabia were the tribal migrations and the perpetual exodus from east to west which Cætani remarks on as a persistent phenomenon for 6,000 years. The Beni Helal migrations, the Hyksos invasions, wars with Greeks and Romans, the Assyrian campaigns, the Egyptian campaigns, and much later on the colossal Arabian conquests which swept through North Africa, overflowing into Spain, France and Italy—if we think of such upheavals and remember that in each one of them Arab horse stock was left behind we shall realize the important part played by the hot-blooded root stock from early times. This is also revealed by many records which relate to the early trade in Arabian horses carried on by the sea-trading Phœnician and other enterprising merchants, and by the records of many a Royal stud in Asia and all over the ancient world.

It is not known yet for certain when Britain received its first Arab horse, but it is possible that it was introduced by the Phœnicians.

A study of migrations, wars and trading connections taking Arabian horses will show their universal distribution. Beginning with the collection of seafaring Arab traders, the Phœnicians, they travelled all over the world as far as France and England. The ships had Arab horses heads carved at the prow. The Hyksos invasion of Egypt, *c.* 2000 B.C., coincides with the appearance of Arab horses on the monuments, and the traditional migration of Beni Helal from Arabia, via Egypt to the Barbary States, is approximately dated at this

Arabian rider in the Battle of Rameses, 2000 B.C.

time. The Hyksos dynasty lasted 500 years. The main facts and dates are as follows: The Hittite Kingdom dates from *c.* 2000 B.C. and the Hittite treatise on horse racing was written about 1360 B.C. Kush (Arabia) sent red horses to Tutank Amen in 1400 B.C. The Arab dynasty of Kings in Assyria lasted from 1431 B.C. to 1176 B.C. There were Arabian Phœnician settlements in Greece and Spain, 1300 B.C. The Chaldeans came from Bahreyn and Yemama and (says Cætani) were firmly fixed well before 1000 B.C. King Solomon gathered tribute of horses from Coa (Central Arabia),[1] Nejd and Saba in Arabia, 1000 B.C. Dido went to North Africa from Tyre (Phœnicia), 822 B.C.—the coins show a type of horse more Greek than Arabian; the Sabaeans from Central Arabia conquered North Arabia, 733 B.C. Sargon II took tribute of horses from Arabia, 722 B.C. Sennacherib captured 7,200 horses from Arabia in one campaign, 705 B.C. The Saracen Arabs conquered Persia, 650 B.C. and the Persians invaded Greece, 499 B.C. and stayed there fifty-

[1] See *Thoroughbred Racing Stock.*

four years. Greece and Egypt were also connected, 645 B.C. Habakkuk describes the wonderful Chaldean horses, 626 B.C. Saracens conquered Egypt, A.D. 641. Saracens conquered Persia, A.D. 651, and were Masters of Persia for 500 years from middle of eighth to thirteenth centuries A.D. Saracens in North Africa, A.D. 703; Spain, A.D. 708; France, A.D. 714 to 732; Crete, A.D. 823; Sicily, A.D. 827 onwards; Thessalonica, A.D. 912. Crusades lasted from A.D. 1060 to 1270, brought home Arab horses. Tamerlane who conquered Persia, A.D. 1387, distributed Arab horses in millions to Central Asia and India which he invaded, A.D. 1398. Mohammed II took Constantinople A.D. 1453 and invaded Italy. Turks overran Syria and Egypt, A.D. 1515–17. Nadir Shah took Syria, and distributed countless thousands of Arab mares among Turkoman tribes, A.D. 1736–79.

No. 3.   THE INTERMEDIARY OR WARM- AND COOL-BLOODED TYPES

Mixed Blood, Hot and Cold

The mixed derivatives from the fusion of North-Western and South or Eastern root stocks can be divided into two classes, each class varying in type according to whether the hot or the cold blood predominates, yet each will vary only within the limits of its main characteristics.

(A) *Equus Caballus Ardens* where the hot blood predominates. This mixture will produce light breeds and racing stock and has in the past evolved the best types of Greek, Indian, Assyrian, Hittite, Egyptian, Barb and other light breeds.

(B) *Equus Caballus Frigicalidus.*—Here the predominating heavy ancestry produces a crossbred of heavier slower type with a smaller eye and more hair on the heels and a larger heavier head, thicker skin and heavier bone. The number of ribs and lumbar vertebrae as might be expected varies between the two extremes, as in the Thoroughbred whose blood is mainly hot but with an unrecorded cold slow strain, and whose ribs vary from the usual eighteen to the Arab seventeen or the cart horse nineteen.

PONY STOCK

NORTHERN AND SOUTHERN FOUNDATION TYPES

No. 1. *Northern.*—The early Celtic, Islandic and Norwegian ponies resembled those which are seen in the cave paintings of South-West Europe. At one period those of Norway were characterized by a dun colour, light mane and a black dorsal stripe. Like other European breeds they have been much improved by Arab blood. The Celtic ponies were all of much the same build but the type varied slightly in England and Scotland according to the amount of common or oriental blood diffused among them.

The pony stock of the British Isles seems to be descended from the small nimble chariot ponies (seen on *pre-Roman* coins). They were probably universally distributed in a semi-wild condition, but the ponies of Wales, Cornwall and the Southern counties would be those which would be most likely to be well bred, possibly from Arabian root stock, as they existed in those districts which are said to have been visited by Oriental traders. However this may be, English pony stock was certainly "improved" by Arabs immediately after the Roman conquest, as the Roman auxiliary cavalry brought with them horses both of Spanish and of Arabian type. In later times the pony stock of the north was doubtless influenced by a Scandinavian cross. At one time common blood had ruined most of the feral stock in England but the importations of Arabs caused it to improve and in modern days the resulting types have been divided into Dartmoor, Exmoor, New

Norwegian ponies

Forest, Fell, Dale, Highland, Rhum, and so on, but we must not forget that these are not ancient types but artificially improved ponies based on Arab infusions into Celtic stock. There is therefore no such thing as a pure Exmoor, pure Dartmoor, pure Welsh pony, any more than the ancient remains of E. Agilis-Adamiticus Plicidens, etc., represent definite species. More than others Icelandic, Norwegian and Highland ponies retain the ancient type. The Exmoor is the most mixed as the moors are unfenced and over-run with crossbreds. (See p. 206.)

The Shetland Pony stands apart from all others as an original prehistoric type of its own. Early representations show it piebald or skewbald and with a small refined head. The modern fault of Shetlands is having a head much too large for their size. The Irish Connemara ponies are another made up breed with the same history of Spanish, Arabian, North-West African, Scandinavian and pre-Roman blood. The Spanish ambling gait can still be seen.

No. 2. *Southern.*—The parti-coloured type of pony which appears in the cave drawings of Spain as the only prehistoric derivative of Southern type to be found so far in Europe, is connected with those Arabian records of speckled and parti-coloured ponies which are mentioned in later days in descriptions of the Musjid breed. Some were also taken to America by the Spaniards. The larger types are still bred in U.S.A. under the name of Colorado Rangers and Appaloosas and some are recorded in the American stud book. Spotted ponies are also still to be found in the Himalayas and are said to have come in old times from "the Erithrean Sea."

The multi-coloured Tanghans of Tibet are illustrated in the *Naturalists Library*, and can still be seen in India.

The great breeder, Ruy d'Andrade, still preserves in Coruche, Central Portugal, descendants of an original type of wild pony, very small (1 m. 40), mousy yellow with a dorsal stripe, barred legs and sometimes striped also on the head and neck. He tells me this is indigenous to the country and *aboriginal*.

There are of course natural barriers beyond which horses cannot go. In early days seas or impassable mountain ranges limited migration and even when artificial transport resolved these difficulties there were still insuperable barriers of climates and conditions fatal to horse life. The tsetse fly and horse sickness for instance, or arctic or tropical climates. There were no horses originally in Australia, New Zealand, America, the Argentine, the Tropics or South and East Africa. In some of these countries they have been introduced and acclimatized in modern times, but in others they can only survive under artificial conditions or not at all, even where Zebras thrive in a wild state. d'Herbelot records that as late as 1697 there were no horses in Zanzibar; the population rode cattle, even in war, as battle chargers, and in Malay there was not even a word for a horse.

There are no early remains of horses in Scandinavia and horses only appear in Denmark in the Bronze Age.

The Swedes had good horses in the sixth century B.C. As I have said there are no pre-historic remains of horses in Libya which was entirely horseless till after the Arabian migration through Egypt.

ICELAND

Horse fighting was a great sport in Iceland and horse flesh was a staple diet. In the Saga of Burnt Njal a match between two famous horses ended in a fight between the owners in the course of which one horse had his eye knocked out by a bystander who was promptly killed by the owner.

The Scythians started the practice of castration. They were the earliest known "waggon dwellers," fore-runners of the gypsies, and they lived on mares' milk and blood drawn from living horses. In East Africa the natives still live on the blood and milk of their cattle. It is of course a disastrous practice with any livestock, draining their vitality, so horses and cattle treated thus are wretched specimens.

34

CHAPTER II

THE GREAT HORSE OF EUROPE

THE Great Horse of Europe was the most distinguished representative of the roman-nosed, Northern type; and he and his descendants have been so closely linked up with European military, social and economic history that it is of the greatest interest to follow his career through the centuries as battle horse, as parade horse, and as the foundation stock of all our present-day agricultural and heavy draught breeds.

AS BATTLE HORSE

Before the days of heavy armour and through long centuries B.C., the Great Horse of Europe patiently plodded on his way bearing heavy burdens, dragging great weights, and generally performing all the drudgery of mankind in peace and war. In A.D. 378 the Goths defeated the Romans at Adrianople and Sir C. Oman tells us that this must be regarded as "the first great victory won by that heavy cavalry which had now shown its ability to supplant the heavy infantry of Rome as the ruling power of war," and which inaugurated "that ascendancy of the horsemen which was to endure for a thousand years." He also notes that from the middle of the sixth century onwards armour gradually became usual, first among great men and then among "all the wealthier classes."

It was when men took to protecting themselves from top to toe in plate armour, c. A.D. 1300, that the Great Horse in Europe had to carry the full burden and glory of battle, but as early as A.D. 1200 King John imported 100 dray stallions to blend with local English stock. Richard II imported to England vast numbers of Continental battle horses, c. 1377.

Writing of the "Days of Chivalry," another historian says, "We must rid ourselves of the popular notion of the Knight as a headlong, galloping cavalier . . . the attacks of the man-at-arms could not be very rapid . . . the shock" (of their charge) "was rather that of a ponderous column moving at a moderate pace than of a light line charging at high speed."

Vivid descriptions and pictures of those knightly battles can be found in medieval chronicles which abound with accounts of men and horses in victory and in distress. The battles of Crécy, Poictiers, and Agincourt furnish terrible examples of the fate of men and of Great Horses in defeat. For when the arrows of the English archers pierced through horse and man the great stallions, maddened with pain, plunged, reared, and stampeded into the dense ranks behind them bringing confusion and death to the struggling masses on every side.

LIGHT CAVALRY

From the earliest days it was the custom of generals to include a certain number of light horsemen in their armies and not long after the battle of Crécy, when the Black Prince fought the Spaniards at Najera, in 1367, a Castilian chronicler mentions that there were men-at-arms supported by light horsemen or Genetors, in the Spanish forces. Thus we see how in England the word genet or *jennet* came into use; not to describe the riders but the mount. We also learn that the celebrated Spanish jennet so often mentioned in the seventeenth century was not in any sense a racehorse, but merely a Spanish battle horse of the lighter type, and later an ambling palfrey.

Not only the heaviness of the Great Horse, but the weight of armour possessed great disadvantages in certain fields of warfare; for instance, during the crusades, when the writer of the *Itinerarium* describes how "the Infidels not being weighed down with heavy armour like our knights but always able to outstrip them in pace, were a constant trouble. When charged they are wont to fly, and their horses are more nimble than any others in the world; one may liken them to swallows for swiftness."

The crusaders were able to bring home specimens of these Arabian flyers from time to time and though in England they probably left isolated well-bred descendants yet these were destined to be swamped by the tremendous impetus given to heavy horse breeding during the reign of King Henry VIII. Faced with a serious shortage of Great Horses to carry his armoured soldiers and no doubt prejudiced by the needs of his own ever present Royal bulk, King Henry passed laws which compelled every man to concentrate on the weight-carrying breeds, which ended in the wholesale massacre of all horses under 15 hands. To further this end many horses were imported from Holland, Germany and Italy—to say nothing of the proverbially coarse Flanders mares! Contemporary pictures of the Cheval Anglais and of a heavy cart type labelled "Britannus" shows how far this policy was successful in providing suitable mounts for the army, and these strong, serviceable horses helped to form the foundation stock of the fine Shires and hefty draught types that we see to-day.

EXCESSIVE COST OF HEAVY HORSES

There were so many Great Horses in 1310 that an Archbishop denounced the excessive cost of their keep in his list of abuses, saying that each horse cost the outrageous sum of 2s. 7d. a week "which would keep *four or five poor people*"! He also quotes the groom's extravagant wages of three ha'pence a day!

The Earl of Lancaster spent £484 4s. 3d. on Great Horses and Hugh Spenser kept forty mares and foals and a hundred carriage horses. Hollinshed describes the "Agricultural" horses of 1558 as being easily able to carry 4 cwt. There were farms for breeding cavalry Great Horses and farm horses which were divided into cart and plough horses known as Stotts affers or avers. They followed the use of oxen for ploughing and mixed teams were used. Wheeled vehicles were used in the time of Richard II, 1377, called chares, cars, chariots, caroches and whirlicotes, and we read of carts and wagons. The breeds were famous for their "ambling pace," very gentle and comfortable for travelling and Mary Verney once complained of having to ride pillion on a "cruel trotting horse" instead of the usual ambler which took her baby on a cushion.

TRAVELLING

The King and his lords travelled on horseback; carriages were considered a luxury reserved at enormous cost for the aristocracy. The best seem to have been modelled in the shape of a glorified cross between a furniture removal van and a bus. They had four wheels and were drawn by three or four horses with a postillion. Solid beams rested on the axles and above this clumsy framework rose an archway rounded like a tunnel—an ungainly structure but ornamented elegantly with painted beams and carved wheels. The inside was hung with dazzling tapestries, while embroidered cushions and sorely needed pillows adorned the seats. Square windows opened along the sides with silk curtains.

LUXURY VEHICLES

The "luxury" seemed rather relative than actual as the vehicle is described as groaning and proceeding by violent jerks, bounding all of a piece over ditches, coming down with a shattering thud which must have jolted the passengers like peas in a bottle. Springs not having been invented till 1690 it is not surprising that after nearly two centuries of springless jolting we still find Queen Elizabeth complaining of aches and pains after a long drive.

These luxurious vehicles were nevertheless family heirlooms and Roger Rowland charged £400 for making the Queen's Chariot in 1397 and thirty-four years earlier "Lady Eleanor's" carriage cost £1,000 (the value of 1,600 oxen). Ornamented horse litters supported on poles like sedan chairs were carried by shaft horses before and behind and there were farm carts for agriculture, but most people rode.

Queen Mary's coronation was described in Stow's *Annals*. "The last of September, 1553, Queen Mary rode through the City of London towards Westminster, sitting in a chariot of cloth of tissue drawn with six horses and trapped with the like cloth of tissue. She sat in a gown of purple velvet furred with powdered ermine . . . after the Queen's Chariot, Sir E. Hastings led her horse in his hand: then came another chariot, having a covering all of cloth of silver, all white, and six horses trapped with the like. Therein sat the Lady Elizabeth and the Lady Anne of Cleves . . ."

Besides those two "chariots" the procession had numerous people on horseback and "two chariots covered with red satin and the horses trapped with the same."

The first coach in England seems to have been made for the Earl of Rutland in 1555, by Walter Ripon, the Queen's servant. The Queen's Dutch coachman, Guilliam Booner, was the first to bring them into notice and Ripon made her a "hollow turning coach with arches and pillars." The term "caroach" was used for a town carriage, and coach for a country one.

MAILS ON HORSEBACK

In about 1600 the mails from London to Edinburgh were conveyed by a man on horseback blowing a horn and depicted in fur-topped boots called "spatterdashes," and a headdress like an earl's coronet. This journey took ten days. The horse is a prancing one with hair on the heels. The rider was required to blow his horn three times in every mile and whenever he met anything or passed through a town. The postmaster was required to keep four horses and two horns ready and he had the right to commandeer other people's horses for the service if necessary. The stages were ten miles for each horse. The post riders were not allowed to take more than thirty pounds weight of mails or to ride faster than seven miles an hour in summer and six in winter.

The charge was 2d. to $2\frac{1}{2}$d. a mile and was raised to 3d. in 1609, but the varying lengths of the mile made the charges uncertain.

Abuses were general. Horses were seized, bribes taken, stables broken into, and chaos reigned. Horses were over-ridden and killed to such an extent that England was accused in an Italian proverb of being the hell of horses and purgatory of servants and the paradise of women. As to the latter one may be tempted to doubt it when one considers the hoops and crinolines, the starched ruffs and suffocating cages of iron corsetry in which they spent their lives.

According to a letter from Mr. Carrod to Lord Wentworth, Hackney coaches had been started in London by a sea captain called Baily and in 1636 there were already 6,000 of them—they were called Hackney Hell Carts which does not suggest much comfort! The horse jobber was called a hackney man and a hackney horse was a roadster.

COACHMEN'S WAGES

Private coachmen were paid about £4 a year and had to sit on the pole, a rather precarious and tiring position!

The innovation of hired coaches brought a storm of protests. They obstructed the streets and "the earth trembled and shook and the casements went shatter-tatter from the tumbling din."

The coach horses were of the Great Horse shire breed or Flemish mares which in the country were used for agriculture as well, and oxen were used to pull coaches out of quagmires. The Flemish horses fetched £18 to £42. In 1680 the Countess of Sunderland paid £100 for a pair of the finest largest grey coach horses, "the stateliest and most dappled persons" her agent could get. A pair of blacks cost Pepys £50.

Lady Wentworth in the *Nettlestead Papers*, December 1708, wrote to her son:

> Mr. Arundell has a payr of the pretyist coach-horses I ever did see. They are very dark; almost lyke black with white mains and long white tailse and they goe brydling and prancin along that al peoples from the highest to the lowest stairs after them. Several has inquired of the coachman whether his master will part with them. I wish you had six of them I am sure you would be in love with them did you see them."

Condemned prisoners of high rank were allowed to travel by coach to Tyburn, a gracious concession, in return for being hanged, drawn and quartered. Common folk went in a cart or sledge.

Postboy

There were stage cloth-hooded waggons for conveying luggage and goods drawn by seven or eight horses in file with bells and feather plumes. They also seem to have been the prototype of the charabanc which held twenty to thirty people.

INVENTION OF SPRINGS

By 1690 springs had been invented and glass coaches were used by the nobility. The new stage coaches were called "flying machines," so great was their speed covering fifty miles a day in twelve hours, sixty-five miles a day being the record! Luggage was often lost, and an advertisement for the recovery of silver laced petticoats and gold and silver stays appeared in the *London Gazette* of 1882. Horses of lighter build had been introduced from Spain and everything speeded up.

John Cresset wrote a violent attack on stage coaches in 1673 complaining of sitting all through summer days choked with dust and stifled, or starving, freezing and choked with fogs in winter, always too late for supper and too early for breakfast, in constant company of ancient sick people and screaming children, crippled by boxes and bundles, or wading up to the knees in mud while coaches were pulled out with broken axle trees. Exhausted horses, surly, ill-tempered coachmen, and irate passengers completed the picture of his vexation.

DANGEROUS SPEED

This dangerously rapid method of travelling was also attacked as a means of escape for criminals who eluded capture with a breakneck rapidity which set the law at defiance.

In his description (1577–78), Harrison says of the horses of England that "though not so large as some others, yet they are of an easy pace, and altogether hard to beat." He also mentions importation of the Spanish jennet, the Neapolitan heavy "courser," the Irish hobby, the Flemish roil, and the Scottish nag. According to another contemporary (Blunderville) the breeds of horses known in England in Shakespeare's day were: the Turkey horse, Barbarian or Barb, Sardinian, Neapolitan, the high Almaine or German horse, the Friesland, the Hungarian, the Flemish, the Sweathland (Swedish) horse (of a mean stature and strength) and the Irish hobby. It has often been said that in the plays of Shakespeare one can perceive the reaction which set in towards lighter horses after the plethora of heavy animals seen during the reign of Henry VIII. It is also said that Shakespeare's own preference was for the horse from Barbary, and he must certainly have seen and may have owned such a horse in 1592 because from that time onwards it is always the horse of that type which he dwells on in his historical plays. Be that as it may, we hear from Gervase Markham that still for all forms of general service the "true English horse . . . of tall stature and large proportions" was held to be the best.

So we learn that "Britannus" was no racer! He was a heavy horse and, at the beginning of the seventeenth century, both in England and on the Continent animals of his stalwart build still had to bear armoured men into battle, but at this period they were no longer the knights of chivalry but were the cuirassiers. Their armour was no longer to make them arrowproof but bulletproof and very cumbersome it must have been!

"It will kill a man to serve in a whole cuirass!" complained Sir Harry Verney, when summoned in 1638 to campaign against Scottish rebels "as a cuirassier in russet arms with gilded studs and nails!" Fortunately for both man and beast this method of warfare soon began to grow obsolete; cuirassiers began to be ridiculed as regiments of lobsters and by 1645 General Monck declared in his *Observations* that he did not think it necessary to give instructions as to how such a man should be armed because, said he, "there are not many countries that do afford horses fit for the service of cuirassiers." In a book called *Cromwell's Army*, Sir Charles Firth describes in detail how these changes came to pass and how in 1645 the Protector formed his new model army with lighter cavalry composed of "harquebusiers" and dragoons.

AS COACH HORSE

Cromwell's wars had furnished him with ample experience of the good and weak points of both heavy and lighter cavalry. A keen horseman himself, he not only rode, raced and imported Arabians, but he also experimented with the heavier breeds and there are accounts of him driving a coach and six in Hyde Park. On one such occasion he had a nasty accident as he lost his temper and lashed a team of five Friesian horses, which bolted, throwing him on the pole, the concussion firing off a pistol in his pocket. (These horses were presents from the Duke of Newcastle, and may have been of the Oldenburgh breed.)

AS PARADE HORSE

In such glimpses we see the beginning of a new era for the Great Horse once he began to be freed from the heavy responsibilities of armoured war. Crossed more frequently with the hot-blooded Arabian and other Southern derivatives, in some cases he became a matchless post horse trotter like the French Percheron and our own post horses, or a slow, high-stepping parade horse like the Spanish horses when at their best. He would retain his massive qualities and yet would learn in the manège so beloved of the Duke of Newcastle—to prance, turn, and parade, and to thunder in mimic warfare showing himself possessed of far greater mobility than in his old unimproved days! In 1360 cart breeds were still ridden.

But as long ago as Edward II English breeders had been struck by the dash of added quality which Spanish and Italian horses seemed to show and history is full of the English importations of these horses and of appeals from progressive men in almost every century who, like Cromwell, believed that an infusion of hot blood (Arabian at best, and Barb when that proved unprocurable) would improve the heavy breeds to a remarkable degree. The effect of these crosses soon showed itself and the influence of Oriental blood became increasingly popular as the battle horses were transferred from the army to the needs of agriculture, while lighter horses for riding and post-chaises replaced the massive "double saddle" horses and heavy coach breeds.

HEAVY HORSES OUTPACED ON THE ROADS

It was small wonder that soon after the Restoration and the wholesale Arabian importations, speeding-up in England became the order of the day! Foxhunting, coaching, road-travelling, cavalry training, all became swifter and racing assumed a paramount importance. Men began to specialize in the production of horses for "The Course, Chase, War, or Travel." In 1700, Dutch cart horses were still being ridden, but on the other hand, racing was introduced into Holland.

By 1727 so much foreign blood and so many mixtures were at a transition stage that Bradley exclaimed, "The true bred English horse hardly exists, unless we may account the Horses to be such that are bred wild in some of our Forests and among the mountains." Yet he need not have lamented, because it was still the blood of "Britannus" (that horse of lofty stature and large proportions) which was helping to evolve the celebrated draught, harness and agricultural breeds for which this country is renowned to-day, and which have been bred up from their foundation on the old native cart and Great Horse stock, improved, not only by that strong heavy-horse stock imported in old times by Henry VIII and some of his predecessors, but also by the infusion of Arabian blood during the late seventeenth, eighteenth and nineteenth centuries. Latterly Thoroughbred blood seems also to have contributed its share. Eventually coach horses became galloping post horses of oriental appearance.

MODERN DRAUGHT BREEDS
CLYDESDALES, SHIRES, AND SUFFOLK PUNCH BREEDS

There are three modern specialized long-standing breeds of draught horses in Britain. The white-legged Clydesdales and Shires and the chestnut Suffolk Punch. Clydesdales are the product of Scotland and the North—Suffolks came from the Eastern Counties, and the Shires were called Shires because they were chiefly bred in the Shires and were called so already 400 years ago. They are the biggest of all breeds in the world, seventeen to eighteen hands and weighing not less than a ton, one indeed reached nineteen hands. Two famous stallions, Glancer and Thompson's Black Horse, are notable in the foundation line of the present Shire.

The Clydesdales are an even more impressively handsome breed with four white legs and blaze, and both breeds are descended from the mixed continental stock varying in type according to the countries of origin. Fifty years ago there were fine teams of piebalds. Glancer and his seven sons, with Darnley and Sir Walter Scott, stand out as sires.

Lanark has long been connected with the breed which was crossed with Flemish stallions. There are many studs of these horses and stud books for both breeds were started in 1878 and the Clydesdale of to-day is almost too famous, for too many have lately left the country. In 1911 no less than 1,617 horses were exported and the prices were high. Flashwood, sold as a yearling for £900, was resold at ten years old for £1,000. The stallion Baron of Buchyro fetched £9,500 and his son £5,250, while Danure Footprint commanded a stud fee of £120.

The Suffolk Punch was mentioned in Cauden's *Britannia* in 1506, the breed is now uniformly chestnut, the bays having been bred out. This chestnut colour has been quoted as evidence of purity of blood, but as two chestnuts are by hereditary colour-law bound to get chestnut, any mongrel chestnut would equally get chestnut if mated to a chestnut.

They are now a good-looking, short-legged, heavy-necked breed, and have a Scandinavian-Norwegian appearance and they may have originated with the Norsemen who settled in the northern counties in the ninth century. They show no sign of Spanish blood. They were not originally good looking, as Arthur Young described the Suffolk of 1760

Clydesdale stallion

as: "Sorrel, very low in the fore end, with a long misshapen head slouching heavy ears a great carcass on short legs." An uglier horse, he says, would be impossible to view. Another writer calls them "half horse half hog," but they were always stalwart weight pullers and plough horses.

Professor Ridgeway traced both Shire and Suffolk to a chestnut variety of the Great Horse of Upper Europe, blended eventually with oriental blood but there cannot have been much oriental blood at the time of the description of 1760. It is evident that superior blood must have eliminated the hideous head very effectually since then.

43

In the eighteenth century hauling competitions for large stakes were held when the horses were set to pull waggons full of sand with the wheels partly sunk in the ground and wood blocks placed in front of them to increase the strain. Sometimes bearing reins

Half-bred Percherons

This is claimed as the world's biggest horse, weighing 3,030 lbs.

were used and sometimes not. It is said that these fearful weights could not be moved till the horses went down on their knees, a cruel test, which must have ruptured many. There were also crazy competitions, attaching the horses to growing trees and forcing them to pull till one of the horses collapsed.

Lord Stradbroke was the first to recognize their merits and by improving the type sold six of his mares for £1,200. The earliest sire to which all pedigrees go back was a light chestnut coaching sire of the eighteenth century called Crisps Horse of Ufford, height 15.2. A Lincolnshire trotter improved the action and in the next century two foreign sires were introduced. There were still bays in 1872, but now there is only every variety of chestnut with a small "race" and perhaps one white foot.

Shire horse

PERCHERONS

The Percheron is a grey French breed of Arabian origin introduced into England (1916) and gradually being appropriated into our British quartette of draught horses. It is easily the handsomest of all heavy breeds. It originated as post horses and hunters descended from Arabians brought by Crusaders and again by the Saracen invaders and probably was part of the Norman cavalry.

In 1753 the breed was crossed with Danish, Belgian and English mixtures. The grey Shire horse of the period being exactly like the Percheron it is probable that an interchange took place. In 1820 Napoleon's two grey Arab chargers, Godolphin and Gallipoli were to the Percheron what the Darley and Godolphin Arabians were to the racehorse —an undying influence stamping it with their type and colour and giving it the beautiful large eyes, splendid head and crest, and noble appearance. The level quarters and high set tail must be insisted on as the original type, any divergence from which shows base

45

Ordinary cart-horse type

46

blood, and the black colour sometimes seen is due to an inferior cross of Nivernais, and if really black (not the black which turns grey) should be taboo.

Georges Trolet in his book on the Percheron horse says that a famous stallion, Jean le Blanc (much admired as the strongest and finest Percheron ever seen) was a direct descendant of Gallipoli. He died in 1836, so was probably Gallipoli's son. Breeders should keep to the grey colour and avoid ugly heads and drooping quarters like the plague.

Fine type of Percheron

Permanent black is a sign of an inferior Nivernais cross. Grey is as typical of the true breed as it is typical of the Starlight strain of Welsh miniature ponies (see p. 228).

THE CLEVELAND BAY

The Cleveland Bay is a "light-heavy" harness horse based on foreign breeds and crossed with the celebrated Spanish coach horses of which large numbers were imported by the Duke of Buckingham, together with Spanish riding Hackneys of the jennet type. They also have Thoroughbred and Arab blood through the Darley Arabian and Godolphin, and are allied to the Yorkshire coach horse and trotting horses of Dutch origin.

THE FARM HORSE OF MIXED BREED

Strong farm horses of mixed breed have been extremely useful to British farmers ever since the day when they first began to replace oxen at the plough.

At the beginning of the twelfth century they were yoked with the oxen, being sometimes driven together in teams of sixteen and twenty, and by the end of that century they were in use for ploughs, sledges and carts.[1]

A hundred years later the value of a "cart" horse had risen from 6s. to 18s. The smaller packhorse and farm animals (rounceys, stotts, etc.) had fetched from 3s. to 11s. 8d. in the preceding period.

Early "Books of Husbandry" contain many references to horses, and picturesque descriptions of a farmer's life. One author writes of the plough as "a divine work for which we ought to thank Heaven," another proclaims the virtues of a good waggoner as one who is "Experienced, modest, and not wrathful, skilfully directing his horses and not overloading them." A third devotes himself to the discussion of the relative merits of oxen and horses for agricultural purposes. From the seventeenth century to 1886 no less than 1,200 books were published on veterinary practice, farriery and horse breeding alone. For many years veterinary science was at the blood-letting stage and horses used to be bled every spring and often twice a year. There was a craze for bleeding, just as there is now a craze for inoculation, but the choice of a dunghill as an equine operating table recalls the days of Job. Restive horses were bled in the hunting field to calm them for the comfort of their riders, and one was even driven into a pond to be sucked by leeches. Male goats were kept in stables, the smell being held a preventive against staggers in horses. It might conceivably have the reverse effect upon human beings! In 1340 there were also complaints of the (still surviving) curse of rabbits on the Sussex pastures. Hundreds of acres of crops were annually "annihilated" by the Bishop of Chichester's rabbits and those of a nobleman with the appropriate name of Lord de Warrenne. Weasels (stoats) were trained as domestic pets and are said to have retrieved their catches like dogs.

Henry VIII flooded the country with enormous continental horses. The Berkshire farmers drove teams of six stallions. In Sussex strings of bells adorned the harness, the jangling of which was said to warn people coming along the narrow corkscrew lanes of the weald.

In 1651 cart horses were a mixture of Germanic breeds, mostly dun and white, and crossed with Belgian, Italian, Spanish and Barb or Arab blood.

In 1680 William III imported a large black breed of Dutch cart horses which are erroneously now referred to as the "Old English black horse" or Fen breed, and often said to be the origin of the Shire, but the Shire was already known in the time of Henry

---

[1] Hollinshead (1587) says: "Our cart or plough horses (for we use them indifferently) are commonly so strong that fifty foot of timber, forty bushels of salt or four quarters of wheat is considered a normal load. Horses used for turning millwheels were blinded by having their eyes bored out."

VIII, and the *Shire* horses of the Fens were not black but parti-coloured or chestnut and grey; the black horses were also known as the "snail breed" on account of their slowness.

At the end of the eighteenth century, Bakewell of Dishley, a celebrated sheep and cattle breeder, set about improving it by intensive inbreeding to horses whose pedigree he kept a close secret. By a process of three new blades and two new handles he got rid of the long thick hairy legs described by Defoe, but in 1788, Marshall, who had praised one of Bakewell's stallions four years earlier, still wrote lamenting the disastrous infiltration of the "Howden muck" into the Vale of Pickering, condemning the whole breed as a plague, adding "The breed of grey rats with which this Island has of late been overrun is not a greater pest than this breed of black Fen horses." Proverbially slow and ugly they were very powerful, the largest reaching eighteen hands and able to draw three tons, but it is perhaps not surprising that either Bakewell entirely transformed them by crossing, or the type died out with the vast influx of later importations. Bakewell's mystery horse may have been the Lincolnshire trotter referred to elsewhere as having been introduced to counteract the snail's pace and to speed the plough. Importations from the low countries had reached two thousand in 1862 and rose rapidly to such a degree that by 1872 they had reached twelve thousand yearly, and John Bull was burnt in effigy by the Flemish farmers who resented their horses going overseas.

The results of all these foreign breeds, some good and some bad, have only been properly sorted out since the stud books were started late in the last century.

In the agricultural horses of to-day we have on the one hand these special breeds— Shires, Clydesdales, the Suffolk Punch, the Cleveland Bay and so on, and on the other we have the still varied collection of farm horses of mixed breed, and allied types, all useful horses of recognized general type.

Farm horses may therefore have Shire or Percheron or any other heavy blood in them and all are of mixed origin. A similar mixed origin is responsible for the lighter van horses and tradesmen's ponies, for not only leading sires of the best heavy breeds, but also many Thoroughbred hackney and hunter and pony stallions have travelled the country for years and have modified all stock to a certain extent, producing heavy hunter types, light hacks, polo ponies, etc., according to what mares were brought to them by farmers.

Even as I write this the menace of almost total extinction by machinery hangs over all harness breeds in this country. The show ring and the racecourse may conceivably end in being the only surviving horse centres. Hunting is already being severely squeezed by barbed wire entanglements and the house building octopus, and when it comes to a master of hounds writing to a landowner to ask leave to bring a shooting party to *shoot foxes* on his estate, things have reached a somewhat startling state since the days when a man who shot a fox ran a risk of being lynched.

Pihiri horse

CHAPTER III

RACING

RACING (like fighting) being a primeval instinct both in men and animals, is a common cause of rivalry and quarrelling. Neither horses nor dogs can bear to be beaten, and as for motorists, they constantly risk death for no reason whatever beyond the instinctive dislike of being outstripped in speed! It is therefore not surprising that we find racing competitions recorded from time immemorial. As the earliest horse

Egyptian Chariot, 2000 B.C.

racing began in the Middle East, it will be necessary to review its progress in Assyria, Egypt, and Syria, and to follow it to Europe in the wake of the oldest racing type, the Arabian horse.   Except in Central Arabia (where wheeled vehicles never existed) racing competitions began with hunting and war chariots drawn by two horses. The first of these are seen on Egyptian monuments *c.* 2500–2000 B.C. In the Hittite treatise of

50

Kikkoulis there are detailed instructions for training, sweating and feeding racehorses. The Assyrian lion hunts, *c.* 800–750 B.C., show the kind of galloping chariots drawn by an Arabianized type of horse, some better bred than others. It will be noted that these galloping chariots did not appear till after the arrival of the Arab Kings of Assyria.

RACING IN ARABIA

Riding originated in Arabia and the first representation of a ridden horse is a statuette found in Egypt of an oriental riding an Arab horse primitively modelled, but of unmistakable type, dating from *c.* 2000 B.C. Another rider is carved on an Egyptian axehead and a seal, to which the same approximate date is assigned. It was only as the Arabian horse spread into neighbouring countries that races were run with riders. The first Egyptian hieroglyph is the horse of Pihiri, a perfect Arabian (see p. 50).

Races were first run in Arabia with loose horses kept thirsty and trained to race to the nearest water. There are details of the celebrated pre-Islamic race of Dahès and El Ghabra in which Quays was tricked into matching his horses against the horses of Hutheyfa over fourteen miles for a stake of 100 camels. His honour was pledged without his consent by an unprincipled sort of pristine bookmaker going by the romantic name of "the Rose." Factional ill-feeling fostered by "the Rose" and his racing confederates reached such a pitch that while the rival owners watched the race, hurling jibes and insults at each other from the hill tops, the supporters of Hutheyfa set upon the favourite, Dahès, belabouring him with sticks with such violence that one of the assailants had a paralysed arm ever afterwards, and though the horse escaped from them when they thought it was too late for him to regain lost ground, and by sheer speed overtook and passed all the horses except his partner El Ghabra, the grey mare being first at the water, both were driven off the winning point in a free fight which gave the rival horses time to come up, and the judge, whose relatives had backed these horses, and who was a member of the opposition tribe, hastily awarded the stakes to Hutheyfa and faded out together with "the Rose," leaving the bystanders to fight it out, and fight it out they did. It is perhaps, hardly surprising that the outraged owner vowed eternal and sanguinary reprisals. Everyone started killing each other and after a lurid career of treachery, violence and murder, the hypocritical and unprincipled Hutheyfa, who double-crossed enemies and friends alike, met a well-deserved death uttering pious lamentations, and vain appeals for "mercy and justice." His death did not end the war and the "Riders of Death" continued reprisals for some 100 years.

There was racing in the Kingdom of Hira, A.D. 120, and King Bahram, who had 40,000 horses, used to test them by racing. The Prophet conducted Arab racing in Hejaz from A.D. 624–687, and was a most enthusiastic racehorse owner. His admiration for the Arabian breed was unbounded. He wrote reams in its praise and allowed a double share of spoil to riders of pure bred horses (Kehilans) in war. He owned several mares, but the reputed "Five" ("El Khamsa") belong to the same category as Greek Mythology and are not authentic but symbolic. The Arabian invasions carrying Islam right through North Africa to France brought myriads of Arabian horses with them, and after the victory of Charles Martel, A.D. 722, the local breeds were flooded with oriental blood.

EASTERN STUDS AND RACING IN PERSIA

Some idea of the colossal breeding establishments of the East can be realized by the records of those kept by Kings and Sultans. At the Rupture of the Duke of Mareb, A.D. 120, the King of Yemen took refuge in Syria with 80,000 parti-coloured Arab horses; and the Caliph Motassem, A.D. 840, had a stud of 130,000 spotted, speckled, and dappled Arabian horses of the type seen in the Persian MS. After the Arab conquests as late as 1614 the Kings of Persia had collected studs of 50,000 mares, and Nadir Shah's Stud seized by the Turks at his death in 1736 had thousands of mares. At the conquest of Persia in A.D. 1387, Tamerlane distributed thousands of Arabian horses in Persia and India, Turkomania and Asia Minor. At the death of Sultan el Naseri in 1342 he left 7,000 racehorses in his Egyptian stables. Caliph Hersham el Ommiade had a stud of 4,000, while Malek Shah had 40,000. One of the Kings of Yemen had a racing stud of Golden Arab horses with white manes and tails, a colour now called Palomino. Races in Persia were run over not less than twenty-four miles.

RACING IN EGYPT

Racing, which had been firmly established in Egypt since the ninth century A.D., having come from Syria and Arabia, was then in full swing and quite as popular a sport as it is now in England. Under Sultan El Naseri, A.D. 1290, it reached a fabulous importance and prices comparable to those now given in England for thoroughbreds were paid for racing Arabs topped by a price equivalent to £67,200 paid by the Sultan for the racing El Karta filly which remains a world's record paid by any one man for any horse up to the present day. All the tribes in Arabia were commissioned to look for the best they could get. He would give £84,000 a day for horses and paid £30,000 for a famous stallion and at his death left 7,000 horses. All the Emirs were racehorse owners and vast hippodromes were built for playing Tennis ("Tchigan") on horseback, reputed a most dangerous game and the origin of Royal Tennis. It was introduced into Europe via Spain as "Pelota" and to France as "La Paume" by which time it was played on foot and was brought to England by the Kings as an almost exclusively Royal game. Being exceedingly complicated and necessitating professional markers and a great deal of expense it was

Origin of polo
The Persian game of Savlajan

eventually displaced by Sir William Hart Dyke's invention facetiously called "Spheristrike" which became lawn tennis, with racquets as another offshoot, at the end of the nineteenth century. Polo was another variety of Tchigan, originating in Persia and played out of

Early Egyptian sculpture, probably the first representation of a ridden horse, 2000 B.C.

doors. It can be seen in old Persian MS. illuminations and was called "Savlajan." El Arifi makes it clear that the implement used in Tchigan was not a polo stick but shaped like the crescent moon.

Racing spread to Greece at an early date and assumed a leading part in the Olympic games as will be seen in the chapter on Greece.

Persian Arab mares. Note the looped rope round horse's neck attached to the other mare's hock

Horse-headed boat from the Shah Nama
These boats were used by the Phœnician Sea Traders

CHAPTER IV

RACING IN ENGLAND

PREVIOUS to the Roman invasion 50 B.C. the Britons were not horse riders but expert charioteers, turning and wheeling with a speed and skill which amazed the conquerors. Local British horses were small, swift and agile chariot ponies. They are seen on coins of British workmanship as two types. In the coins of the Iceni a pure Arabian type with and without rider, arched neck and very highly carried tail (sometimes a triple tail) accompanied by a palm branch which is not, as was at first assumed, a copy of the Roman Stater, but suggests oriental craftsmen. (Details will be found in *Thoroughbred Racing Stock.*) The other type is the Celtic pony. The coins show no chariots and we only know of them from Cæsar's account of them and excavated remains of a small light type. The Iceni seem to have had their headquarters near Newmarket.[1]

That there was an Oriental element in Britain is evident enough in the existence (and modern survival) of gypsy wanderers, which at one time were exceedingly numerous. Their oriental type, language and habits and dark complexions are well known and may be a link with the old Phœnician Saracen traders, traces of which still exist in the West of England and the word "Sarson" was the local name for the old inhabitants who worked in the tin mines of Cornwall and Devon, and "Saracens Stone" was a name given to the large blocks of hard sandstone called Greywethers of Cornwall. Headlands and other places have Arabic names such as Ras de Catte (Cat's head) on the opposite French coast and many other local names. "Corn" or "Korn" is itself a promontory or "horn." Horse riding and racing were introduced by the Romans and their foreign Syrian legions, but details are lacking leaving only a few bare facts. The best Roman cavalry was the Thamudene Arabian section. All we know is that in the fourth century A.D. there were special covered training hippodromes in which Arab horses were raced at Rushborough, Dorchester, Netherby, Carleon and Silchester, and that altars were erected to the goddess

---

[1] Ancient excavations have brought to light metal work in Early Britain from 100 B.C. The horse bits are all snaffles of two-link and three-link type of small size for ponies and several are of bronze-coated iron made in Eastern Britain. Two, probably from the Thames Valley, have links of solid bronze but the rings are hollow. One, a two-link bit probably from a south-west workshop is solid bronze. It shows a plastic design which is new to Celtic art history in England and is of very delicate workmanship. It was designed for a two-horse chariot.

of horses. Horse racing is incidentally mentioned in the Anglo-Saxon era when the Saxon boys of fifteen strove to excel in riding. Bede describes one of a party who came to a plain adapted for proving the riders of the swiftest horses. This man, in trying to clear a hollow, was thrown and stunned against a stone.

In the ninth century Hugh Capet, suitor for a sister of Æthelstan, sent him a present of "running" horses with gold ornamental caparisons, but these were hacks. "Running" meant ambling.

FIRST NAMED RACEHORSES

The first racehorses we know by name were Arundel, an Arabian stallion imported from the King of Armony and owned by Sir Bevys of Hamptown, and Truncefice, an Arab mare from Bradmond, King of Damascus, which raced over a seven-mile course for £1,000 at the Court of King Edgar, in London, A.D. 957. The race was won by Arundel, and the mare, "Swiftest Truncefice," was celebrated in verse as a proverbially renowned

Pre-Roman British coin. Cunobelin Arab type
Note the palm branch

example of a brood mare 600 years later. Another Arundel belonging to Sir Alured de Vere beat a horse owned by the Prince of Wales, afterwards Richard II, being later sold to him for £20,000 in 1377. This was an incredible price in those days when horses were valued in pence and Richard, who was of a vindictive temper, may have nursed a grudge for he took the first opportunity of sending Sir Alured to Tower Hill, though horses were not mentioned in this connection. William the Conqueror brought over Normandy chargers and Spanish stallions.

At quem Romanis dudum non cognita tellus,
Insula ab undoso quæ tunditur undique ponto,

Nutrit equum, placidis gressu, facilisque lupatis
Ducier, haud dorso sessorem verbere vexat.

Early British horse, not a racing type

We are told that Richard II loved his horse Roan Barbary as an only son, and was furious when Bolinbroke took the horse to ride to Westminster to be crowned. He was a fine horse but had a bad temper except with King Richard.

"COURSERS" AND "RACES"

There was no *indigenous racing breed* in England. I have gone into the matter very thoroughly, and the more one studies the old records the more evident it becomes that the existence of a breed of racing mares of English *blood* or indeed an English breed of any sort is a fallacy as even the heavy horses were continental, and the idea has been based on a misconception of terms and on the principle that kittens born in a henhouse are chickens! The old word "Courser" was not a racehorse but a battle horse or heavy charger, a "charge" in a tourney being called a "course." It only very gradually changed

HORSMANSHIPP

To the Rt. Honble. Sr. John Skeffington _____ of Fisherwick in Staffordshire Bart.
Baron of Loughneagh, Viscount _____ Massereene, Custos Rotulorum &c.,
Governour of ye County of Londond___ and Towne of Coleraine & one of
the Lords of his Maties. most Honble _____ privy Councell of ye Kingdom of
Ireland &ca.
    This plate is humbly _____ dedicated by Richard Blome

to mean a horse for coursing hares and eventually became of modern use for a racehorse, and has now dropped out altogether. A "race" too, was originally neither a breed nor a competition in speed, but a stud, and a "race of coursers" was not a breed of racehorses but a stud of heavy cavalry horses. In the same way a "running horse" was an ambler, usually a travelling hack, but races were run occasionally between amblers whose legs were described as "moving in pairs together on the same side." The terms have rather naturally been misunderstood and quoted as evidence of an indigenous racing strain, but examination of contemporary stud books dated from the sixteenth and seventeenth centuries clearly proves that the "races of coursers" were studs of non-racing continental breeds and remained so till the advent of oriental importations.

TYPES—HUMAN AND EQUINE

Under Richard I racing was popular but suffered violent interruptions and vicissitudes. As I have already said, a curious fact is that the type of horse bred in different countries is often influenced by the human type which breeds it. Coarse, heavy Teutonic nations breed coarse horse stock. Refined, mercurial Latin nations like a refined, active horse, and the ultra refined, exquisitely modelled horses originated among the hot-blooded, hawk-eyed, slender-boned tribes of Arabia. England has been much influenced by the types of its reigning monarchs. Henry VIII, of massive bulk, made havoc of all racing types. His standard seems to have been based on his own Royal bulk plus armour, and he issued an edict slaughtering all light horses with the same ruthlessness as he slaughtered his wives. His ideal horse was a cart horse of colossal strength, unwieldy as it must have been in battle, but it seems to have been used as a sort of equine battering ram to ride down infantry. No doubt some of the hill ponies escaped only owing to the impossibility of catching them in the inaccessible mountains of Wales and Scotland, but all Crown lands were completely cleared. See p. 203.

The Scotch horses of the fourteenth century were described as small pacers, but Scottish laws prevented the development of horse racing.

Henry VIII was not always fat in youth, for he is described as very fond of tennis "at which game it was the prettiest thing in the world to see him play, his fair skin glowing through a shirt of the finest texture."

SIXTEENTH CENTURY

The subsequent weight of this ponderous monarch can be judged as the Venetian Ambassador in 1519 described that Henry VIII when hunting invariably rode several horses and never took the diversion without tiring eight or ten horses which he picked up as he went along. At Eltham the stud consisted of eighty-six coursers, hunting geldings, hobbies, Barbarics, stallions, mail-bottel, pack "Besage," and two stalking horses.

English horse was not a racing type

Heavy courser in England

In 1606 Lord Essex gave a gold snaffle as a prize. A Statute of 33 Henry VIII, C.5 enacted that Dukes and Archbishops should maintain seven trotting stallions for saddle, Marquises, Earls and Bishops five, and Viscounts and Barons five. Subjects with lower incomes had to keep two, and men whose wives wore silk gowns, French hoods or bonnets of velvet, or pearls and other ornaments were compelled under severe penalties to keep one trotting stallion. Evidently finery had its drawbacks. Englishmen were forbidden to sell any horse to Scotland or overseas.

In 1579 Prospero d'Osma scheduled the horses in the Royal Tutbury and Malmesbury studs as cavalry chargers (Coursers) and Jennets (small coursers or amblers). At Hampton Court there were Spanish Jennets and Barbaries (foreign horses). In 1598 Tutbury still had battle horses and amblers and Italian heavy chargers, but Queen Elizabeth had a separate racing stable of forty Arabs, Barbs and Turks at Greenwich. Her own personal stables consisted of geldings and that mysterious animal the "bottel" horse. Contemporary writers describe King Henry's stud as "a mixture of bastard breeds," Flemish roiles, Scottish nags, Jennets and battle chargers.

In 1620 the Malmesbury stock comprised Polish, Danish, Flemish, Spanish, Turkish and Arab mares. In 1624 the Royal Tutbury Stud had Polish mares, Jennets, battle horses and Arabs.

The whole aim of horse breeding was for war, not racing, the country being torn between the military dictators and the people who had a sneaking liking for sport.

Cartright's Admonition to Parliament, 1572, complains of the "Indecent hurrying through the morning prayers. The Minister pasteth it over as fast as he can gallop, because there are some games to be played in the afternoon as lying for the Whetstone, heathenish dancing for the ring, a beare or a bull to be baited or else a jackanapes to ride on horseback."

SIXTEENTH–SEVENTEENTH CENTURIES

Queen Elizabeth was a bloodthirsty huntress and loved to see the deer torn to pieces. Her huntsman Selwyn once gave her a wild-west show, jumping from his horse on to the back of the hunted stag, keeping his seat in spite of the animal's frantic efforts to throw him off and guiding it by a hunting knife gashing its neck, brought it round to the Queen and then plunged the knife into its throat so that it fell dead in a fountain of blood at her feet. This so delighted her that she favoured him greatly ever after. The incident is recorded on a monument at Walton-on-Thames.

Shakespeare's description suggests the better type of hack:

> *Round hoofed, short jointed, fetlocks shag and long,*
> *Broad breast, full eye, small head and nostrils wide.*
> *High crest, short ears, straight legs and passing strong,*
> *Thin mane, thick tail, broad buttock, tender hide.*

The horses of the seventeenth century were fed largely on hay and bread and thorough-bred stallions were given eggs and oysters!

Horse bread was made with beans, wheat and rye, kneaded with bran and water, and baked into loaves but was not to be given until a day old. Toast steeped in "muskadue" or oatmeal on the morning of a race and vinegar was spurted into the horse's nostrils.

Under Edward VI horse stealing was a capital offence without benefit of Clergy, and many extremely vexatious laws were in force. No Catholic could own a horse worth more than £5, whether his wife wore a velvet bonnet or not!

In spite of the colossal difficulties of transport countless numbers of Arabian and oriental horses were imported in the seventeenth and eighteenth centuries. They took months and indeed years to arrive. A list of named horses is published in *Thoroughbred Racing Stock*. The fame of Arabians as the fastest horses in the world had spread from Egypt where they had been racing for centuries. Travellers brought back glowing accounts of the flying "Kocklanis" (Kehilans) which commanded "intolerable" prices and no trouble was deemed too great to secure them. Imported under the name of "bred horses" (Kehilans, i.e. thoroughbreds) they were variously termed Arabians, Barbs, Barbarys, Turks and Turkomans. I have shown that Barbary was a term used loosely for horses from barbaric, i.e. foreign countries, not necessarily from the Barbary states as explained by Leo Africanus in the seventeenth century, and it is important to remember that a "Turk" always meant an Arab as there was never a Turkish native breed beyond pack animals and the Turkish Pashas always collected Arab horses by force or fraud or purchase. A Turk was an Arabian imported from or through the area then known as Turkey which comprised all Irak, Syria and North Arabia, and many Arabians imported via the North African trade route through Barbary to Europe were styled Barbs, as also were those imported from the *Arab* studs of the Sultans of Morocco and the various Beys and Pashas occupying Algerian and Tunisian areas. The Barb horses were, as I have said, a crossbred native pony of great merit for work but smaller than the Arab (called by the Duke of Newcastle "a mere Galloway" under fourteen hands) and of cosmopolitan origin, which enjoyed a reflected glory in Europe owing to its Arabian blood but despised in the East where all royal studs were Arabian and a Barb was considered a "kadish." The Godolphin Arabian evidently got confused by historians with Lord Godolphin's brown Barb, an apparently real Barb which appears in his stud book as a Barb, while the Godolphin Arabian is entered and referred to throughout as "his lordship's" Arabian. From other sources we know that his name was "Scham" and that he was of the Jilfan strain, misspelt "Guelph." This stud book is now in my possession, together with the only contemporary picture of the horse painted at seven years old.

SEVENTEENTH CENTURY

James I built stables at Newmarket and began breeding racehorses on a large scale with oriental blood including the Arabian horse Rupert. The Markhams were horse dealers and imported several Arabians which Markham praised in enthusiastic terms, but the one purchased by James I for £154 was a case of "give a horse a bad name and hang him." Some men and some animals get attached to some silly story and no one ever mentions the "Markham Arabian" without pouncing on the Duke of Newcastle's casual remark that he once saw him and did not think much of him, and that he ran badly, but the fact remains that he was the leading sire at the Royal Stud for many years and that the stud lists show thirty-nine of his progeny including his unbeaten son, Frisell, and his thirty-six descendants. The Duke of Newcastle was a High School enthusiast and was more concerned with demivolts and semilunes than with racing. He alternately extolled different breeds as the world's best horses, Spanish, Neapolitans and Barbs, according to which could spring highest and do it oftener than other breeds.

THE DUKE OF NEWCASTLE

His point of view is well known in his own words, "As poor as I was in those days I made shift to buy four Barbes, five Spanish and many Dutch horses all the most excellent horses that could be and among them a grey leaping horse, the most beautiful that I ever saw who went exceeding high and just in leaps without any help at all, as also upon the ground, and 'Terra à terra' beyond all other horses and he did look as if he had been above the Race of Horse kind."

He praised the Spanish horse as the best all round horse in the world and also the English mixed breeds, and he called Barbs and Spanish horses the gentlemen and princes of their kind. In fact his opinions could not be relied on for two minutes together. He frankly admitted he knew nothing about Arabs except that according to "many, many merchants, noblemen and gentlemen" their reputation was high and their price incredibly and even unbearably high, running from £500 to £3,000. "Therefore" said he "I recommend you to the Barb for breeding as even a Barb that is a jade will get better racers than any English horse." The Turkish horse is then praised as the best in the world but hard to procure and costing £150.

We may here note that some years later the Newcastle stud at Welbeck Abbey was entirely composed of the intolerably expensive Arab breed, with the Great Arabian and the Little Arabian as leading stallions.

The Duke of Savoy presented the Duke at the age of seventeen with a Spanish horse and he bought two Barbary horses for the circus for £200 and £100.

In 1644 at Hamburg he was very hard up and was always in fear of imprisonment for debt. He had left England with only £90 in his pocket and started a horse circus in Antwerp. He got eight horses and his wife wrote of his great affection for them and their devotion to him.

Having obtained credit he forsook his waggon for a coach and nine horses of Holsatian breed for which he paid £160. He presented seven of them to H.M. Queen Mother of

England and kept two for his own use and the Princess of Oldenburg gave him a Friesland horse. His return journey to England took six days and nights at sea.

THE BLAZING STAR

Meanwhile an alliance was projected between Prince Charles and the Infanta Maria of Spain. The Duke of Buckingham, otherwise known as the "Blazing Star," had been sent over with the Prince to negotiate with the Spanish Court. The Prince however made a

Spanish Andalusian, 1870

bad impression and the Princess considered him hardly appreciably more desirable than Lucifer himself and in their anxiety to get rid of the unwelcome heretic suitor (who was more concerned in extracting diamonds from his father to give to his mistress than in the matter of his proposed bride) the Spanish Court seems to have paid off Buckingham with ship loads of horses, fine linen and gifts of every kind, including camels, mules and bright-coloured birds.

SPANISH CONNECTIONS

The horses were Spanish harness horses and hackneys as well as oriental breeds. Buckingham seems to have distributed the coach horses among his friends at home as they do not appear in the Royal Stud lists, though there is some evidence that Charles kept a brood mare or two before his accession, and James continued to breed from the despised

Markham Arabian. Whatever were his merits or demerits however has no bearing on our present-day racing stock as the Royal Tutbury Stud was sold up and dispersed to the four winds in 1651 but certainly the Arabian breed suffered no discredit for all subsequent writers praised it as "the only breed to get racehorses."

King James frankly stated that the mere sight of the Great Horses bored him to tears owing to their clumsy appearance, so he must have been terribly bored when the Archduke sent him "a dozen gallant mares with foals, four horses and eleven stallions" all heavy Neapolitan Coursers which arrived at Greenwich Palace on April 3rd, 1605.

Racing and hunting fill the historical records. Races were run in Hyde Park in 1635 where thousands gathered and squandered their money. The chief race was the St. George's Cup. Riders, twelve stone—entrance stake, 2s. 6d. and the winner had to contribute 6s. 8d. or 3s. 4d. for the prisoners in North Gate jail! Neither the entrance fee nor the prisoner's dole appear excessive. We wonder what Lord Derby would have said if Wormwood Scrubs had claimed a bonus on Hyperion's Derby stakes!

In the days of James VI there was pony racing in Scotland, the chief race being won by Lord Hamilton's pony on Solway Sands. Silver bells were given at a Chester meeting and the winners had to deposit security for these annual trophies lest they should be tempted to make away with them. In 1624 the cup winner was allowed to retain the bell for the first time.

King James I preferred sportsmen to politicians and was foolish enough to say so. Everyone began gambling heavily and lost their estates to pay their debts. In 1605 the river Ouse was frozen over and Drake tells us that the King organized a race meeting on the ice, the course being from the Marygate Tower under the great arch of the Bridge to the Crane at Skelderten Postern—we are not told how the horses kept their feet.

PURITAN AGITATION

An anti-gambling fanatic called Hinde began a crusade against racing as the cause of profanity, cursing, brawling, quarrelling, bad example and idleness, but he produced little effect beyond bringing the profanity on to his own head.

JAMES AND SPORTSMEN

James rebuked the spoil sports, declared games and dancing lawful, and established Public races especially at Newmarket. Before this, horse matches between owner-riders over any convenient stretch of turf had been the chief form of racing. Superstition was rampant and sick animals had a wretched time being exorcized for evil spirits, one sick foal being left out all night to die in a snowstorm to get rid of the devil, and the owner thanked God that its satanic influence had been removed! Witches prescribed nostrums and in Ireland a wall-eye was considered an evil fate. James laughed at superstition and laughed also at his own accident when after a lively dinner he rode alongside the New

Neapolitan "courser" (charger)

Le Superbe Cheval De Spane.

"The superb horse of Spain" (eighteenth century)

River and was flung off on to the ice, disappearing in the crash head first. Sir Richard Goring seeing boots sticking out of the river rushed to the rescue, and, in spite of much water swallowed, the King mounted and rode back to bed and he rewarded his rescuer by something more substantial than handshaking. He founded a Royal Stud at Tutbury, chiefly composed of Arabians, Frisell, an unbeaten son of the Markham Arabian, and a number of orientally bred mares.

He wrote a long treatise in which he praised games on horseback and the noble sport of hunting, but called shooting with guns and arrows a "thievish sport."

MORE PROTESTS AGAINST RACING

In the reign of Charles I, Sir Edward Harwood presented a petition in forcible language warning the King against the decline of Great Horses, saying that if 2,000 were required at short notice they would not be procurable. He went on to point out that the French horses were in every way superior to ours, and could rout ours in battle on even terms, inflicting heavy loss. The King feigned surprise and asked why, and Sir Edward pointed out that our horses were being neglected for racing and hunting, the landed proprietors devoting all their time to breeding these instead of essential war horses.

Charles I said he would take steps to remedy this scandalous state of things, professing to be surprised and shocked, but nothing was done, for racing was by now beginning to get a serious hold and we find General Lord Fairfax, in great fear that the supremacy of the cavalry in war would suffer, protesting vainly against "the over-valued pigmy baubles," much as Herodotus declaimed against the "pampered jades of Asia."

PAMPERED JADES AND PIGMY BAUBLES

In a lengthy treatise dated 1644 he made it clear that all breeds large and small were of foreign origin, such native horses "as might be called English" being of a slow common kind, and even these had continental blood. Being essentially a cavalry man, and judging horses by avoirdupois weight, he extols the large slow foreign heavy breeds for war and deplores the recent craze for oriental racehorses as not comparable to the powerful armour carriers, and calls them "over-valued pigmy baubles" only useful for the despicable pleasure of racing and no good for heavy armour; yet even he cannot resist advising a cross of Barbary to warm up the phlegmatic local stock. It really was not surprising that the non-military horsemen should have got tired of this perpetual influx of cart horses due to the influence of Henry VIII and the heavy armour of the time and turned to the Arab, whose racing reputation was already established as early as 1300 B.C. It is amusing to think that the horse which has given the name of Fairfax an eternal fame in the General Stud Book was one of these identical "over-valued pigmy baubles," the "Helmsley Turk," otherwise the Fairfax Morocco Barb (an Arab from Morocco).

The upheavals which cost Charles I his head upset horse breeding and finally scattered all the previous racing stock. Sir John Fenwick, stud master to Charles I, with a salary of £200 a year, possessed more rare racehorses than anyone in England, and almost all the racehorses in England were from his stud and breeding and all were Arab and Oriental. The Parliamentarians confiscated his stud in 1648 to the great grief of his stud groom.

James D'Arcy's stud also disappeared in the same way; the Tutbury Royal Stud was put up for sale. An inventory was begun in 1643 and finished in 1649, which seems to have been rather a prolonged process.

TUTBURY ROYAL STUD DISPERSED

The stud was valued at £1,982 and included the Villiers Arabs imported by James I, also two twelve-year-old mares and thirty-three colts by Frisell,[1] thirteen of which were grey. Sir A. Hardrigg, Col. James and Lord Thomond bought, or were given, some of the Tutbury horses but they were never traced in the search made by Charles II. The sale was finally completed on January 6th, 1651, when the Council of State handed over the money to Mr. Frost. All the colts had been sold on July 3rd, 1650.

Six of the best horses went to the Duke of Ormond in Ireland but were apparently wasted as though he improved the local Kilkenny stock he seems to have failed to breed racehorses. He crossed Galloway pony mares with Spanish, Arabian and English mixtures; when he left Ireland he appointed Sir W. Fowler his manager and wrote in April 1668, "On Monday next a groom will go hence with an Arabian horse for a stallion for this year but he must cover only the largest and strongest mares. The Spanish horse I had from Lord Dungannon gets no likely colts yet he may serve to help the neighbourhood to mend the ordinary breed." Later on he handed the stud over to his son Lord Arran saying that he had been so unlucky or so cheated with horses and horse breeding that he was resolved to be troubled with them no more. The O'Briens seem to have made more use of some others as they got a certain reputation as racehorse breeders.

Cromwell was an enthusiastic sportsman but he was obliged to humour the fanatics by temporarily forbidding racing, cock-fighting and bull-baiting. Horse racing was prohibited from February 26th to August 1654 because of the threatened Royalist rising at the next race meetings, and again in 1659. Every racecourse was closed, thousands were thrown out of work and owners of racehorses had to sell for what their horses would fetch. (It is notable that this has happened more than once in America with disastrous results.) The prohibition included hunting, hawking and football.

CROMWELL FOUNDS ORIENTAL STUD

The setback was only temporary for we find him taking energetic steps to import Arabian horses and his buff-coated Ironsides without armour soon superseded the Great Horse in battle.

[1] Son of Markham Arabian.

Cardinal Mazarin presented Lockhart, his Ambassador in France, with four exceedingly fine Arab horses for the saddle which Lockhart said were the finest he ever saw and that the Lord his master would be mightily pleased with them (*Thurloe State Papers*, Vol. V). He maintained regal establishments of huntsmen, stud masters, falconers and gamekeepers, and owned the White Turk, called after his stud groom Place, who afterwards stole the "Coffin mare" and concealed her from the Royalist agents on Charles II's return.

Soon Cromwell disregarded the Puritans altogether and at one crisis in his life, when a deputation from Parliament visited him on the matter of the crown he kept it waiting two hours while he inspected a "Barbarie" horse in the garden! He swept out all the monumental "destriers" for he knew that with the passing of plate armour we had a surfeit of the Flanders breed and needed the fineness of the East. Every agent on the Mediterranean shores had a roving commission to buy Arabian horses from Aleppo and the best Eastern horses available, for Arabian horses had been famous *as racehorses* in Syria and Egypt for over a thousand years. This is a point which has never been understood by those who write on racing history but was well known at that time. I make no excuse for repeatedly insisting on it.

The following is one of many typical contemporary letters from Mr. Longland, Cromwell's agent at Leghorn, to Mr. Secretary Thurloe (June, 1655. *Thurloe State Papers*, Vol. III, 526):

> "I now have advice from my friend at Naples that His Highness commission for the two horses and four mares is completed, I hope to His Highness full content; my next may bring you an invois or factor of theyr cost and charges; as also a description of each; their race or pedigree, collour, age, height, quallity and condition. . . . I gav order to the man I sent over for Tripoly to redeem the English captives, to bring a mare thence, which he did; but 'twas so small a thing, gentile and thin, the legs little bigger than a hynd's, that I thought not worth your acceptance; for a good mare to breed should be as well tall and large, as clean limb'd and handsome. I know not yet whether I shall speed in the commission I gave to Aleppo for a horse, but if I do I am confident the world has not better horses than that place affords."

The promised letter cannot be found.

Richard Cromwell also favoured horse racing and sport and the origin of the modern thoroughbred racehorse begins with Oliver Cromwell for on Charles II's restoration he found the new foundation material ready to hand, and within an hour of his return to England had seized Cromwell's Arab stud. On May 26th, he ordered that the Sergeant-at-Arms "forthwith seize all the goods of such persons as sate as Judges upon the late King and that the seven horses of Oliver Cromwell, said to be the best in England and such other horses as are seized of or belonging to such persons be carried to the Mews for the service of His Majesty." (*Parliamentary Intellygencer*, 1660.)

PRINCE CHARLIE AS A RIDER

It is not generally known how good a horseman was Charles II. In 1637 the Duke of Newcastle had been appointed Governor to Prince Charlie (later Charles II) with special orders to teach him to be a good rider which was not difficult as he was a natural horseman and looked as if he had been born in the saddle, graceful, strong and good tempered. He

Snowball, Darcy White Turk   [*Milbanke Collection*

never dragooned a horse or ill-treated it, and there was a magic understanding between himself and his horse, and he never over-rode a horse. He was particular to have horses with good shoulders and quarters.

At the age of ten he could ride the most intractable horses and leap them over obstacles with a skill which made him the centre of attraction as a master rider and he would wager to ride any horse brought to him, even barebacked. The Duke who never spared criticism was intensely proud of his pupil.

Of Prince Charlie he says, "When I was his Governor I had the honour to be the first to sate him on horseback and did instruct him in the Art of Horsemanship. It is a great satisfaction to me to make mention here of the joy I had then to see that His Majesty made my Horses goe better than any Italian or French riders (who had often rid them) would do and hear him say that there are very few that know horses; which was knowingly said and wisely judged of His Majesty."

[old J. Sartorius, c. 1684

Charles II, Royal mare

It is not therefore surprising that after a vain search for the vanished Tutbury horses he set his agents to work in earnest. He realized that it was not only necessary to import stallions, but that mares were just as important, and it was the Arab mares brought from the Levant (the tradition of whose purchase still lingered in Arabia a century ago) which from 1660 onwards were known ever after as Royal Mares, together with their progeny. They appear in John Cheny's Contemporary Stud Book, 1727, and were incorporated in the Oriental section of the subsequent publication of Weatherby's General Stud Book for one hundred years. The mares were evidently obtained from the Levant Company organized by Louis XIV's Minister Colbert who reorganized French horse breeding from top to bottom. This Company was stationed in Cairo and other Eastern ports and had a contract to supply the King with ten Arabians of the highest class annually—these and their progeny were ever afterwards called Royal. They were stamped with a Crown and an L on the thigh. Colbert's brother, Charles Colbert, was closely connected with Charles II, being his ambassador, and Evelyn's diary describes his magnificent arrival at Whitehall in a richer coach than had ever before been seen. Both brothers and Lord Winchilsea were co-directors of the company. It will be noted that King Charles' Royal mares from the Levant were described by Cheny in almost the same words and were undoubtedly from the same source at the same time. The painting of one of them, 1684 or earlier, has a background of palm trees and pyramids. King Charles kept large studs and spent colossal sums yearly on importing oriental horses. In addition to enormous sums paid to his agents the annual fixed sum spent on horses was £16,640, which his enemies denounced as extravagant beyond belief. But this was a mere bagatelle to the floating expenditure. He rivalled Sultan El Naseri in his determination to get the best at all costs. King Charles rode in races himself carrying all before him.

Sir Robert Carr wrote March 24th, 1675, that His Majesty had ridden three heats and a course and won the plate by horsemanship as all four were hard run and closely contested. He was fond of hunting as well and never lost his nerve over a country, but he preferred racing and used to entertain all the jockeys to dinner.

Charles was also a finished "Whip" and encouraged his nobles to drive their own horses instead of using postilions and advocated breeding coach horses of high quality.

DEVOTION TO VICE

Thomas Shadwell, a playwright, *c.* 1660, alludes to the great wave of passionate devotion to vices of various kinds in England during this reign when the talk was exclusively of horses, cocks and dogs and cards. Lord Campden's son, Mr. Noel, lost £2,500 at tennis in one day to Lord Rich (afterwards Carnarvon).

PRIZES FOR RACING

The racing prizes which began under James I with bells were changed under Charles II to cups and jewels, while hunter plates were introduced by Queen Anne who founded Ascot in 1712. At Chester the original prize was a wooden ball embellished with flowers given on Shrove Tuesday annually. A silver bell value 3s. 6d. was substituted in the thirty-first year of King Henry VIII. Under Charles II the Sheriff of Chester offered a piece of silver plate. The High Sheriff borrowed a Barbary horse from Sir Thomas Middleton and won it himself barring the horses of Sir Philip Egerton and Mr. Massey from competing, saying they had arrived too late for entry! A bit of sharp practice which caused great ill-feeling.

The general horse stock of the country was described as a mixture of "all the horses of all the Nations," and as having degenerated through running wild and uncared for on the moors and in the forests at the mercy of any jade pony or cart stallion or jackass. The mules so bred would, of course, come to a natural end, but the heterogeneous horse mixtures were condemned as a disgrace to the country.

Dr. Fuller writes in 1662: "Our English horses have in a mediocre degree all the necessary good properties—neither so slight as the Barb, so slovenly as the Flemish nor so fiery as the Hungarian, nor so airy as the Spanish Jennets, nor so earthly as those in the low countries and generally all German horses. For stature and strength of middle size and are both seemly and serviceable, and while the seller praiseth them too much and the buyer too little the unbiassed bystander will give them due commendation." He continued that Yorkshire bred the best by keeping them on steep and stony ground, but there is no word of racing merit concerning the Yorkshire stock and beyond commending their good feet compared with those of horses bred on marshy fens, they seem to have been good serviceable working horses, his view being that horses were bred for cavalry and he admits that all the mixtures, good or bad, were of foreign origin.

LANGBAINE, 1685.

"First, therefore, I advise you to buy either an Arabian horse (if you can procure him), a Spaniard, a Turk or a Barb for your stallion that is well shaped to beautify your race and well marked to agree with most men's opinions."

To begin with the Arabian he quotes the high prices: "Notwithstanding their great value and the difficulty in bringing them from Scanderoon to England by sea, yet by the care and at the charge of some breeders in the North the Arabian horse is no stranger to those parts. Where Persons who have the curiosity may I presume at this day see some of the Race if not a true Arabian stallion." This seems to have been the origin of the reputation enjoyed by the "breed of the North."

He goes on to quote the Duke of Newcastle's praise of the Spanish horse for all-round perfection, whether for manège, pad, hunting or running, and that the best are from Cordova, but he adds that "though he do prove an Extraordinary good horse by the time he arrives at your own home he will likewise prove an extraordinary dear one." The prices fetched are given as £300 to £1,000.

"The Turk" he says "is about equal to the Spanish in beauty but somewhat odd shaped, his head being somewhat like a camel," this seems to indicate a concave profile, "he hath excellent eyes, a thin neck excellently risen. They never amble but trot very well and are accounted at this present better stallions than Barbs for gallopers.

"Some merchants affirm that there cannot be a more noble and diverting sight to a lover of horses than to walk into pastures near Constantinople about sailing time when he may see many hundred gallant horses tethered and every horse has his attendant or keeper with his little tent plac'd near him to lie in that he may look to him and take care to shift him to fresh grass as occasion requires.

"The price of a Turk is commonly £100 or £150 a horse and when bought it is difficult to get a pass.

74

"The Barb is little inferior in beauty but too slender and ladylike to breed from, with no action, and in the North they prefer Turks and Spaniards, but he is sinewy and excellently winded and good for a course if not over weighted.

"The Mountain Barbs are best belonging to the Allarbes who will not part with them except to the Prince of their Band. It is only the ordinary sort which are to be met with commonly in the hands of English Nobility and Gentry, and they may be bought in Languedoc and Provence in France for £40 or £50. In Barbary they may be bought for £30."

This account shows the difference between the horses of Morocco (Mountain or Desert Arabian Barbs) and the ordinary sort commonly imported to England and it is just this which makes the difference between the Arabian *Moroccan* Barbs of our stud book fame and the native cheap ruck of imported horses which could not by any possibility have impressed themselves on posterity. We do however still see the underbred Hispano = Barb head in the inferior types of thoroughbred chasers.

Buffon, 1755, demonstrates the process of producing racers clearly and prophetically saying that "in order to breed good horses foreign ones are essential, 1st Arabs, 2nd Barbs and Andalusians, failing these use fine English horses as these are derived from the former and have *not much degenerated* from them.

"Arabs are the finest in the world, Barbs are commoner. The Spanish have thick necks with much mane, head rather large and convex, long ears, thick shoulders, broad chest, big round quarters, narrow blocked-up feet, fiery eye and noble bearing. Horses of pomp and ceremony. English horses of the best kind are like Arabs and Barbs, they are big at *least 14.2, some in fact reaching 15 hands but they are not as good as the Arabs being more suitable for hunting than racing*." The abnormal height of 15 hands is amusing. English writers say much the same.

EIGHTEENTH CENTURY

Osmer, a veterinary surgeon, wrote in 1761: "Arabian horses and their descendants when properly chosen are preferable to all others whether you are to be carried a mile or a thousand, let the weight be what it will, nor have other horses such true courage or calmness of temper, nor can they bear fatigue with equal fortitude as our *severe discipline of training* will in some measure help to show." He then draws a comparison between them.

"Now it has here been allowed that the Arabians are the best kind of horses we know of from whom it can be expected to breed a racer or in other words the most perfect horse. Arabian horses being better constituted for action than other horses do by means hereof excel all others.

"The sinew of the mountain (desert) Arab is like a bar of iron hence the degree of difference between him and some other Asiatick horses and all other horses of the world. But we understand so little about the matter that these very horses are called weak cat-legged things and our great coarse brutes with hairy legs, thick skins and lax fibres, are considered much the strongest. . . . The attachment of some men to what is commonly called 'a good English horse' is as absurd as the objection of sportsmen to blood, i.e. cat-legged things.

"As to Barbs I mean those only which I have seen, all have a particular cast or turn in their hinder parts from which they may in general be easily known by the observant eye." His eye for this drooping quarter makes his description of the Godolphin Arab's wonderful loins all the more valuable as evidence of his Arabian conformation.

FOUNDATION OF THE JOCKEY CLUB

It is interesting to note that our highly aristocratic English Jockey Club started as an anything but respectable coffee house called the "Star and Garter" where all the fast titled young men congregated to bet and drink. Dukes and earls and minor nobles gambled, quarrelled and fought and it was here that Lord Byron's great-uncle quarrelled with and killed Chaworth for which he was brought to trial. Good cooking, expensive wines and high prices were the rule. The actual Jockey Club began as such in 1753, and two-year-old racing was sanctioned in 1770. The club showed off its authority by warning the Prince Regent off the Turf on account of his jockey Chifney's riding of Escape.

The family of Tattersall owed their name and fortune to Highflyer to whom they built a memorial mansion called Highflyer Hall. They started as unsuccessful newspaper proprietors and very successful auctioneers, and the firm holds the world's most famous and wealthy business as such, which yearly increases in fame as prices rise to unprecedented heights.

The twelfth Earl of Derby founded the Epsom Derby and Oaks in 1780, but it was many a long day before the Earls of Derby ever won the race themselves. The late Lord Derby has however amply made up for lost time.

NO OBJECTION TO FOUL RIDING

Going back to its inception, crossing and jostling were allowed as part of the sport if no special agreement was made to the contrary, and they were not prohibited till 1792, amid violent opposition from Denis O'Kelly who boasted he could drive his opponents off the course by sheer force and was highly incensed at the restriction of his activities. Yearlings were raced in 1786 and continued to be raced for ninety years.

LONG COURSES

In the early eighteenth century, races varied from four-mile heats to twelve miles and the horses did prodigies in the way of stamina, three four-mile heats in one day were quite ordinary.

There has always been a recurring anti-racing element which associates racing with the devil and all his angels. To some people a pack of cards, a bottle of whisky or a sweepstake ticket are the emblems of degradation and depravity, and a sweepstake ticket is still taboo in England, which will not even allow a sweep to support its own hospitals. It is something of a miracle that racing has survived.

The Duke of York, son of George III, who was rebuked for driving to Newmarket on a Sunday replied with a spice of humour that he always carried a Bible and Prayer Book with him in the carriage.

SPORT TRIUMPHS

Love of sport had triumphed. All the efforts of military men and Puritans failed to stop racing and in 1755 the "Over-valued Pigmy Baubles" had established themselves as the world's only racing breed—the "bred" or thoroughbred horse destined to become England's finest achievement—the horses whose magical speed has electrified the world.

ORIGIN OF THE WORD THOROUGHBRED

The English thoroughbred is now called English because of his long residence on English soil and the skill with which he has been developed by English breeders who have every reason to be proud of having produced the world's most famous racing miracle. He was at first called only Thoroughbred because of his oriental origin, the word thoroughbred being a literal translation of the Arabic "Kehilan" which is the generic term for the Arabian breed and was introduced to England by the first importers. A "bred horse" was an Arabian horse of pure descent and the imported mares were sometimes distinguished from the ones foaled in England by the word "Natural."

The exasperating Arab custom of not giving a horse a name, but naming him after his successive owners or places of residence, was also introduced into England and has been a source of infinite confusion to historians. Mercifully the Darley, Godolphin and Byerley sires did not constantly change ownership but the Alcock Arabian did and went by no less than ten different names, notably Dorchester Turk, Brownlow Turk, Akaster (Ancaster) Turk or Arabian having been owned by the Duke of Ancaster.

The Darcy White Turk or Sedbury Arabian was an Arab imported from Aleppo and the Darcy Yellow Turk, also called the Chestnut Arabian, was imported from Damascus. Both exercised an enormous influence on modern pedigrees and we know their names, shown in the Milbanke collection as Snowball and Orange. The Leedes Arabian exceeds the Darley Arabian in the bulk of pedigrees.

Every Thoroughbred in the world is descended in direct male line from one of four oriental sires, the Darley Arabian, Godolphin Arabian, and Byerley Turk, the Helmsley Turk, and from a number of Oriental mares, and all the grey thoroughbreds are descended through some twenty-six generations in direct, though not exclusively male, line for over

77

two hundred and fifty years from the grey Alcock Arabian. Moreover, these pedigrees are saturated with other Arabians which quite overwhelm even the Darley Arabian's colossal

Byerley Turk

Old Morocco Barb (Helmsley Turk, Fenwick Arabian)

influence when taken in bulk, notably the Darcy, Lister and Leedes Arabians, and above all the super saturating influence of the Arabian mare "Old Bald Peg" to the tune of hundreds of thousands of repeats. Blue Peter alone has 252,383 of these to 40,503 of the Darley Arabian. There is in fact no evidence on paper of anything whatever except Oriental

78

Leedes Arabian. This picture is miscalled "Leedes Son of the Arabian,"
but the marking identifies it as the Arabian himself

Dormouse, son of the Godolphin Arabian

blood. The living breed, however, shows obvious reversions to some unrecognized and unrecorded bars sinister of non-racing cold blood. As all the Bruce Lowe taproots are accounted for, the only unexplained reversion must be attributed to something outside his calculations and inevitably regarded as blots on the escutcheon, there being no known possible sources of origin unless we discard the stud book altogether and are blind to the difference between hot blood and cold. Otherwise we have a pure Oriental pedigree. Bruce Lowe did not trace his forty-three taproots to their ultimate origins and if this is done they can be reduced to only eighteen, as the main bulk of them trace back to the same sources. This is sound logical deduction, but we have more than this for the contemporary descriptions and pictures of the horse stock of England are legion, and we cannot get away from the fact that for four centuries all writers unanimously described the so-called True English Horse as a coarse, non-racing, heavy-headed horse of all work for "service, travel, and burden," and the Arabian as the "Sole and only breed for getting racers." When they describe the English horse he turns out to be entirely foreign, Continental, Neapolitan, Flemish, Spanish, Danish, in fact anything but English.

GREY COLOUR TRANSMITTED FOR TWO HUNDRED AND FIFTY YEARS

There are certain horses which stand out from the rest in the world's memory, either for their performance or their progeny though some of these have had astonishingly little opportunity of achieving fame. Who would have thought, for instance, that a grey Arabian horse which some two hundred and fifty years ago passed from hand to hand, known only as somebody's Arabian or Turk, would transmit his grey colour in unbroken sequence to this present day—a colour curiously allied to the speed which has brought it into everlasting fame through the Tetrarch, Tetratema, Mumtaz Mahal and Mahmoud. He served very few known mares but the Akaster Turk mares must be included with his progeny as Akaster is an obvious misprint for Ancaster, originally often spelt Ankaster, the Duke of that name having been one of his owners, the horse appearing as leading stallion in his stud book, whereas Akaster does not elsewhere occur and "Turk" was indiscriminately used for Arabs. Even so his progeny were remarkably scarce and must have been of outstanding merit to survive through two-and-a-half centuries. The tenacity of the colour is all the more remarkable because in some cases almost every generation the grey was mated to bay, brown or chestnut; and as grey once lost can never reappear this overriding of other colours shows a tenacious hereditary power.

DARLEY ARABIAN

Then, who would have imagined that the bay colt with "a blaze something of the largest" purchased as a yearling at Aleppo by Thomas Darley and sent to England three years later with the pious hope that he would not be too much disliked in England, would have seven thousand brood mares registered in our last volume of the General Stud Book, all saturated with his blood. We know that he was of the Managhi strain but he too had no name but his owner's. He was just the Darley Arabian and the hope that he would not be much disliked reads amusingly in view of his subsequent world-wide celebrity.

GODOLPHIN ARABIAN

In the case of the Godolphin Arabian we do at any rate know that his name was Sham, which is Arabic for Damascus, but here again it is the name of the place he came from, i.e. Damascus Arabian. We know that he was of the Jilfan strain (anglicized Guelf) and that his only contemporary picture done from life, named, signed and dated by J. Wootton when the horse was seven years old, shows a pure Arabian type with tapering head, small ears, a large full eye, level quarters and high set tail. All other pictures, especially the so-called Morier, so widely disseminated, must be ignored as they were posthumous and (there being no photography in those days) purely imaginary. There is not the remotest ground for the modern suggestion that he was a Barb. I have Lord Godolphin's original picture by Wootton and the original MSS. of Mr. Coke (Lord Leicester) and Lord Godolphin's stud books in which he is entered as an Arabian throughout. He was registered as such in the General Stud Book and remained so for 133 years till as late as 1891 the General Stud Book for the first time produced a suggestion that his Arabian origin was in dispute and that an unspecified portrait favoured his being a Barb. As a cat is mentioned as appearing in the picture the horse seems to have been the spurious animal with the hook nose and lop ears in the Morier picture which was prophetically inscribed by the artist with the names and wins of his progeny dated long after his death, conclusively proving that it was not done from life. A fancy copy of still later date has no more claim to accuracy.

The fact that the Godolphin horse was Lord Godolphin's leading stallion and was painted by the leading artist, J. Wootton, disposes of the nonsense that he was teaser to Hobgoblin who was not at stud but racing till 1734, four years after Roxana's death. In the Godolphin stud book the Arabian was mated to Roxana in the ordinary stud routine and Hobgoblin was never leading stallion. The whole story of the battle with Hobgoblin for Roxana and the story of the water cart were disseminated by the crazy novelist, Eugene Sue, the anonymous "frenchman" who is quoted in the General Stud Book. He got the idea from a Spanish fairy tale story of the seventeenth century, and his reputation for veracity in France was "romance first and to hell with facts" (*"tant pis pour les faits"*). His fantastic "Penny Dreadful" romance should have warned Messrs. Weatherby against taking him seriously.

How Lord Godolphin's genuine picture was overlooked until I discovered it is a mystery, though Lord Godolphin Osborne did once mildly suggest that if his picture was right all the others were hopelessly incorrect.

In the same issue of the General Stud Book, 1891, there is a further statement that the Darley Arabian was probably a Turk or Syrian. This shows ignorance, both of facts and of breeds. There is no such thing as a Turk or Syrian breed—in old days both meant Arabs and now they both indicate mongrels. Here again there has been a confusion in the pictures, as the genuine original reproduced by Pick in 1822 as being at Aldby is

The Alcock Arabian

now in America, and the one now there, so often reproduced, is certainly not the same. Henry Darley stated that it is only a copy. It is done in a similar pose but is a crude painting looking like a cardboard hunter. The Darley Arabian is the most famous of three out of the four foundation sires from one of which every thoroughbred in the world is descended in direct male line. The Godolphin Arabian and the Byerley (misspelt Byerly) Turk were the other two. But none of these approach the Leedes Arabian or Sultan (sire of Old Bald Peg) and the Darcy, Helmsley and Lister "Turks" and Old Bald Peg herself, whose repeated crosses in the pedigrees taken in bulk represent a staggering total. All these were Arabs as their pictures clearly show, and the word Morocco stamps any horse from there as Arabian from the Arab tribes settled there.

Tregonwell's Natural (wrongly called Barb) Arabian mare
Copied by Lady Anne King from a picture at Halnaby

Darcy Yellow "Turk"

ECLIPSE

In considering Thoroughbred history so many speculations have been based on the so-called skeleton of Eclipse that it is necessary to point out that any conclusion based on it cannot be relied on as its authenticity is extremely doubtful. At one time there were several "authentic" skeletons of Eclipse and a bewildering number of "undoubtedly genuine" hoofs being hawked about for sale entailing a centipedal ancestry! and the

[by kind permission of Major Paget

Lister Turk

skeleton now in the British Museum has no more claim to authenticity than the others. In fact its component parts lay about for some hundred years in cupboards with other horses' bones and do not correspond with the careful measurements made from the horse's skeleton immediately after death by the veterinary surgeon, St. Bel. Its identity was questioned at the time of its first appearance as a saleable commodity in the hands of Bracy Clark, who took twenty years to palm it off on the public. Moreover it was later in an incomplete and decayed state and reconstructed. Professor Pycraft experienced great surprise at the coarse texture of the bone, saying it did not suggest that of a Thorough-bred horse. Judging by the state of things when I once visited the skeleton department during a spring cleaning, some years ago, no man on earth could have identified the specimens afterwards heaped as they were loose in drawers, unnumbered and unlabelled, or scattered about anyhow together with human skulls and bits of whales! It shattered my belief in Eclipse as a historical relic. The department has since been reorganized.

84

THE DARLEY ARABIAN

BRUCE LOWE

An Australian, Bruce Lowe, adopting the Arab system of counting the strain by the female line, traced every thoroughbred back to one of forty-three foundation mares which he numbered according to the numerical superiority of their descendants in classic races. They really number only eighteen as I have found that the rest trace back to previously numbered mares. The theory is interesting but obviously an unsound breeding guide as a pedigree of twenty-six generations represents 134,217,726 units. It is in fact a mathematical absurdity when we consider that our pedigrees are now nearing twenty-nine generations which equals 536,870,912 units, so that one mare on the bottom line represents only 29 to 53,670,883 against her! She would be quite negligible unless incessantly repeated, as in the case of the Arabian mare No. 6 Old Bald Peg, which swamps the pedigrees even when not on the bottom line, just as the Leedes Arabian and others eclipse the male line sires in the bulk of ancestry.

Further, in calculating the number of classic winners from each taproot, no account is taken of the vast bulk of identically numbered losers, thus invalidating the whole theory.

VALUE OF BLOOD

Latterly there has been an increasing tendency to confound location with blood. This unscientific principle would entail the conclusion that the Ethiopian can change his skin and the leopard its spots by sheer lapse of time and change of habitat. Eternity would not do it in breeding livestock. Personally I am not prepared to argue that black is white. Blood is blood and always will remain so, a fact which is of incalculable value to horse breeders, and forms the one immutable law on which it is really safe to rely.

The theory of modification and alteration of a species by environment or employment independent of individual artificial selection is negatived by the now accepted fact that acquired characteristics cannot be inherited. Underfeeding may stunt stock to an unnatural size. Force-feeding may develop its latent powers prodigiously but no amount of cropping ears or docking tails has any effect on progeny, nor can wounds, blemishes or fractures be inherited. Pre-natal impression may produce distortions by a shock causing arrested development of the foetus before birth but with all due respect to young Jacob and his rods, no mare will produce striped foals by being kept in sight of zebras, or spotted ones by looking at leopards or cows. It is certainly a fortunate provision of nature that this is so, otherwise stock breeding would be a disorganized gamble of accidents. Telegony, i.e. the influence of a previous sire on a mare's subsequent progeny, is also disproved. Reversion to an ancestor is of course a fact and quite unpredictable in its incidence, and some characters once lost never revert at all, notably the grey colour and any colour which has been lost in breeding chestnuts.

The theories were amusingly reviewed by Professor Ewart's daughter Jessica as a child in 1895:

Thoroughbred brood mare and foal, bred at Burton Park Stud

A French idea of British behaviour when Fille de l'Air won the Oaks

"Last night the two great authorities on Telegony and Reversion Sir W. F. and W. T. dined with us and they had all the old arguments over again and ended in exactly the same position as they had begun. It is a subject in which Scientists never agree and they argue each others heads off. Some declare Telegony and Reversion go hand in hand; others wont hear of any resemblance. Others again swear that Telegony is simply imagination and quote the Bible story of Jacob and the rods, and others say it is simply throwing back to a far away ancestor. Some take one side and some the other and nothing will make them alter their opinion. The question was neatly summed up by Milne the Stud Groom in strict confidence: 'They Scientific gents is that obstinate there's no sense in argyfying with them and that's a fac. If a foal prodooces stripes or no stripes each claims his Theoriums proved'."

After listening to all this learned conversation, discreetly sitting in a corner one evening, Jess Ewart repaired to the kitchen next day to explain things to Cook. "Good morning Cook, she said, do you back Telegony or Reversion, or Jacobs speckled cattle?" Cook replied with great dignity "Well Miss since you ask me I dont go for to back neither o' they horses with their outlandish names, but Jacobs speckled kine is different as its in the Bible Miss, but howsomnever its not got nothing to do wi horse racing and such like ungodliness."

After Jess had explained that it wasn't a bet and expounded the scientific theories, Cook proclaimed herself strongly in favour of Reversion as she minded well how Mr. and Mrs. Janny Broon of good old Bamfshire stock "perdooced a baby girl as was black" and it turned out her great-grandmother was a Hindoo. "My!! Mr. Broon went on something awful and said as Mrs. B. had deceived him and boasted about her grandmother being a great Spanish beauty and the poor lass replied she had always been told so and how was she to know contrariwise. Anyhow the child turned oot an awful wee devil as vicious and greedy an the biggest liar and thief" . . . so of course she backed Reversion every time! Milne supplemented it by: "Well Miss it always gives them clever Scienteefic folk somat tae arg bargy aboot an its a wise child that kens its ain father." From which it may be deduced that he held a fourth independent theory of direct inheritance and no nonsense about it. In fact his attitude was much that of the Irishman when the Scientist's wife produced a black baby owing, said the Scientist, to the prenatal terror of having been chased by a blackamoor, and whose dry comment was "Faith yer honour and are ye sure he didn't *catch her?*"

THE BLOOD FACTOR

The physical blood factor is the unchangeable element which cannot be got rid of except by mixing it with alien blood after which the ramifications of heredity become unpredictable with any certainty.

Medical science has proved the enormous importance of blood groups and these differences are insisted on by Dr. Brent (lecturer in forensic medicine at Charing Cross

87

Hospital). "These blood groups," he says, "are more fundamental than any racial characteristic yet recognized." It has been proved that certain blood groups are antagonistic so that transfusion may cause death. They cannot be reconciled, thereby demonstrating the futility of any theory of automatic nationalization of a type by transference to another country. Blood is not only a phrase, it is a fact. It cannot and does not change with environment or climate any more than the bony structure of a convex or concave skull. A negro remains a negro however many generations he may be bred in Europe. Even the progeny bred from allergic blood groups are very adversely affected.

THE NATIVE ENGLISH MARE'S-NEST

In the last few years there have been attempts to minimize the Arabian influence in our pedigrees, and these must be corrected, for not only has Arabian blood been the only source of speed but it has overmastered an alloy of cold slow blood on the foundation line.

We have outlived the strangely inverted mirage of a mythical bay breed with star and bracelets as the progenitor of an Arab which wasn't an Arab but a Barb from Libya. We have duly squashed the unjustifiable doubt thrown on the Godolphin as "probably a Barb" (after a hundred years' registration as an Arabian). But the agitators are still busy. The latest moonshine of disordered fiction is the Osborne–Robertson Mare's-Nest, an ornithological oddity which claims that all foundation mares in thoroughbred pedigrees whose origin is unknown are *ipso facto* a famous old native English racing breed so famous apparently that no stud book, public or private, or any contemporary writer ever so much as mentioned it, and no artist ever portrayed it, but on the contrary, records and pictures proving the exact contrary are legion. This arbitrary interpretation of silence is certainly quite unprecedented in the history of stud books. Silence in pedigrees is seldom golden, and to assume that all mares whose origin is not stated are English is just as silly as to say that all mares whose colour is not stated must have been piebald—with no evidence whatever of the existence of such a colour, and it may be noted that these female myths have no male counterparts and nowhere is an English racing stallion recorded.

It is quite bad enough to have the Godolphin Arabian changed to a Barb as well as the Tregonwell Arabian mare, Snorting Bess, considering that both were registered Arabians even before the first volume of the General Stud Book existed, and that their pictures confirm their registration, but when it comes to claiming without verification a whole breed of non-existent and unregistered English racing mares, some protest has got to be recorded before they follow the Godolphin into Weatherby's pages by sheer force of blind reiteration. This is a very serious danger. The racehorse owner Thomas Wharton, in 1648 known as "that most profligate impious and shameless of men reputed to be the world's greatest liar," once said to a protesting friend: "Are you such a simpleton as not to know that a lie emphatically told and well believed is as good as if it were true?" The English Mare's-Nest is a perfect example of groundless statement emphatically repeated and well on the way to being well believed.

I have given minute details of every one of the foundation mares in my books *Thorough-bred Racing Stock* and the *Authentic Arabian Horse* and it is necessary to repeat most definitely that none of these mares were English by blood. That dogmatic self-constituted "Professor," the late journalist J. B. Robertson (*Mankato*) not only invented a catchphrase title for himself but invented the equally unfounded catchphrase of "Our Native English running mares" for all mares whose origin was not stated in Weatherby's General Stud Book.

The construction of this astonishing Mare's-Nest began with a casual tentative suggestion by an unknown American which would have passed unnoticed as any other guesswork had not J. Osborne revived it and laid the first egg as "Origin Unknown, so may have been English." The incubation process being as follows: "Probably English," "May certainly have been English," which in Robertson's hands rapidly became "Unknown and therefore *proved* English." "Our Native race mares." "Our old *breed* of English running mares." "Our celebrated native racing breed" culminating with the hatching of that winged brood of our world-famous unrivalled breed of "*Yorkshire* running mares!"

The unknown quantity thus rises from the ranks to the full blown glory of Plantagenet blue blood!

This is the assertive process of elimination by addition. Following on this we have the same process applied to elimination by subtraction and Mr. Burton's Natural Barb Mare (No. 2 taproot) is dealt with by successive elimination of the word "Natural" (pure bred imported) then the "Mr.," then the Burton, and finally throwing the word "Barb" into the waste paper basket she is henceforth listed as "this famous English Mare." A Byerley Turk mare of well-known oriental parentage suffers the same dehydrating process succeeded by inflation and becomes Mr. Bowes of Streatham's celebrated *Yorkshire* running mare. Pictures of both these mares show them to have been Eastern. This truly unwarrantable progression is unsupported by any evidence but was adopted by the Osborne-Robertson mare's-nesting enthusiasts without verification. In fact it was a case of: "What's good's English, all that isn't, ain't!" (Lowell.) Such an arbitrary interpretation of a blank in the pedigree is certainly without precedent in the annals of stud records and in this instance is often flatly contradicted by positive evidence in existing records showing some of the mares to have been Oriental.

This quite unpardonable juggling with pedigrees has got to stop or we may as well scrap stud books altogether. Neither the Jockey Club or Weatherbys themselves have ever laid claim to any such brood of phantoms and no self-constituted authorities have any official mandate, but they are nevertheless a recurring bore. The recent persistence of some of them, coming on the top of the renewed agitation about the Jersey Act suggests a wish to excuse the barring of American horses on the ground that our stud book blanks represent a marvellous racing breed to which their similar blanks can lay no claim. No good purpose can be served by bluff of this kind.

It really is hardly credible that Robertson should treat the daughter of the Leedes Arabian out of a daughter of Pelhams Arabian as an English mare. In another case he says: "the mare is unknown which is *plain evidence she was of superior English breed*." The adoption of "unknown" as a proof of excellence, thus arguing "*ex silentio*," is indeed a principle emphatically condemned by the "Jersey Act" by which the Jockey Club barred horses with blanks from any future entry in the General Stud Book. They voiced in no uncertain way their opinion of blanks as a bar sinister "unknown and therefore flaws." Were the Jersey principle to be retrospective some of our foundation strains would be taboo. The Derby winner Mahmoud is an instance. It is indeed difficult to explain the few really unknown blanks except as flaws of inferior blood as there is clearly common blood to which some of our thoroughbreds revert showing itself in coarse heads and lumbering limbs; certainly not traceable in the General Stud Book records, which on the contrary all go back to oriental sources. Otherwise one would have to suspect some illicit subsequent *mésalliance*.

In *The Field*, 1947, Mr. J. Loder openly admitted that in his opinion Robertson deliberately discarded the word "natural" (imported, or pure eastern) from the General Stud Book record of No. 2 mare. If correct this *suppressio veri* is just what rules Robertson out of court as an unbiased historian. However excellent his knowledge of modern racing may have been we are compelled to resist his accuracy on pedigrees, for on referring to *Flat Racing* we find him systematically carrying on the same arbitrary process in other cases.

Posing as an authority under the fancy title of "Professor" of the Royal Veterinary College (which enquiry proves to have been as mythical as the rest of his claims), he misrepresented thirteen of the Bruce Lowe taproot mares, putting them under the heading "English mares," in some cases not only disregarding their oriental sires but supplying an English Dam, which in the case of Byerley Turk, mare No. 3, is a pure figment of his imagination, as she was by the Selaby Turk out of a Hautboy mare (Hautboy by the Darcy White Turk ex a Royal (Arab) mare) out of a full sister to Morgans Dun by a son of the Helmsley Turk out of a mare by Dodsworth (Arab), her dam being Mr. Burton's Natural Barb mare No. 2. (See p. 91.)

As to "running" there is no *evidence* that they ever proceeded faster than a walk and certainly none of their having raced!

Natural was used for pure Easterns bred in England, like Crabbet Arabs, but this would not make the mare English, or all Crabbet Arabs are English at that rate!

Robertson ignored Mr. Curwen's signed statement that No. 9, the Vintner mare, was sired by his Arabian and all similar evidence. Again he did not know that families Nos. 2, 3, and 22 are the same, and that No. 8 goes back to No. 4, which includes Nos. 10, 12, 17, 18, 19, 28, 31, 35 and 40, which all trace back to Mr. Layton's Barb mare Violet (see Pick), No. 4 which he elsewhere treats as he treated Mr. Burton's Natural Barb mare No. 2, eliminating both her owner and her name in order to call her an English running mare. The word "running" being his own interpolation in both cases, as well as the word "English." This invalidates his whole list of winners descended from numbered families and his deductions as to their respective value so that his section on foundation stock is not worth the paper it is written on. Some numbers which he treats as dying out, or inferior, being actually very much alive.

Not only have we the positive evidence of countless contemporary writers, but we have the negative evidence of the total absence of any mention of English racing mares

Mr. Burton's Natural Barb (Arabian) mare

from all the contemporary published and unpublished stud books. Why this conspiracy of silence about such an outstanding breed? Why no pictorial evidence of a racing type? Pictorial records are not confined to painters of oil portraits as some people seem to think.

There are many prints of sixteenth- and seventeenth-century English horses, all hairy-heeled, heavy cart-blooded types, exactly corresponding to their written descriptions (see the British horse, 1579, the Welbeck brood mares and Markham's "perfect Horse") and others in my books, where there are also pictures of early foundation mares, all oriental, from the Milbanke collection.

However primitive drawings may be, the type always emerges, even in the rock carvings of fifty thousand years ago, and those of Arabia and Egypt 1800 B.C., where type is quite unmistakable.

Having published the detailed pedigrees and history of the foundation mares which definitely disprove the Mare's-Nest theory I cannot allow that anyone is justified in trying to incubate its manifestly addled eggs. I have been misquoted to the point of inversion as saying the Thoroughbred is "wholly Arabian in origin." I never mind a fair fight, but I object to being pilloried for what I have not said. I have said nothing of the sort, in fact I have insisted on exactly the contrary not once but many times. What I did say, and repeat, is that it was entirely *foreign*, which does not necessarily mean Arab or even Oriental, but may include all or any of the cold blooded slower continental mixtures imported to England and which (with the exception of Orientals) formed the whole of England's horse stock at that time, including the agricultural and heavy battle horses which were also from abroad. My conclusions are based on historical records and masses of documentary evidence and perhaps I may be allowed to quote some of it from my own words.

Thoroughbred Racing Stock, p. 256: "There are undoubtedly strains of common blood in our racehorse." P. 259: "We are still striving to rid ourselves of the common and cart blood, every drop of which acts as a clog on the speed which it is our object to increase. It is not from the Arab that we get bad temper, unsound feet, short wind and defective stamina. These come from the flaws in the pedigrees. The dominating stock was Arabian (the only fast blood in *those* days) and though there are evidences of other cheap imported elements which still reappear in the ruck of our degenerate throw-outs at Tattersalls, all these were inferior to the Arabian and the unwelcome heavy heads, pig-eyes or goose rumps are reminders of the undoubted blots on the escutcheon from foreign coach and cart horse alloy. These coarse types are partial reversion to the cold blooded slow stock."

Authentic Arabian Horse, p. 47: "Possibly some of the coarse heads and common characteristics come from the unknown foreign element of continental cross breds. In fact one is forced to that conclusion, the written pedigree revealing no common blood." P. 51: "The coarser strains seem to have been chiefly from the Italian and Spanish horses which were used as war chargers, hunters and carriage horses."

Mr. Prior, the greatest and most reliable authority on old pedigrees, whose researches have entirely superseded those of Sir Theodore Cook and Sir Walter Gilbey, quoted by Mr. Loder (their theories were only theories as opposed to Mr. Prior's facts), says of the lists of horses drawn up by the Duke of Newcastle, *c.* 1660: "A perusal of them tends to show how entirely Eastern origin was the racehorse of the hundred years immediately after the Restoration, the studs being virtually composed of pure bred Arabians, Turks and Barbs."

No one can possibly accuse Mr. Prior of being carried away by enthusiasm for the Arab horse, yet, as a result of his judicial enquiry, he goes further than I do, as he does not admit any except oriental blood in the racehorse. He gives the pedigree of Pacolet, 1763, as an instance and he is right in this, that, judged on *paper*, no stud books record English blood of any sort.

In support of this, we have unanimous contemporary testimony, and can follow the records through the ages from one century to the other in an unchanging chorus. Blundeville, 1588, describes the English breed as very indifferent, strong, heavy, slow draught horses, ending by describing the English horse as a coarse bastard Neapolitan war charger and utility "courser" described elsewhere "as more fit to break a neck than a lance," and the "true plaine English mare" as a similar crossbred.

Markham, 1593, "The true stallion whose wonderful speed both in short and long courses may make our English Prickers hold their best runners, but Baffles, who by nature has all things perfect, nothing defective, and this is only the courser of Arabia."

He here explains his use of the word courser and follows it up with a panegyric of the breed. ("Baffle" was used for a worn-out jade.)

J. Crouch, 1636, laments that "our best horses in England are reserved only for coach horses. The rest, arrant jades, scarce one of 'em serviceable; badly kept, and miserably neglected, saddle-galled geldings, nagges and cart horses," and says that "as a horseman, having served overseas," he is convinced that "no nation in Europe is more backward and careless in breeding and managing horses than we are in England."

There was evidently no racing breed at that time.

General Lord Fairfax, 1664: "There are no horses accounted English, which are not full of foreign blood to counteract the cold phlegmatic type by crosses nearer the sun."

About a decade later we find the Duke of Newcastle warning breeders that "even a *bad Barb that is a jade is better for getting racers than any English horse.*"

Bradly, 1727: "The true bred English horse hardly exists unless we account the horses to be such as are bred wild in some of our forests and among the mountains."

Buffon, 1755: "Arabs are the finest in the world. Barbs are commoner . . . English horses of the best kind are like Arabs and Barbs. They are big, at least 14.2 (!), some in fact reaching 15 hands, but they are not as good as the Arabs, being more suitable for hunting than racing."

Seventeeth-century saddle horse

Osmer, 1761: "I do here lay it down as certain truth that no horses but such as come from foreign countries or which are of extraction totally foreign can race. In this opinion every man will readily join me and thus opinion be confirmed by every man of experience and observation. The constituent parts of foreign horses differ as much from all others as their performances."

He reiterates that: "Arabians are far the best," that "high-bred" always meant "foreign" and that "for racers the blood must be totally foreign."

The "good English horse," he says, "is a coarse half-bred, with hairy legs, thick skin and lax fibres. The Arab excels all others and is the only horse for getting racers, in other words, the perfect horse."

Bérenger, 1771: "English horses are infinitely inferior to Arabs and Barbs, having stiff inactive shoulders, sullen tempers, and lack of suppleness in limbs, cold, indifferent, tame, lifeless and unanimated." He also mentioned that the contrasting fire of the foreign horses was "like the sparkling fire of generous wine."

Alken, 1815, contradicts the "very erroneous ignorant notion" that the thoroughbred was a mixture of Oriental and northern stock in order to combine the height and weight of the north with the speed of the south, saying that the increased size is due to good feeding, and that some accidental crosses were immediately detected as such crosses could not race, the Oriental being the only fast breed.

Napoleon, in 1820, said the Arabian stallion is the world's best horse, far better than any thoroughbred for the improvement of all other breeds.

Quotations could be multiplied *ad infinitum*.

In this continuous chain of evidence we have no talk of a superior English racing breed but the plain, unvarnished reiterated truth that no such thing existed, the best "English" stallions are definitely condemned as worse than the worst Barb, and this would apply equally to "English" mares. In this connection we may note that the common Barb, then so extensively used to improve our stock, had a very convex head from its mixed Spanish and North European ancestry and that its occasional reversionary appearance in the thoroughbred is not surprising.

Even as late as 1800, Weatherby, in the General Stud Book, says: "English horses are by no means as beautiful as the Arab though *next to him* as the world's best horse."

No Native racing breed could have survived the edict by which Henry VIII, 1535, ordered "the *killing* and *burying*" of all horses as were not likely to produce stock fit for profitable *labour*, agriculture and heavy cavalry. (See pp. 203, 231.)

Rice comments: "To this enactment we may attribute the dying out of the smaller native breeds, and the universal appearance in their stead, of useful stout animals well able to take part in battle, the chase or the pageant, and to carry their heavily weighted riders with credit."

Moreover, the height minimum of 15 hands would ensure the slaughter of all racing types which were scheduled from 12.2 with an extreme limit of fifteen hands, then considered "too big for racing."

Holinshed says of Henry VIII's stud that it began well but soon lapsed into "a mixed breed of bastard races." Sir Walter Hungerford's "courser" with which he challenged all comers, was a battle horse; and the word "race" was often used for a stud, not a competition in speed. A "race mare" was a stud mare. This has misled many writers, as also the word "running" horse which, at first, meant a pacer, and only gradually changed its meaning. "The legs moving in pairs on each side like a camel." They were described as "swift in running but in gallop false and full indifferent." (See p. 200).

I have been asked to explain why none of the early Arab importations achieved distinction on the racecourse. The earliest (the two Arundels and Truncefice) certainly did, and remained celebrated for centuries, and the immediate descendants of the later

Old Bald Peg   [*Milbanke Collection*
(Foundation Arab Mare)

ones, pure Arab on both sides, were many of them unbeaten, and G. Markham, 1607, says the imported oriental horses were used exclusively for racing and were swift beyond all others at our English Bell courses on hard ground.

There are however reasons which may explain why many imported horses were not raced at all, and why the Markham Arabian failed to win though his son Frisell was unbeaten. Wilfred Blunt describes the treatment of Arabian stock destined for sale:

"Starved before birth, weaned at a month or at most a hundred days, and never allowed to run with his dam but kept tied up by the hock to a tent rope. In his first autumn turned out to shift for himself on what miserable dry herbage he can find, heavily shackled with iron handcuffs to prevent his being stolen. At a year he is like a wretched half-starved cat. Sold to dealers on the edge of the desert he is put into close and filthy stables and fattened for sale. During all this time he has probably never had a gallop, being closely hobbled day and night, one hind foot drawn up to within a couple of feet of his forelegs. When all his bones are set to short paces he is imported to England and suddenly put to race against the specialized product of expert English trainers."

"Surely," said Mr. Blunt, "even the produce of Doncaster and Rouge Rose might be excused for failure if treated so." Yet even so we find Markham in 1593 saying that his brilliant speed put all our English racehorses to shame.

At the longest reckoning horse history in England goes little beyond Roman times and all the light horse breeding between Cæsar and Henry VIII is of purely academic interest

Tulyar winning the St. Leger. Reputed sold for a quarter of a million sterling

owing to the wholesale elimination of light stock and its replacement by ponderous imported weight carriers.

May I once more repeat? I have never said the thoroughbred was of wholly Arabian origin, but all evidence shows he is *totally foreign*. I do say that there is overwhelming evidence against the existence of any native racing mares, English by blood, and, like the Jockey Club and the Bedouin breeders, I shall regard blanks as flaws of common blood, not merits, until further proof is forthcoming.

On the other hand it cannot be denied that there is a colossal amount of Arab blood in vast preponderance. I have compiled a dictionary from which it is possible to work out the proportion of bulk figures of ten tap roots in the pedigree of any registered thoroughbred as in the following table. The results of analysis are positively staggering

96

A vexatious argument

[Photo : Daily Mirror

Pinza, Gordon Richards up
after winning the Derby.

and are concentrating more and more with every generation owing to early inbreeding which fixed the type exclusively bred for speed and will soon reach supersaturation.

It must be remembered that a pedigree of twenty-six generations represents 134,217,726 units against twenty-six units of the top or bottom line taken singly. The bulk therefore counts more than the direct male and female descent.

Name of Winner	Godolphin Arabian	Darley Arabian	Byerley "Turk"	Leedes Arabian	Darcy White "Turk"	Darcy Yellow "Turk"	Lister "Turk"	Helmsley "Turk"	Old Bald Peg Arabian Mare	Sultan Arabian
Big Game ..	28,232	44,079	64,032	187,197	90,420	294,508	63,832	109,946	367,162	367,162
Sun Chariot ..	42,079	68,394	94,706	169,899	230,307	279,293	60,717	102,912	233,579	233,579
Hyperion ..	15,594	23,998	32,199	31,426	181,182	111,938	22,350	41,003	138,827	138,827
Fairway ..	14,931	22,734	33,188	58,350	50,252	92,804	18,662	34,478	113,740	113,740
Windsor Lad ..	25,376	38,944	61,783	93,573	103,753	152,544	30,366	56,880	184,091	184,091

This table shows the number of repeat crosses of some foundation sires of our classic winners showing also the repeat crosses of the Arabian mare, Old Bald Peg. "Turk" was an alternative term for an Arabian and was often used for horses imported from Syria which was occupied by the Turks and for a time called Turkey.

Sun Chariot's direct sire line is the Darley Arabian and she belongs in direct female line to No. 3 Bruce Lowe family which traces back to the same as No. 2 Burton Barb mare. Big Game is from the same sire line and he descends in female line from No. 6 the Arab mare Old Bald Peg, so not only is she his tap root, but he has over a quarter of a million repeat crosses of her.

I have been asked to explain the increase in size of the early English racehorse if no "Native English" cross was used; the only native English stock at that time consisted of small ponies which had escaped King Henry's massacre of the innocents. The racing events were then for ponies 12.2 to 13.1. The Arab was the biggest as well as the only fast breed then known, and the reply is that he always tends to get stock bigger than himself because in his own country his growth is stunted by starvation and hardship. Good feeding, selection and specialization increase the size of the English-bred pure Arab to 15.2–16. One might as well however ask why in the last half century, without any outcross at all, the modern Thoroughbred seems to have made a sudden further spasmodic increase in height as compared with the average of the previous 150 years, an increase which does not seem to carry a corresponding all round improvement and is sometimes suggestive of running to seed as, except in a few notable cases such as Hurry On, it seems allied with increasing unsoundness of wind and limb and loss of stamina. The sons of Hurry On, though high-class horses, seem to have reached the end of their excellence and have mostly failed signally to transmit their merits though some of his daughters do so. It is a matter for reflection that our best classic winners and sires of late years seem to be reverting more to the Arab size of about sixteen hands or under, which appears an excellent size for bloodstock. The tallest three-year-old to win a classic race is Ki Ming, 17.2, winner of the 2,000 guineas, 1951.

THE WORLD'S TWO MOST FAMOUS JOCKEYS

In connection with Thoroughbred racing, mention must be made of two outstanding miracles of modern race riding. In Derby winning the late Steve Donoghue was supreme with six Derbys including a Derby hat trick of three wins in succession. It is unlikely that this will ever be equalled.

Gordon Richards has the all-time highest record for number of races won in one season, having well surpassed Fred Archer's previous record of 246 wins. He reached an unprecedented pinnacle of fame in 1953 by winning the Coronation Derby with many lengths to spare on Pinza (see p. 98) and being the first and only jockey ever to be knighted. Sir Gordon and Lady Richards are to be sincerely congratulated on both honours.

Lady Wentworth's Fleeting Storm, yearling filly by Ballyogan, sire of Ki Ming

Olein. Sold at Newmarket in 1943 for 17,000 guineas

Festoon

Masaka

CHAPTER V

GREECE

THE original Aryan races do not seem to have been horse breeders but collected a mixed lot from the countries they passed through. No fossil remains have been found to indicate that horses were ever indigenous to Greece. The country was mountainous and only suitable in parts for horse breeding but wars and trading brought horses from outside. Fact and myth are so mixed up in Greek history that it is often impossible to disentangle fact from fiction, but Scythia, Persia, Arabia and Africa were probable sources of supply. The Greek legend ascribes the horse as a gift from the Sea God Poseidon, and the gods of the sea and the sun were credited with celebrating the first Isthmian games together. The fact that the sun horse gods (which were the Arabian deities) combined with the sea god suggests overseas and oriental origin for the most prized breed. The Persian invasions found Greek warriors still fighting on foot. The Greeks not being a nation of natural horsemen they prided themselves on the term "swift of foot," Mercury the Messenger and god of speed being depicted neither riding nor driving, but progressing by the speed of his own winged heels. Foot racing long preceded chariot racing. Lasthenes is extolled for winning a race reckoned at forty-five miles on foot against a horse.

Light and heavy horses seem to have existed side by side in Greece as well as in almost all other countries except Arabia, where the racing type alone was bred. When the Greeks did take to horses it developed into a dominating passion. The rich and noble families bred racehorses and horse racing and sport became their chief interests. A victory at one of the great meetings was regarded as one of the highest glories that life could afford and famous poets were commissioned to celebrate it. This view of horse racing was at its height from the sixth to the fourth centuries B.C. Again during this period most of the larger Greek states had cavalry but the mainstay of the armed forces were the infantrymen; cavalry tactics, generally speaking, were not highly developed and the cavalry horses were of inferior quality to the racehorses and the prizes given for war horses were less valuable. In the fourth century the Macedonians under Kings Philip and Alexander made more extensive use of cavalry. The Parthenon horses were sturdy pony-cobs, their size may be calculated by the fact that their rider's feet hung down almost to the horse's knees. Similarly Xenophon (seventh chapter, fourth century B.C.) instructs pupils to mount by seizing the mane near the ears which could hardly have been done except with a pony about 12.2 to 13.2 in height. The ponies exhibit both Southern and Northern type and are very similar to the Assyrian wild ponies shown in Assyrian sculpture being caught with lassoes. Their necks were typically pony type and their heads straight with small ears low in the mane which is hogged, whereas the racehorses' manes are often described as flowing in the breeze.

The hogged manes had a bottom row of what looks like some sort of plaiting which is difficult to identify.

Thracian horses were much esteemed and were brought in by an oriental people—probably Hittites. According to Homer these were the fairest horses ever seen, whiter than snow and in speed like the wind and swifter than the storm, shining like the rays of the sun at dawn. The colour of the chariot horses was described as "Xanthos" which Pietrement translated golden chestnut, often in England translated "dun," but dun is a dull colour and belongs to non-racing breeds and could not by any possibility be described as shining like the rays of the sun. "Phœnix," dark red, properly purple, which might otherwise be called red bay or the deep purple-chestnut with fair mane and tail, called in Arabia "Kumeyt," may have come from the Phœnicians, but Xanthos might far more probably have been the golden chestnut with flaxen mane called in Arabia "Ashgar Muharrak" (fiery chestnut) now called Palomino. There were also parti-coloured horses. Dun might also be a younger shade of grey in the transition stage as it seems most unlikely that dun was ever a racing colour.

The earliest representations of horses in Greek lands are of about 1600 B.C.: the war-chariot, drawn by a pair of horses, appears on sculptured tombstones of that date from Mycenae. The use of the war-chariot was probably adopted from the Near East. There are no Greek representations of *riders* till the eleventh century B.C. In Homer (about the ninth century B.C.) the two-horse chariot is used in battle, or rather to convey the warriors to the battlefield, where they dismount and fight on foot. The *four-horse* chariot begins to appear in pictures towards the end of the eighth century B.C. Ancient scholars observed that Homer knew of riding horses (since he mentions them in similes), but did not speak of his heroes (who belonged to a past generation) as riding. This is not quite accurate, however, for in the tenth book of the *Iliad*, Diomedes and Odysseus mount the horses of Rhesus and ride them home, which shows that the Homeric heroes *could* ride, and ride thoroughbreds.[1] Homer also gives an elaborate description of a chariot race, which will be quoted later. There are plenty of representations of chariot races from the seventh century onwards. In these the chariot is usually drawn by four horses. By this time the chariot was no longer used in warfare, but was retained for purposes of sport.

[1] Rhesus, King of Thrace, marched to the assistance of Priam, King of Troy. An ancient oracle had declared that Troy would never be taken if the horses of Rhesus drank water from the Xanthus river and ate grass on the Trojan plain, so Diomedes and Ulysses crept into the camp by night and killed Rhesus and stole the horses, riding them away.

The greatest of Greek athletic festivals took place at Olympia in the Peloponnese every four years, and the four-horse chariot race was the most illustrious of all sporting events. The Olympian festival was of almost immemorial antiquity, but it was reorganized

Greek racing type (sixth century)

Greek cavalry horses (cross-bred ewe-necked type)

in the year 776 B.C., and the meeting of that year was reckoned as the first Olympiad. The chariot race, however, was not introduced into the programme till 680 B.C., when Pagondas of Thebes was the winner; but this was probably a revival of an old event which had been discontinued. The riding race was not introduced at Olympia till 648 B.C., when Crauxidas of Crannon, in Thessaly, owned the winning horse. The course at

103

Olympia measured six stades, and in the four-horse chariot race there were twelve laps, making seventy-two stades or about nine miles, with twenty-three turns. With this long course there cannot have been heats, as the equestrian events were confined to a single day. At Delphi one field of forty is recorded, but only one competitor got home. The programme varied at different periods. It came to comprise (besides the chief event, the four-horse chariot race for full-grown horses) a shorter race of eight laps for colts, and the *synoris*, a race for chariots drawn by pairs. The first pair-horse chariot race recorded at Olympia was in 408 B.C., and was won by a local man, Evagoras of Elis.

A mule-cart race was introduced in 500 B.C., but was abolished in 444 B.C. The riding race was once round the course, a short mile. A riding race for colts was added later. In 496 B.C. the kalpe was introduced and lasted till 444 B.C., it was a race for combining horse racing with foot racing, the rider dismounting at a given moment and finishing on foot.

In the *Iliad*, Nestor described a fight with the Eleians over a cattle raid, capturing booty of cattle, sheep, pigs and goats, and 150 chestnut mares with foals at foot. Later he says that four prize winning chariot horses had gone to the Olympic games to run for a tripod and Augeias confiscated them and sent away the driver sorrowing for his horses.

We have less information about the details of the other great Panhellenic athletic festival, at Delphi, Nemea, and the Isthmus of Corinth. More is known about the quadrennial festival, the Panathenæa, at Athens. Here also the chief event was the four-horse chariot race. There were also in the fourth century at least a chariot race for colts, another for what were called "war-chariots," and a "processional chariot" race. The comparative importance of these events can be judged from the prizes. The first prize for the chief event was 140 clay jars of the famous Attic oil; for the colt-race only forty jars, for the "war-chariot" race sixteen, for the "processional" four. Many of these Panathenaic prize amphoræ have been preserved: they bear the figure of the goddess Athena on the front, and on the back a picture of the contest for which they were awarded. The official term "war-chariot" is rather misleading. Chariots had long ceased to be used in warfare: what is probably meant is that the chariot was drawn by army chargers as opposed to the thoroughbreds entered for the principal race. One of the most popular events at Athens was the so-called *apobates* race, a combination of the four-horse chariot race with the foot race in armour. The driver had a passenger, an athlete who wore the helmet and carried the heavy shield of the infantryman: the passenger (apobates—"stepper-off") mounted the chariot in full course, dismounted and ran, remounted and so on. Competitors in the apobates race are represented on the frieze of the Parthenon. One or two Panathenaic amphoræ give pictures of the *synoris*, the pair-horse chariot race, as run at Athens: here the driver did not stand, but sat in a sort of two-wheeled cart which is almost like the American racing buggy.

As to the riding events at Athens, in addition to the chief race there was one for "war horses" or army chargers; and, from the end of the fifth century onwards, a contest of javelin-throwing on horseback, with a target set up on a post.

Another fancy event which came in at Athens about the same time was the torch race on horseback, a variety of the ordinary torch race which was a relay race for runners with the torch serving as baton.

The Greek charioteer stood in a very light and flimsy two-wheeled car. He wore a long robe, and in historic times used a goad (not a whip as in Homer). The finest representation of a charioteer is the bronze statue at Delphi, part of a chariot-group dedicated to Apollo by a victor in the Pythian Games between 480 and 470 B.C. The charioteer was often a professional, but there were amateurs also: occasionally the owner drove his own chariot, and not infrequently the driver was a kinsman of the owner; thus the chariot of Arcesilas, the Greek King of Cyrene in the earlier part of the fifth century, was driven by his brother-in-law Carrhotus. Horses were *ridden* by jockeys, who were always young boys. The winner was always the owner.

Cheating, bribery and a criminal record debarred from competition, the reward of victory was a Crown of Olive. The conqueror returned home in a chariot with four horses and a special breach was made in the walls of his city for him to enter. The games lasted five days.

Iolaus is said to have won the prize at Olympia for chariot racing with the horses of his uncle Hercules.

Whether actual or fabulous it is difficult to say but Oenomaus is said to have run races against the suitors of his daughter Hippodamia from Pisa in Elis to the Isthmus of Corinth, little short of a hundred miles. The legend of Oenomaus is in the best tradition of autocratic fathers as he refused to let his daughter marry any man who failed to elope with her in a chariot with horses fast enough to out-distance his pursuit, the beaten suitor being speared by Oenomaus and his head hung up over the palace door. Hippodamia must have almost despaired of ever reaching an Hellenic Gretna Green by the time twelve heads were adorning her savage parent's portico. But Pelops (grandson of Zeus) arguing that the race is not always to the swift resolved to rely no more on mere speed and bribed Myrtilos the king's charioteer to remove the lynch pin from his majesty's chariot wheel and replace it with a wax dummy which melting in the fury of the chase Oenomaus was killed cursing Myrtilos and the perfidious Pelops who escaped with his bride to Pisa. When it came to paying Myrtilos however he began to think that his promise of half his kingdom, or some say to a share of Hippodamia's favours, was too heavy a price and threw Myrtilos into the sea where he was drowned uttering in his turn frightful curses on Pelops and his whole race. There are several modifications of the fable and the curses did not prevent Pelops from restoring the Olympic games to a new splendour shortly afterwards.

There is another legend concerning Amphiaraus who reigned jointly at Argus with Adrastus. They began with a feud but made it up when Adrastus gave his sister Eriphyle to Amphiaraus in marriage, making him swear that he would in future let his wife decide any point on which they might disagree. Before long Adrastus began pressing Amphiaraus to join a war expedition against Thebes, but Amphiaraus thought it an ill-fated scheme and refused to go, hiding himself from his brother-in-law. Eriphyle, however, coveted a golden necklace which had been given to Harmonia by Venus, and Polynices bribed her with it to insist on her husband going to the war, which having pledged his word he was obliged to do. Before starting, however, he charged his son Alcmaon to kill his mother at once in case of his death. Amphiaraus, though seething with anger at Eriphyle's treachery, fought bravely, and on their way to Thebes they founded the Nemean games and Amphiaraus won the chariot race and throwing the discus. At last only he and Adrastus survived and he fled towards the river Ismenus pursued by Periclymenus but before he could be overtaken the earth opened and swallowed him up and Zeus made him immortal, and he was henceforth worshipped as a hero. Adrastus escaped riding a horse called Arion (the very swift), supposed to be the offspring of Poseidon and Demeter when they respectively changed themselves into a stallion and a mare. Eriphyle was duly murdered by her son when the news reached Argus.

The *Odyssey* makes no mention of chariot racing. Ithaca had no pasture lands but studs were kept in Elis.

Agamemnon's gift to Achilles was twelve prize winning horses.

Chariot races were started with a rope stretched in front of the lined up horses and dropped at the start. This was the method called "Mikwas" in Syria, and from it our starting gate has been evolved.

The first detailed Greek account of a ridden race is 508 B.C., when a mare called Aura whose rider had fallen off at the start continued the race on her own account. The mare having won the race unaided, making her spurt when the trumpet blew and stopping after reaching the winning post, she was awarded the prize, it being thought more meritorious than if she had carried a rider. She was owned by Pheidolas of Corinth.

No women were allowed to be present at the Olympic games, the penalty being to be hurled from a rock, but this appears to have gradually been disregarded as women did appear, not only as spectators but as competitors and some won the crown.

According to Pausanias, Cynisca, daughter of Archidamus, King of Sparta, was passionately fond of the Olympic games and was the first woman to breed horses and win an Olympic victory in a chariot race. It is improbable that she drove the chariot in person, but she appears to have erected a statue to herself at Olympia the base of which has been found with part of an inscription in verse, the whole of which has been preserved in the Palatine Anthology. It runs as follows:

"My father and brothers were Kings of Sparta. I, Cynisca, conquering with a chariot of fleet footed steeds set up this statue. And I say that I am the only woman of all Greece that ever won this crown."

The statues both of herself and the horses, of which another base was found, also signed by the sculptor Apelleas at the beginning of the fourth century B.C., have unfortunately disappeared.

Pausanias also mentioned a statue of another woman which the Spartans told him represented Euryleonis, who had won a victory at Olympia with a two-horse chariot.

Women seem to have had the same pride in excelling male opponents as we see nowadays, and by this standard Lady James Douglas and her horse Gainsborough deserve a statue as the first woman owned combination to win the Derby.

Belistiche 264 B.C. seems to have been the first woman to win the two-horse chariot race, and Amazons appear in Greek art.

Alexander the Great had won his celebrated charger Bucephalus as a boy of twelve, having wagered with his father, Philip of Macedon, to pay the price of the horse if he failed to ride it, everyone else having been unable to do so. The horse was a black Thessalian with a star, so fierce and violent that Philip had flown into a rage and ordered its removal. The boy Alexander derided them all as clumsy poltroons and on being challenged to do better, ran up, took the horse by the bridle and turned him towards the sun, having noticed that his shadow was frightening him. This fear of their own shadows is more than once mentioned in connection with Greek horses which suggests they were of extremely nervous tendency.

Having patted and soothed him he quietly got on his back and rode off in triumph. This so impressed King Philip that he shed tears of emotion and gave him the horse. Later the horse would kneel for him to mount, and when it was stolen in Hyrcania he issued a proclamation that the whole nation would be exterminated unless it was returned which soon brought the horse back. At the age of thirty, in 327 B.C., Bucephalus was killed in battle against the Indian King, Porus, and though bleeding to death dashed out of danger and saved the King's life. Alexander founded the city of Bucephalia in his honour.

The ancient female divinities Eos (Aurora) and Epona (the Gaulish Goddess) were shown on horseback. Selene (the Moon) sometimes drives a chariot and sometimes rides side saddle.

Xenophon warns buyers that there is much cheating among horse dealers. He tells them to examine first of all a yearling's feet as an unsound horse is useless. His feet should be hollow and ring like cymbals. Pasterns should be sloping but not excessively so. Good bone, supple knees, powerful shoulders and broad chest. The neck must not sag (ewe-necked) but be arched like the neck of a game cock as it protects the rider and it can see better where it puts its feet and it is less liable to bolt. Head lean, cheek small, eye prominent (not sunken), nostrils wide, crest large, ears small, withers high, loins short and broad, shoulder high, wide haunches and a double back. Colours, grey, xanthos, dark chestnut with fair manes. "Dappled dun" (so called) is probably a stage of grey; the most popular were white Thessalians, the white horses of Thebes and white horses of Thrace.

Philip of Macedon, 350 B.C., whose cavalry were famous, ran chariot teams and race-horses at Olympia and his son, Alexander the Great, was born on the same day that the news came of his victory in the chief race, which was considered a wonderful omen of his future greatness.

Simon the Athenian, makes a great point of high carriage of the tail. Oppian (second

Winning horse being crowned with laurels by Hecate. Note very small pony size, fourth century B.C.

Greek racehorse, sixth century B.C.

century A.D.) gives much the same points of a charger or hunting horse as Xenophon, stressing the neck arching like the plume on a helmet, forehead broad, thick curly forelock, a double chine, good full tail, fine clean legs and sloping pasterns. "With unflinching courage they rush on the enemy's serried phalanx; they prick their ears and arouse at the call of the trumpet, nor does their eye quail before the flashing sword." Compare description of Job's horse. Oppian says that horses understood the word of command and are the most intelligent of all animals, neighing when their master mounts and grieving at his death.

Ovid says their heart knows when victory is won, remarking on their proud carriage and noble spirit. "If a horse wins the crown in seven laps of a chariot race with what a lofty air he carries his head and courts the cheers of the crowd, or if he comes home with the lion's skin how superb is his action, how grandly does he show off his paces as his hoofs trample the earth under the weight of his heroic spoils."

The various breeds of horse are praised alternately as the swiftest. In speed as the eagle flying, the hawk swooping, or the dolphin cleaving the waves! Like the Duke of Newcastle his views vary. Oppian mentions a breed called the Orynx as very handsome and either striped like a tiger or spotted like a leopard, "but this is artificially produced with a branding iron on very young foals."

Faults objected to by the Greeks (second century A.D.) were: Hoofs with thin horn, or full fat, soft and flat. Heavy fetlocks, shanks with varicose veins, flabby thighs, hollow shoulder blades, projecting (i.e. ewe) neck, bald mane, narrow chest, fat and heavy head, large ears, converging nostrils, sunken eyes, thin sides, sharp backbone, rough haunches, thin buttocks and stiff legs or knees.[1] He also described Cyllaros the horse of the hero Pollux as coal black, like jet, with a white mane and legs. This seems to have been of the Tartar breed called Karabolo.

After the fall of Greece horse breeding seems to have declined, as in modern days there have been no horses there except the sorriest underbred pack ponies, a heterogeneous collection of misfits and drudges.

[1] Varicose shanks strike one as an unusual defect and the habit of riding barebacked fully explains the strong objection to a sharp backbone. Greek and Roman sculptors have been criticized for the unnaturally drawn back open mouths of their horses as incorrect, but this is evidently because the original heads were drawn back by a bit which is now missing.

Greek winning racehorse

CHAPTER VI

ITALY

THE monuments of Northern Italy show that horses were used as early as the Iron age. Horsemen appear on a bronze bucket of the seventh century B.C. Aelian describes the white Venetian horses as small and thick set with "flat noses" and Dionysius of Syracuse got some for his stud, 405 B.C.

They were greatly valued in Sicily by the Sicilian aristocrats. Hieronymus, issuing from his palace arrayed in purple and crowned with a diadem, used to drive in a quadriga drawn by white horses. The sacrifice of white horses to the gods was characteristic of the Teutonic and Scandinavian peoples. The brutal waste of horses wherever idol worship prevailed is one of the more curious consequences of human devil worship. Millions of valuable stallions were thus wantonly killed in India, and even in Arabia a mare would be hamstrung and left to die on her master's grave.

The numerous Roman coins give us some idea of the early Roman horses which were mostly of the heavy type though the conquerors picked up many Arabian horses, the Thamudene Arabian Cavalry being their best troops. For their light cavalry regiments they hired mercenaries from Syria, Arabia and North Africa, and Cæsar hired the Arabian Nabataean King with eight hundred horsemen. Early in the Christian era the horses for war were the Northern breeds, Huns, Friesians, Burgundians, Dalmatians and Cappadocians for chariots; Persians for saddle, and Sicilian, Spanish and African breeds for the circus. Symmachus got nearly all the Roman chariot horses from Spain. From 29 B.C. to the fourth century A.D., all writers agreed that the model horse should have "clustering locks," thick flowing crinkled heavy manes, long thick tails flowing out behind, arched necks, mighty tossing crests, small heads carried high, flashing eyes, fiery nostrils and an impatient restless temperament.

Following on the Roman conquests racing spread to Italy taking with it the Arabian and mixed North African horse. The great Circus Maximus between the Palatine and Aventine Hills was an amazing structure, 2,121 feet long and 404 feet wide, with tiers of seats which in the time of Cæsar held 150,000 and under Titus held 250,000 spectators, and in the fourth century was enlarged to hold 380,000. Horse races, gladiatorial fights, and athletic contests were held there, but the chariot races were one of the chief attractions. A low wall ran down the middle of the arena with turning posts at each end. The ordinary length of a race was seven laps or about $7\frac{1}{2}$ kilometres and twelve to twenty-four races were run daily during the festivals. Sometimes as many as four dozen races were run from sunrise to sunset. So great were the crowds that even in those days the habit of paying a man to wait in a queue was prevalent and in the time of Augustus one thousand

Italian coursers (not racehorses)

people were killed when the top wooden seats collapsed. The laws of fairness insisted on in the Olympic games seem to have been absent. Accidents were common and tempers ran high. Some thirty thousand people perished in one of the race riots in the time of Constantine. Four-horse chariots were driven by slaves, the reins wound round their waists, each carrying a knife to cut loose in case of accident, each also carried a double lashed whip and the prizes were a gold and silver wreath and a palm branch. They made large fortunes and could retire in comfort if they survived to do so, but their social position was low and there were no rewards such as free seats and exemption from taxation like those enjoyed by Greek victors. They might however cheat and steal with impunity.[1] No expense was spared in training, but the games were of a savage barbarity very different from the sports of Greece. Wild beasts were pitted against each other and set on to tear to pieces a man tied to a stake. The alternative amusements were people burnt alive or otherwise tormented and the greater the agony, contortions and screams of the victims the greater the public applause. Bulls, elephants, bears and tigers were set to fight each other or against men armed only with a lance.

Sometime round about the year 531, Theodoric the Goth returned to Ravenna, and there "he delighted the hearts of his subjects by the pageants which celebrated the marriage of his niece Amalaberga with Hermanfrid, the king of the distant Thuringians. This young prince, whom Theodoric had adopted as his 'son by right of arms,' had sent to his future kinsman a team of cream-coloured horses of a rare breed, and Theodoric sent in return horses, swords and shields and other instruments of war, but, as he said, 'the greatest requital that we make is joining you in marriage to a woman of such surpassing beauty as our niece.' "

Cassiodorus described the cream horses in these words. They were "of a silvery colour, as nuptial horses ought to be. Their chests and thighs are adorned in a becoming manner with spheres of flesh. Their ribs are expanded to a certain breadth: their bellies are short and narrow. Their heads have a likeness to the stag's, and they imitate the swiftness of that animal. These horses are gentle from their extreme plumpness; very swift, for all their bigness, pleasant to look upon, yet more pleasant to ride. For they have gentle paces and do not fatigue the riders with insane curvetings. To ride them is rest rather than labour; and being broken in to a delightfully steady pace, they have great staying power and lasting activity."

Chariot races and race riding on one horse leading another or with riders leaping at full speed from one horse to another were very popular, and Julius Cæsar had horse and bull fights with Thessalian horses, which were of Arabianized type as shown on the coins. The chariots were four-horse ones, and four teams competed, distinguished by red, white, blue, and green colours, which represented four great racing companies and Domitian added two new ones, purple and gold, later absorbed by the blues and greens. Pliny laments the effect of colours on the populace and expresses surprise at seeing so many thousand people possessed with the childish passion of seeing a parcel of horses gallop and men standing upright in the chariots. "If" he says "it were the swiftness of the horses or the skill of the men which attracted them there might be some pretence of reason for it but it is the dress that takes their fancy." He adds that if the contestants were to exchange colours their partisans would follow, not the horses, but the colours.

[1] The charioteers of the fifth and sixth centuries, such as Porphyrius, had been the idols of Constantinople and imperial politics were swayed by racing intrigues; but three centuries later their popularity declined and amateur prowess took the place of paid professional skill. Basil, the Macedonian, was a slave boy found naked on the steps of a church and presented to Theophilus. He attained fame by taming fierce horses and eventually murdered the Emperor and took his place. In the tenth century Philoræus, a stable boy, captured the Byzantine public by galloping round the circus standing on his horse and playing with his sword. Later the Hippodrome was used for knightly tourneys and later still for polo.

"Such mighty charms, such wondrous power reside in the colour of a paltry tunic." It is certainly difficult to make sense of this form of frenzy which seems to have been the instinctive effect such as that of a red rag on a bull. Feeling ran so high that the competitions ended in wholesale massacres and executions and in A.D. 445 the rival factions had a pitched battle in the arena during which both spectators and competitors were killed and the city was set on fire.

Dacian in A.D. 166 produced eleven thousand wild beasts in the arena; lions and tigers, elephants and bulls, rhinoceri and bears, were common events, but the great sport was to put an unarmoured man with a lance against wild beasts, but if he fought too well and the end was too prolonged the man was tied to a stake for the beasts to destroy. Seneca alone protested against this blood lust. Panthers, stags and lions were trained to harness.

Racing in the streets (sixteenth century, Italy)

Chariots with two horses and a leader, or seven or eight horses were used, and the Prætor Aulus Fabricius appeared driving a team of dogs; celebrated horses were treated with royal honour, their hoofs were often gilt and they were given money and presents. Volucris the favourite horse of Lucius Verus received a bushel of gold pieces. We are not told who spent them for him. Hadrian erected an inscribed tombstone for his horse Borysthenes.

Caligula often took his meals in the stables and gave his horse Incitatus a house with furniture and slaves and insisted on his friends dining with him, and himself had him to dinner. Having been made Pontifex he associated Incitatus with himself in the priestly office and gave his charioteer Eutyches a gift of £17,000. The charioteers took a second, but nevertheless a very important place. Every excess was allowed them and in one case a man had his mother raised to consular rank.

Many inscribed tablets to Eastern winners still survive, notably one to Aquilo which ran 262 races, won 137 and was placed in them all. His grandson Hirpinus ran 234 races winning 140 and being placed in the rest. On a monument to a charioteer, first century A.D., there are the names of thirty-eight oriental winning horses. They were imported from Barbary and Spain but there are no records of racing in either country at that time.

Most of the world's coinage was based on Alexander the Great's "Stater," but the type of horse represented is not by any means a slavish imitation. It differed with the types of horse in the countries which designed the coins and a study of these coins shows how realistically these types were reproduced by the metal workers, and that they were as representative as the types of the kings, emperors and other rulers who had them minted.

Frederick II, Emperor of the Holy Roman Empire, 1194, was a great horse breeder and imported Barbaric oriental mares for his breeding stud in Apulia. From the age of fourteen when he was boy king of Sicily, he rode all over his Empire at top speed on a series of wonderful horses, and was for ever warring against Popes and rebellious subjects. His favourite horse was called Dragon and he is described as appearing at Malfi mounted on a red horse coming to snatch peace from the earth. He became a legendary figure. If he rode a white horse he was aping the Saviour and accused of blasphemy; if a dun horse he was called death, and if a black one men trembled before the judge with the balance.

Popes kept large herds of wild horses and Europe was full of them. In A.D. 752 Pope Gregory III forbade St. Boniface to allow people to eat horseflesh, either wild or tame, but this seems to have been forgotten, as in A.D. 1000 the monks had a special blessing for the flesh of wild horses.

In 60 B.C. Virgil's points included a preference for glossy bay:

> *"And to the white or dun prefer the grey*
> *As yet a colt he stalks with lofty pace*
> *And balances his limbs with flexile grace.*
> *Light on his airy crest his slender head,*
> *His body short, his loins luxuriant spread."*

A muscular chest, flaming nostrils, quivering restless limbs, and a thick, full, fair mane, flowing over the right side of the neck. A double back and solid hoofs complete the picture. He, however, like many moderns, confuses grey as different to white, unless it was a way of saying the young horse is preferable to the old one.

The Duke of Ferrara's horses have been quoted as having contributed to our racing blood, but it is impossible to trace any racing blood of Italian origin in our English records. Only one Neapolitan mare is mentioned in the General Stud Book, though private stud records show many of them in non-racing stables. The Mantuan chargers imported by Henry VIII were heavy double deckers for pillion riding and armour carrying, and the racing Ferraras were small ponies as can be seen in the stuffed horses of the Ferrara palace, and there is no record of their having been imported to England. In any case they would have been eliminated by King Henry with the rest of the smaller breeds. The Neapolitans are never mentioned by any writer in England as racehorses.

Pillion riding was universal and horses were expected to be able to carry more than one rider. Roman horses of medieval times were mostly heavy war horses such as those seen in the Plaza San Marco and later in Donatello's famous statue.

The Italian light horses were a complete medley of Arab, "Turk," Barb, Spanish and local stock. Hackneys are mentioned as greatly esteemed and sent by Henry VIII to Italy.

In the Middle Ages horse racing took place in a Piazza at Siena, a semicircular brick paved area surrounded by a road of stone flags which formed the racecourse on the edge of a shallow basin. It included a steep descent and dangerous turn, and horses were often killed or injured. The festival was semi-religious and the winning banner bore a picture of the Virgin Mary. Races, bull fights and tournaments were held in honour of the saints.

The horses were chosen by casting lots and the riders did their utmost to unseat each other, and wore crash helmets to protect themselves against the furious blows of their rivals. The "palio" was a canopy which formed the prize but was usually replaced by a cup or money, and eventually races were called "palios" and seem to have begun in the thirteenth century.

In Florence the races were run through the city which was packed with people. The church bell tolled three times to call out the horses and the palio of brocaded crimson silk velvet, gold and ermine, was carried on a triumphal four-wheeled car adorned with carved lions and drawn by two horses ridden by postilions and the piazza was draped with blue velvet and yellow lilies, but in some of the races the horses were most wretched half-starved things brutally beaten, jeered at and abused.

Prizes were lengths of scarlet cloth, or farm animals from oxen to geese, the latter being derisively given to the third prize winner with a bunch of garlic. At Siena the horses were of high quality and were bred at Maremma.

The races at Siena were at first run with riderless horses. Buffalo fights were most popular and highly dangerous to the spectators, and a celebrated bull-fighter, Morello, rode the bulls in the ring, and buffalo-ridden races followed. There were also pitched battles with asses in which the team which managed to seize an ass and ride it twice round the square won the prize. Riders were hurled off and seldom kept their seats for more than a few yards, all rolling together on the ground. It seems to have been a game of all-in wrestling from which men and animals emerged only as battered wrecks. If a hostile company carried both donkey and rider out of the ring it was all in the game—the only thing forbidden was the *soaping of the animals*!

In 1581 an extra "palio" was competed for and among the riders was a peasant girl called Virginia, who though she did not win either the first prize or a silver cup, won the hearts of the young men who fell head over ears in love with her, and even the Governor of Siena was so enamoured that he presented her with a horse.

The races were started to a trumpet blast, a rope stretched across the course fell and the race was won on the third lap. The festivals were enlivened by magnificent cars representing the teams of contestants. A bad horse was jeered at, ill-treated and often beaten and left without food. The custom of reviling the wretched losing animals is referred to in early racing in Syria. No one had any use or mercy for a loser.

Even in modern days, as late as 1898, jockeys were allowed to administer a hail of blows to other jockeys and their horses, and even attacked each other with heavy whips before they started. The din of the battle was inconceivable and the "fantini" (jockeys) even when hopelessly beaten, continued to belabour all and sundry. They were even allowed to seize and drag each other off their horses and were left struggling on the ground, fighting to the death while the horses bolted, and on one occasion the cunning owners of an old horse which knew the course but could not win under a rider's weight, ordered the jockey to fall off and the horse won, all attempts to stop him having been frustrated by his bridle being made of breakable cardboard!

A story is also told in 1864 of a lady spectator in a stand overlooking a dangerous turn leaning forward and seizing one of the jockeys by the hair, knocking him off and bringing his rival down with him, while the horses went on and duly cashed in as first and second.

On another occasion in 1788 two factions were so determined to prevent each other winning that they attacked each other before the start with their whips and then got off their horses and fought with such fury that soldiers had to be called in to stop them. Meanwhile, a rank outsider won the race.

Jockeys, once engaged to ride, were imprisoned or went about with a guard to prevent bribery, but having won they became the object of fanatical idolatry from delirious crowds of admirers and were not likely to end the day sober.

Whether the saints in whose honour these wild festivities were held would have entirely endorsed their accompanying murders and cruelties seems, to say the least of it, doubtful, but the people of Italy have never considered human life very much and animal life not at all. In 1626, at Messina, many races were run both by footmen, mules, ordinary horses, and Barbs (or "ginets" as they call them in Syracuse) with the usual circumstances of throngs of people, ladies at the windows, gentlemen on horseback and in coaches about the streets.

The pernicious habit of calling horses bred in a country "native" is now spreading to Italy—Italian writers referring to imported thoroughbred stock afterwards bred in Italy as "Native Italian" and "indigenous sires," which may be very misleading to future historians. Italian and French breeders have been more successful than those of Germany in getting good *type* as to conformation. The remarkable success of Cavaliere Ginistrelli in breeding Signorinetta, winner of the English Derby and Oaks, gave a strong impetus to breeding and the breeders have spared no expense in securing the best blood. The Tesio Incisa stables won leading races in Italy and played a prominent part with Donatello, sold afterwards to M. E. Esmond.

Italy is not only ready to buy the best but is also willing to sell the best, so as to raise money, and Mussolini himself sanctioned the sale of Donatello when he heard that the exchequer would profit by it, it was the taxation which beset the new owner which caused him to resell the horse to England for a record price of £60,000, afterwards topped by an even higher price secured by Signor Tesio for the unbeaten horse Nearco sold to Benson for £62,000 and now a leading sire in England. Most of his stock are sprinters, Dante (Derby winner of 1945) stayed one and a half miles but broke down for future racing and had been beaten by Court Martial in the Two Thousand Guineas. Dormello is therefore the leading stud in Italy, followed by Gornate (S. de Montel), Mirandola, Oldaniza, and the National Stud at Mirabello.

[*Photo : Anscomb, Newmarket*

Nearco, bred in Italy

CHAPTER VII

FRANCE

THE Gaulish chieftains 400 B.C. were buried seated in their chariots with their horses and trappings; some have been dug up in the Champagne district. The Gauls fought against the Romans 292 B.C. with a thousand chariots.

When Hannibal (218 B.C.) reached Italy he defeated the Romans with his Spanish cavalry and Numidian horsemen who rode without saddle or bridle. The Gaulish envoys to Italy in 170 B.C. brought back twenty-two horses and we know from Cæsar that the Gauls certainly imported horses from other countries and paid highly for them and that horses bred in France were greatly superior to the bad and ugly German stock.

France is a country well suited for breeding horses of all sorts and was saturated with Arab blood from the Saracen invasions and horses brought back by the Crusaders. Normandy had much the same reputation for horse breeding in France as Yorkshire had in England. From the earliest days the Lords of the Abbeys in Normandy and Brittany were stocked with Arab, Barb and Spanish horses, and in A.D. 1260 the town of Brest was exchanged for a white Arabian mare and 100 livres of rent. Nine Arabian horses were brought home by the Crusader, Vicomte de Rohan, and let loose in the forests, where herds of semi-wild horses of Saracen origin were already established and founded a famous breed. In the Middle Ages, Valognes and Saint Lo were noted for cavalry. The horses of the Camargue were half-wild grey stock of Arab origin, introduced 125 B.C. in the neighbourhood of Arles. Later the Limousins were the pride of old France, as Royal saddle horses, but the Government studs were perpetually being overset by wars and political tornados which either swept the studs away or so dislocated the management that they ended in being a bewildering mixture of cart horse and oriental blood.

Le Merlerault (Orne), rich and well watered is, perhaps, the best county for brood mares. It was in this region that Louis XIV founded the Haras du Pin, the most celebrated of all French National Studs. A most important reorganization of horse breeding took place under his Minister Colbert who founded the Levant Company, and whose brother, C. Colbert, was Ambassador to Charles II. He distributed stallions of all the best Continental agricultural, harness and saddle breeds to serve different districts. The Levant Company stationed in Egypt and Syria was under contract to supply the King annually with ten Arabian horses of the highest breeding. These were specially valued and marked with a crown, and they and their progeny were by Royal command called "Royal" and kept exclusively for breeding. This is particularly important as Charles II was doing precisely the same thing in England at the same time and his "Royal mares from the Levant," "ever afterwards called Royal" in the same words as quoted by Cheny, undoubtedly came from the Colberts from the same source.

Purchases of horses in the Levant continued but the cost and transport difficulties increased in 1775. Louis XVI sent his two stud masters to Cairo to buy Arabian horses. On arrival in 1777 they were informed that they would have to go to the King of Yemen who was the only source of supply. Finding that horses would have to travel thence via the Cape, they went instead to Damascus where thirteen years before the previous Royal stud master had purchased seven Arabians in South Syria. They also purchased a few of the best and biggest horses from North Africa.

Anjou boasts not only of having supplied England with Plantagenets but of having founded in the reign of Louis XV the great cavalry school of Saumur, which ranks next in order of merit to the great National Stud which preceded it by about fifty years.

Navarre is called "the Arabia of France," for what reason it is difficult to explain, as Houel blamed the mild climate for its failure to produce first-class racehorses, but many good horses have since been bred there, though Normandy remains at the head of horse breeding.

A hundred years ago a number of studs were founded in the Navarre and in South-East France, and even in the vicinity of Paris, but the four great regions of horse breeding were in the West and South-West before the Revolution of 1789.

RACING UNDER LOUIS XV AND XVI

In 1681, coinciding with his importation of Royal Arab mares through the Levant Company, Louis XIV started racing in France with a plate valued at 1,000 pistoles, run at Echère, near St. Germain. It was won by a horse brought over from England, which the King offered to buy for its weight in gold. The owner refused to sell but offered the horse as a gift which ended in an interchange of "beaux gestes" on both sides.

In 1766 a match was run in the plain of Sablons near the Bois de Boulogne between two thoroughbreds belonging to Count de Lauraquais and Lord Forbes, each riding his own horse. The first-named owner is said to have made many enemies in England and had at one time owned Gimcrack. There was close contact between the French and English Courts, and in 1768 Lord Carlisle wrote to George Selwynn, "I am really sorry for my Newmarket friends who are overwhelmed by all these Frenchmen," and Hugo Meynell, annoyed beyond bearing, exclaimed in a fit of ill-temper that he had come to the point of "wishing peace to the devil and a good old war with France!" Under Louis XVI a certain method in racehorse breeding and racing began to be practised.

In 1783 there was rivalry between Vincennes and Fontainebleau. English aristocrats sent their horses to run in France. The chief owners were the Comte d'Artois (afterwards

Charles X), the Duc de Chartres (later Duke of Orleans and better known as Philippe Egalité) and the Dukes of Lausun and Fitz-James. These sportsmen also returned the compliment by running their horses in England. The Duc de Chartres[1] in 1785 ran the two-year-olds Rouge Vert and Glow-worm, bred in France. In 1784 he ran Cantator in the Derby and continued racing until his tragic end. Just before the Revolutionary cataclysm, excellent stallions were imported from England; Comus, Barbary, Glow-worm, King Pepin, Pyrois and Teucer and a number of brood mares.

In 1782–83 the great orator Mirabeau visited England to study racing, and published a pamphlet under the name of "Mr. Grossley." He was not apparently impressed by the appearance of the racehorses of the time and he makes a curious comment on the jockeys. "The groom who almost lies upon the neck of the horse holds the handle of the whip fixed before him." This description differs entirely from the pictures of race riders of the period who were depicted sitting upright and not "nearly lying on the horse's neck," so we must assume that they crouched more than the artists drew them.

The early history of studs in France was of constant importation of Arabians and the formation of huge breeding establishments which were broken up and reconstructed till in the Revolution all method was lost and all results scattered. The Pompadour stud was founded by Louis XV with a mixed lot of Spanish and Limousin cross breeds.

In 1764 the Prince of Lambese, Grand Equerry of France, was set to collect and organize breeding stock. The best oriental sires and thoroughbreds were imported and Pompadour was inundated with Arab blood. Normandy and the Limousin, which furnished cavalry and coach horses, attained a high reputation and continued to be among the most important trading centres.

On January 29th, 1790, the Revolution suppressed *all studs* by decree, in spite of the harassed protests of many officials, including Mirabeau, whose intervention was ignored. The decree was due to the financial crisis on January 19th, 1791, and the destruction was soon completed. In a couple of years the work of centuries was annihilated by the blind stupidity of fanatics. Just as has since happened in Russia, this ruthless destruction was speedily followed by bitter realization of the irretrievable error. The pressing need created by the dearth of horses is shown by the fact that in the midst of the ruin of all national institutions, the first to be re-established were studs, long before colleges or any other bodies.

In a frantic effort to replace the lost material, a law was passed in the third year for the establishment of seven stallion depots, but unfortunately they forgot that these organizations cannot be replaced in a moment and that mares are necessary to produce foals! Everything was lacking. Men and horses were alike missing. Destruction and degeneration were rampant and there were neither stallions nor brood mares, nor grooms to look after them. In the sixth year further desperate consultations took place.

It was the extraordinary feats of the cavalry at Stettin in 1806 that decided Napoleon, "the world's greatest Cavalry Commander," to reorganize horse breeding and repair the

[1] The Duc de Chartres' Hawker is known as the sire of one of our foundation mares.

damage as best he could and in 1838 the French Jockey Club was founded. "A good Arab stallion," said Napoleon "is the world's best horse, far better than the Thoroughbred for improving all breeds" and he proceeded to place first-class Arabs at the head of the studs and removed the Arab Stud at Deux Ponts in Bavaria to Pompadour in 1814. (It was revived in 1815.) Thoroughbreds were appreciated, but Arabs were everywhere proving the best improving sires. Napoleon imported numbers of them from his Egyptian campaign and must have had some of the best from the celebrated stock collected by Mohammed Ali. The type can be seen on the coin minted to celebrate the English victory in Egypt.

It was the period of Egypt's greatest celebrity in horse breeding, but the whole of this priceless stock was afterwards swept away, the last of them disappearing with the death of Ali Pasha Sherif at the end of the century. The Egyptian Agricultural Society has collected some, from the Crabbet Stud in England which got the best, but those bought by Mohammed Ali (the present Prince) were all sold to America in recent years.

But Pompadour was doomed to destruction, for once more breeding in France was dislocated and it sank to be a mere stallion depot. Again in 1833 it was officially reinstated —commissions were sent to Syria to buy Arabs and a few English thoroughbreds from England and the Anglo-Arab strain was founded.

Spanish horses were tried but failed as sires and eventually only the oriental horses were preserved. Promiscuous crossing had gone on for nearly a hundred years, and though an attempt was made to separate the breeds the stock was never pure. The first Great World War made havoc of breeding: the complete disruption of France and the wholesale looting of studs by Germany in Hitler's world war has brought final disaster, and it will be many years before the destruction of stock can be repaired—some in fact is irreparable. The Thoroughbred stock was however eventually salvaged and occupied a prominent position in 1949 racing, in fact French horses have swept off our best races and great is the outcry at home. The French winning horses (notably Arbar) are marked by their pronounced Arab heads and staying power and have compelled a partial revocation of the Jersey Act.

THE MARTINVAST STUD (THE GREY REVIVAL)

BARON DE SCHICKLER

PERIOD UP TO 1914—CRADLE OF THE LE SANCY STRAIN

To this ancient and royally imposing domain is due the great "Grey Revival" which will live in history as a faint spark which had flickered almost to ashes and sprang suddenly to a glorious flame destroying the rooted British conviction that grey was not a winning colour.

Of German origin, and owner of vast wealth, the Baron's great rectitude had earned him a great and unexpected tribute from a Frenchman, Baron d'Estreilles, in 1873, speaking of the honour in which his white jacket and cerise cap were already held among sportsmen.

Baron Schickler began by importing mares of the best English strains and a very beautiful grey stallion, The Nabob, from which he bred the famous Vermont and Bois Roussell, winners in the same year of the Grand Prix de Paris and the French Derby in 1864. In 1868 Suserain (The Nabob—Bravery) won the French Derby.

The stable then passed through one of those inexplicable bleak periods when nothing goes right, and which lasted for twenty years. A man must be indeed tenacious to survive such a long and grievous collapse, not to speak of the colossal expenditure. In 1886 a semi-victory was at last achieved by Sycomore in the French Derby, dead-heating with Dollar's son Upas.

Soon the sun emerged from the long eclipse with the birth of Le Sancy, foaled 1884 at Martinvast, by Atlantic out of Gem of Gems, and bred back on both sides to Alice Hawthorn. This mare was well named a Gem of Gems.

It is interesting to note that this wonderful colt foal very nearly perished during his first months in a paddock where there was an old form of stile in the form of a V inverted. The colt, examining the obstacle, threw up his head and was somehow caught by the jaws and wedged to the point of strangulation. A passer-by, after frantic efforts, managed to extricate him, but by that time he was lying apparently lifeless. The stud groom, hastily summoned, eventually brought him round but it was obvious that the jaws were dislocated. The vet arriving post haste from Chantilly said that nothing could be done, and it was only after weaning, two months later, that in trying to chew his corn the jaws snapped back into place. He developed late, only coming to his best as a racehorse at six years old when he finally made havoc of all opposition.

At two years he was only second to Frapotel in the Grand Criterium. At three years he beat Frapotel brilliantly in the Prix Daru, one of the best breeders' races of Long-champ, but faded out of the French Derby and Grand Prix, won respectively by Monarque and Ténébreuse, the champions of the Aumont stables, his long stride being ill adapted to these courses.

In the spring he won four consecutive races at Longchamps at four years old over his favourite distance of two thousand metres, but the opposition was not of the highest class and when he met the remarkable mare Bavarde she beat him.

At five years old he first showed remarkable class. After two defeats in the P. des Sablons and Lutece he won ten successive victories, the most conclusive of which was his defeat of Galaor by three lengths carrying $65\frac{1}{2}$ kilos.

A bad mistake was then made of putting him in the 6,200 metres of the "Gladiateur" race entailing a twice repeated hill climb of Longchamp and pitting him against Ténébreuse, the previous winner in 1888, which mare also won the Cesarewitch in England that year. Ténébreuse and her stable companion Sibérie lost him in this effort.

At six years old he won all his nine races, ending his career in a blaze of glory.

Beginning with a brilliant victory in the P. des Sablons, his crown of honour comprised in France: his second win of the Grand Prix de Deauville, where with his great weight of $65\frac{1}{2}$ kilos he toyed with adversaries such as Malagache, Pré Catelan, Saint Pair du Mont and Pourpoint; in Belgium he beat Yellow the great son of Dutch Skater in the Grand Prix de Sart, at Spa. His career makes one wonder how many potential champions may have been discarded and lost for ever for failing at two and three years old. Few owners persist long enough to achieve success at six years old. He went to stud at seven years old in 1891.

The luck of that stud had turned with vengeance. In 1892 the success of Chêne Royal, son of Narcisse, was followed in 1893 by that of Ragotsky by Perplexe, both descended from Vermont, the former through his dam Perplexité, grand-daughter of Vermont, and the latter through his sire Perplexe, sire of Perplexité.

This mare Perplexité bred to Le Sancy the colt Palmiste, winner of the French Derby of 1897. He was followed in 1903 by Ex Voto who ran away with it, in 1906 by Maintenon by Le Sancy out of Golden Rod, a daughter of Bend Or.

New triumphs were won in 1907 and 1911 by the produce of Le Sancy's daughters. One of these, registered by the particularly unpleasant name of Sea Sick, won the French Derby, Saf Saf dead-heated, and Alcantara II out of Toison d'Or also won it. The horses Palmiste and Ex Voto were bred by Schickler Stud, Maintenon and Alcantara were bred by the Vanderbilt and Rothschild studs.

Perplexité had distinguished herself by the victory in 1890 of her son Fitz Roya by Atlantic, and the Schickler colours brought off the double event of French Derby and Grand Prix in 1893 and 1894 with Ragotsky and Dolma Baghtché, and in 1900 Semendria carried off the Grand Prix again. Krakatoa was another stallion for this stud.

The birth in 1904 of Roi Hérode by Le Samaritain out of the splendid Roxelane by War Dance going back to Rouge Rose the dam of Bend Or, was an event of the utmost importance to England, for he was imported to Ireland and sired The Tetrarch, that famous spotted "rocking horse" whose flying races caused Steve Donoghue to call him the world's fastest horse, so fast as to be a freak never likely to be seen again.

Baron Schickler became possessed of Gem of Gems, as follows. He had a mare whose produce, Iceberg, had won several races, and this mare by Chanticleer was due to be sent to Atlantic. In looking up the stud book, he noticed that two daughters of Strathconan by Chanticleer were in existence and enquired if they were for sale. The reply was no for the grey and yes for the chestnut: things had got so far when he received a wire saying the grey was for sale at £1,000. The deal was fixed and Gem of Gems arrived in France in December 1881, in foal to Doncaster. Certainly she was a cheap purchase. She foaled in due course the first-class race mare Escarbouche, dam also of Fra Angelico, which with Chêne Royal accounted for first and second places in the French Derby of 1892.

The Grand Prix should have followed but for an error in tactics of the jockeys. In England these great stables carried off the Eclipse Stakes by three lengths with Justicier.

The crowning triumph of the Le Sancys, however, was destined to disaster in the

123

Mahmoud

Roi Hérode

124

Epsom Derby for Holocauste broke a leg, with the race in sight, after seven false starts. His dam Bougie produced Gardefeu, grey sire of Bruleur.

The grey strain, revived over nearly 300 years from the Alcock Arabian, was established in spite of all the clever writers. Professor Ridgeway said that speed and the bay colour were inseparable, and "Lottery" predicted in his book on racehorse breeding that the grey colour would completely disappear from the track; not to speak of almost the whole racing world which prophesied that no grey horse ever could or would win the Derby. Grey, they said, was a slow colour. Bay with a star was supreme. The first theories have been disproved wholesale by the grey influx of race winners and the unheard-of speed of The Tetrarch and some of his grey descendants, and then both were swept to the realms of nonsense by the grey Mahmoud's sensational win of the Epsom Derby in record time! The fastest time for the whole years of the Derby records. The year 1946 found again a grey Derby winner in Airborne. Nobody had really noticed his existence. He was the only grey in the race, and the world and its wife backed anything and everything else. His victory outraged expert opinion and confounded the prophets and was therefore vastly unpopular. Nobody had a good word to say about it, but the fact remains that he won from an impossible position in slashing style, coming up from nowhere like a rocket to win by a length.

Be it also remembered that Roi Hérode, one of the world's greatest sires, was not an outstanding racehorse and in his day so little was thought of him that the artist who painted a picture of Querido (who beat him by a neck in the Grand Prix du President), merely put Roi Hérode in the distance as a grey smudge. The smudge has left its golden hoof mark on posterity and Querido is a forgotten query.

The Tetrarch

125

CHAPTER VIII

GERMANY, AUSTRIA AND HUNGARY

THE cold-blooded coarse stock of Germany was noted even as early as Cæsar's time for being ugly and bad. Beauty was never a German ideal, and in the time of Tacitus, A.D. 116, they seem to have been inclined to divination, a practice which descended to Hitler. Intuitive horse breeding was a complete failure. Indeed, in 1486 horse breeding was frowned upon by the Clergy and the newly made Bishop of Augsburg, Count Friedrich von Zollern, having asked for his former master's opinion on whether he should take on a Bishop's duties, received a warning, "I tell thee again and again without hesitation if thou wilt follow in the footsteps of the Bishops of our days saying within thyself 'Lo, I will have so many horses,' then fear that which thou hast often heard from my lips." With further admonitions against worldly vanities, Geiler ends, "It would be better for thee if thou hadst never been born."

At one time Germany started a craze for deliberate ugliness and perversion. The Würtemberg stud manager, of sadist leanings, even tried to produce monstrosities by forced crossing of different species of animals, cattle, horses and deer. These grotesque fantasies came to no good, but a depraved taste spread all over Europe nearly obliterating the finer breeds. One astonishing branch of freak breeding was both ingenious and interesting. This was the production of polychromatic horses with amazing spots, stripes, patches and streaks, and abnormally profuse manes and tails, both sweeping the ground.

It was not till the introduction of Arabs that a revulsion of feeling took place and thoroughbreds were also imported to improve the stock.

The Trakhenen Stud in East Prussia was founded in 1732 with a mixed lot of one thousand horses! All sorts were collected, with Arabs as improvers. The Imperial Stud at Weil specialized in Arabs and imported a number of horses from Mohammed Ali's breed, including a famous white stallion called Bairactar and a bay called Tayar from Abbas Pasha's stud in Egypt. It is now the only surviving stud in Germany.

In the eighteenth century all studs were crammed with Arabian importations. Horse breeding commissions were sent to the desert to bring back the best obtainable and the class of horse in Germany, Prussia, Bavaria, and Hungary was transformed and orientalized, and in modern days thoroughbreds came from England. Frederick the Great's cavalry was famous. The Würtemberg Imperial Stud, founded in 1817, was by far the finest and most famous German stud, entirely Arabian of high class.

GERMAN THOROUGHBREDS

In the year 1822 bloodstock breeding began and the first races were run in Germany on the Mecklenburg course. The Mecklenburg Hochadel family founded studs, the original stock being, of course, from England. At first there were only a few races and breeders were obliged to go and compete in England, where the horses Arnim, Fauxpas, Meridian, Turnus, and Seahorse won races. In 1854 Baron Wilamowitz Mollendorf won with Scherz, a three-year-old German bred stallion, which won the Cambridgeshire at twelve to one by seven lengths in a field of nineteen.

Other provinces took up racing, especially in Silesia, led by Count Johannes Renard, who established a big stud and won the Cambridgeshire with Adonis, beating a field of forty-one. Adonis ran forty races winning twenty-seven times, the stakes amounting to M.172,322.

By 1860 Germany had a programme of fifty races, but studs came and went as the expenses were too high and the stakes too small, and there was no betting market. A change took place when in 1857 the Union Klub took over the racing leadership—they organized richer races and all the large clubs followed suit.

The International Klub had started in 1858, but the French had charge of the races and had the best horses, so German owners suffered. The oldest of the more important German races are the Friedrich Franz race, founded 1827; the German Derby, founded 1869; the Henckel race (which corresponds with the Two Thousand Guineas), 1871. Among others, the Union dates from 1834; the Preis der Diana (German Oaks), 1857; the Grosse Preis of Berlin, 1888; the Grosse Preis, 1858; and the Zukunfts, 1859; the German Leger, 1881, and the Leipzig Stiftungs Preis, 1875.

At the end of 1860 bloodstock from Neustadt and Trakhenen was amalgamated with Graditz, which imported stallions to produce a strong cavalry horse. Trakhenen became the headquarters of half-bred breeding. The horses were coarse and the aim was bone, not beauty or speed, but as much weight in the head as in the legs. Oppenheim stallions in possession of the Prussian State, which had hitherto been divided among the Neustadt Trakhenen and Graditz studs, were now concentrated at Graditz which imported stock of good class to produce military horses. The horses remained very coarse. Near Osnabruck was a stud of black Drenthe horses of Dutch origin which supplied London with funeral horses.

At the beginning of the year 1870 Freiberg Edward von Oppenheim started a large stud at Schlenderban, near Cologne, the produce of which equalled Graditz, but it was another twenty-five years before any more big studs were founded such as Weinbergs Waldfried stud and Haniels Walburg stud. At the end of the nineteenth century German

127

bloodstock had declined all over the country, quantity taking the place of quality. Big doubtful foreign horses took the place of good sires.

A change for the better came when the Von Weinbergs bought Festa (St. Simon— L'Abesse de Jouarre) for 1,000 gns. at Newmarket, and she bred five first-class winners in five successive years, each being the best of its year. Of these Fabula, being in England in 1914, was sold by auction as an enemy possession and went to Spain.

In 1913 the bay, Dark Ronald, was brought over from Ireland. Winner of the Royal Hunt Cup he was so outstanding at stud that the Treaty of Versailles insisted on his return. Another sire was the French horse Nuage, by Simonian ex Nephite, by Flying Fox. The quality of German bloodstock derives from Dark Ronald and Festa. In fact this blood is so inbred that the demand for out crosses was imperative.

The war of 1914 stopped all importations, and Germany was thrown on her own resources. The chief stud was still Graditz of mixed thoroughbreds and half-breds. The latter won five Olympic medals in 1936. This stud had been successful on the German turf from 1870 to 1900, a decline then set in though Baron Oppenheim still led the way.

Nereide was considered in Germany the best race mare ever bred there and was bred by the Erlenhof stud founded after the first Great War. No German horses have reached English classic form, and Nereide borrowed on the dam's side from Italy.

It is impossible to say what has become of German horse stock since 1939. We know that vast numbers of horses were stolen from Continental racing studs and lots of others destroyed. At the time of the French surrender there were whole trains of horse boxes all waiting with grooms and tackle to take the racehorses back to Germany which indicates that the date of the surrender had been pre-arranged with Petain, this date had been "prophesied" by Hitler long previously. Hitler's prophetic instincts, when proved correct, always had a solid base which was founded on more than intuition.

The German climate is not very good for bloodstock breeding. During hard winters the young horses have to spend the most important months of their development in the stables, whilst in England and France they can run free in the meadows the whole year round. These disadvantages, also the fact that training must be discontinued for the whole of the winter, necessitating overhaste in preparing the horses for their big events, are hindrances which foreign competitors have not to reckon with. They will probably therefore always remain dependent on new importations. The German nation as a whole has no natural instinct for good horses. Individual breeders have arisen, and the Prussians are the best horsemen, but it is not a universal national gift as in England, Ireland and Wales.

AUSTRIA AND HUNGARY

Hungarian horse stock has been a mixture of cold and hot blood like that of Russia and Poland, but in the fourth century must have had very little but cold blood, being described as having a great hooked head with protruding eyes, a mane to his knees, hollow guts, and a body "full of empty corners." A truly ill-favoured creature of cart-horse type, and a bad cart horse, too. Turkish-Arab blood improved things considerably, and Don John of Austria had a stud of horses from Smyrna in 1595. A stud of completely mixed breeds, light and heavy, was founded at Mezzoheges in 1785 and Babolna followed in 1789. Thoroughbred racing was started in 1822 by Count Szechenyi, and a Thorough-bred stud was founded at Kisber with some Arab blood as well.

Lippizza, near Trieste, was the site of a stud formed in 1580 with Spanish and Arab stock; the Viennese High School horses became famous, they were snow white, of commanding appearance, extremely Arabian in type though with a Spanish convexity of head.

It is impossible to reckon the havoc which must have been wrought by the last war and useless to go into more details of all the various European studs which have probably now ceased to exist.

We must, however, mention the grand mare Kincsem. As a two-year-old she won ten races on ten different courses. As a three-year-old she ran in seventeen races and won them all, among others the Hungarian Two Thousand Guineas and Oaks, and on May 21st, the Austrian Derby, and two days later a two-mile and one-mile race. Following this up she won four big races in Germany, the Grand Prize on September 3rd, and another race at Frankfurt on September 8th. On September 28th and 29th she won two more races and on October 7th the Hungarian St. Leger. Two days later she won a race of a mile, and by October 23rd she had won three more races. At four years old she ran no less than fifteen races, winning them all. She ran her first race on April 22nd over one mile, then a race in Pozsony, one in Budapest and another in Vienna, and by May 30th had won nine races; she was then entered for the Goodwood Cup in England and won, with two horses against her, having started as the outsider.

Baron Maurice Hoeller recorded that Lady Golightly made the running with Kincsem last and that on reaching the rise her jockey held her back for fear she might slip, but on entering the straight Lady Golightly was done with, while the seven-year-old Pageant was a good six lengths ahead. At the distance Madden took up his whip and the "Hungarian Wonder" shot past and won by two lengths. Mr. de Blaskovitch offered £10,000 for her but it was refused. On September 3rd she dead-heated for the Baden-Baden Grand Prize, giving the winner weight, and she won the run-off by five lengths, and then won three more races at home.

As a five-year-old she won twelve more races, and on October 21st she ran in Pest and won in a canter by ten lengths carrying 11.6, beating Illona (9.2), the winner of the Hungarian Oaks and Guineas. She had won in all fifty-four races undefeated, carrying weight up to 12st. 1lb.

One of her descendants, Vatinius, won the Hungarian Derby in 1921. During the Rumanian raid of 1919 they carried off three hundred thoroughbreds and the stock disappeared. The Bolshevists destroyed the Budapest racecourse and it was not reorganized till 1925. Efforts were made to get horses from Germany, but no sooner had a move been made than Hitler's war put an end to further breeding.

CHAPTER IX

RUSSIA AND POLAND

THE original Russian and Polish stock was of Mongolian origin. Russia was conquered by the Mongols in the thirteenth century and the oldest frozen remains of a Siberian burial dating from c. 5000 B.C. have unmistakably "cold" type with erect manes. They are called the yellow mares, so doubtless traces of their colour still remain. Probably they were of the northern dun colour, their heads are big and long and there is not the smallest indication of hot blood in what remains of them. In the reign of Ivan the Terrible (sixteenth century) oriental sires were imported by the thousand, but the Tsars also imported eight thousand horses yearly from the Tartars. The Cossack horsemen have always been famous for horsemanship and trick riding much in the same way as the cowboys of South America. The native horses have remained of a plain small type very enduring and handy under saddle. The better-class horse stock has been influenced by the Arab importations of the Tsars and probably the common stock have a dash of oriental blood with Mongol predominating. There used to be wild herds of these very ugly, asinine, erect-maned but speedy ponies in the Russo-Chinese steppes and deserts, but these gradually became crossed with domestic breeds and are only feral, not truly wild. It is also doubtful if Tarpan crosses remain fertile beyond the first or second cross.

Count Orloff's Russian trotters were the most inbred breed of modern days, repeatedly crossed and re-crossed to its own nearest relation of Arab and Barb blood and a Dutch Hart-draver trotting mare and her son, a celebrated horse called Barss. The saddle section was founded on an Arab and the harness section on a Barb called Smetanka. The Orloff stud was sold on the death of Count Orloff in 1845 to the Russian Government, and removed to Khenovaya. Russia has imported large numbers of thoroughbreds and Arabs since 1919, and during the second World War their cavalry did marvellous work.

POLAND

The Chrestowka stud was founded in 1508. It was a high-class stud of mainly Arabian blood and used to sell Arabians to the Turks and these were called "Turks" and many mares found their way to England as "Turks" or "Polands."

All the pedigree stock both of sheep, cattle and horses was maliciously destroyed during the Great War of 1914 as representative of aristocracy. Horses from the great studs of Antoniny and Slavuta were even tortured, burnt alive and hanged in the market places, their princely owners being massacred and their palaces burnt down.

The Potockis tried to begin again with new blood, but no sooner had they started racing than the studs were once more wiped out in the Greater War so that nothing now remains of the *original* blood, all of which has gone. The sole surviving line was through the Arab Champion Skowronek, imported to England and made famous by the Crabbet Park stud where he was only second to Raseem and Shareer, winners of the World's Champion 300 gns. Gold Cup outright three times in succession. He was full of Abbas Pasha blood as the Potockis had purchased many stallions from Egypt and some from Crabbet, notably Champion Pharaoh, but Euclid, a stallion from India, proved a failure. It seems useless to go into further details of the once fine Polish studs as the Greater War has put an end to them and any reformation will have to be new ventures.

South Russian pony, 300 B.C.

CHAPTER X

SPAIN

ANCIENT IBERIA (Southern Spain) included Andalusia and Murcia and South Valencia (south-east region) and the coastal parts of Valencia and Catalonia and Lower Aragon bounded by the Pyrenees. It was inhabited by several tribes, chiefly builders and metal workers. The whole of Spain and Portugal was originally Ligurian and was invaded by Celts and Iberians, who came from North Africa before 1000 B.C.

The Celts came into Spain about 600 B.C., taking Central Spain and Portugal, and the Ligurians departed to Germany; towards the third century B.C. the Celts and Iberians began to merge into Celtiberians with Iberian (North African) predominance, and we see Celtic types of pony and another with a dash of oriental in some of the Spanish cave drawings.

Liria was twenty-five miles from Valencia. Some Lirian vases third century B.C. are painted with battle scenes with infantry and cavalry and (in one case only) of ships. In hunting scenes the Iberians, both men and women, are shown mounted and on foot, attacking stags with short spears, and on a vase from Archena, Iberian soldiers are fighting another tribe which they caught hunting wild boars. They were good horsemen and rode both astride and sideways with saddle and stirrups, snaffle-bit and reins. The horses are well bred with slender limbs and high tail carriage, one is piebald—there is nothing of the battle horse about them.

The first of the Eastern people to discover Spain were the Phœnician Arab Sea Traders, c. 2000 B.C. They had remarkably gypsy-like characteristics, being described in the *Odyssey* as tricksters, seducers and kidnappers arriving in some small town and dazzling the inhabitants with their wares, golden chains strung with amber beads, and gaudy oriental finery, and their return cargo may have comprised boys or men to be sold in the oriental slave markets. They had the gypsy gift of making life attractive with gew-gaws, silks and commodities unobtainable elsewhere; by 1100 B.C. they had colonized Cyprus, Rhodes, Sicily, Malta, and Sardinia. In all these places they left traces of horses progressing from east to west. Their first landing in Spain was at Cadiz and after a great sea battle in 800–700 B.C. the Iberians came under their dominion and paid tribute to Tyre, which only ceased when Tyre was captured by Nebuchadnezzar 573 B.C. and the Phœnicians abandoned the Peninsula. Greek settlements followed in the seventh century B.C., which were evicted by the Carthaginians a hundred years later. The Phœnicians had an extensive trade also with Cornwall, Ireland and Brittany.

The mixture of horse types must have been general, Greek, North African, Celtic, Andalusian and Arabian, and from A.D. 428 for over a century, heavy Vandal horses with convex heads. The early Iberian vases, however, show distinctly oriental types.

There is a possible connection between the blood-sweating horses of China and the blood-sweating Andalusian, and with the high-stepping Chinese horses. There was extensive trade with Portugal, Italy, and China as early as the last century B.C., but there is no direct evidence of interchange of horses. The Spanish Andalusian appears to be descended from a prehistoric stock, and recent efforts have been made to preserve it from extinction though in the Middle Ages it was nearly extinguished by crosses of all sorts, and has been greatly modified from what it used to be, a faster element has lately been encouraged. Originally it was a magnificent parade, cavalry and coach horse celebrated all over the Continent, and has influenced vast numbers of breeds, including Lippizzas, Neapolitans, Hanoverians and English hunter stock, and some draught breeds. It had masses of curled or waved mane and tail, and was of proud and noble appearance. The famous breeder, Ruy'd Andrade, still preserves the Zapata and Querriro strains of Jerez, which are of big "battle horse" build, and their pedigrees go back to the eighteenth century. They are now used for agriculture. The Spanish Jennet was smaller and lighter, but had the same head, and it is from Spain the Barb got his convex sheep's profile which is essentially a non-eastern feature and very persistent in heredity, suggesting an original foundation breed, just as the concave profile stamps itself on its descendants.

Another type bred for the bull ring at Arrepiado in Portugal is very alert and quick. In Portugal, well-trained horses are required able to dodge and turn, not like the slaughter horses of Spain, which are only there to be killed.

A fourth type is a fine breed called Alter, akin to Lippizzas but chestnut in colour.

At the close of the sixteenth century the Spaniards were making great efforts to breed faster horses, and at one time they gained a reputation for speed which was lost by experimental cart-horse crosses. This speed is now being developed once again.

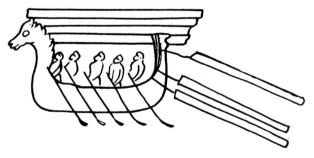

Arab horse-headed Phœnician boat, B.C.

CHAPTER XI

AMERICA

THERE were no horses in America till Columbus landed in 1493, followed by de Soto and Mendoza about forty years later, nor was there the smallest tradition of their ever having existed, the native Indians being panic stricken at the sight of horsemen. In 1539 de Soto landed 213 horses to lighten his ships, but Allyon had already taken over ninety in 1525. Three years later Navarrez had lost most of his horses at sea and had to eat the rest while constructing fresh ships. In 1541 de Soto also lost 150 horses, only saving forty. Thirty-five of these were also killed for food after his death.

The last Spanish expedition left five stallions and seven mares, which in two centuries multiplied to herds of 6,000. The main importations added to these herds were Arabs and Barbs which produced the mustangs and cow ponies. Later on heavy European breeds were imported for agriculture.

The earliest racing began in Virginia on rough tracks a quarter of a mile long which gave rise to the name of "quarter horse," for the mustang-thoroughbred crosses raced on them. The most notable sire was the little Janus, only 14.0¾, a thoroughbred four-miler brought to the Roanoke stud from England. He had extra powerful hind legs, and his progeny were noted as whirlwind sprinters unequalled at "quarter" racing. These horses were coarse and strong, useful cattle horses, and remained famous for two hundred years from 1688. The first-named in the records were Bonny and Watt.

The American Stud Book shows numerous Arabians and Spanish stock of all sorts of queer colours apparently originally of Indian feral foundation, for we do not find these variegated colours elsewhere except in the case of the speckled Appaloosas, golden Palominos and parti-coloured Colorado Rangers and Pintos, which can be traced to Arabia in remote times and occasionally reappear in various parts of the world where piebald and skewbald are fairly common, the others being specialized in America.

Before 1650 there had been desultory importations of heavy horses from England, but it was only at this date that the London Company imported some superior ones. In 1609 there had been importations of Dutch and Flemish horses and later saddle horses from England. New York belonged to England in the fourth year of Charles II and his reign was therefore the start of serious racing in both England and America, where racing began in 1665 and was continued for over a century at Long Island where the first

Greyhound, winner of the world's trotting record

Messenger, imported from England 1786 and was twenty years at stud

135

American racecourse, an oval of two miles, was laid out by Governor Nicolls. One of the first thoroughbreds was Bulle Roch, a son of the Darley Arabian, foaled 1709 and imported by Samuel Gist.

Slyboots, Dabster, and Routh's Crab, and Tryall followed. Monkey, the son of the Lonsdale Arabian, though twenty-two when imported in 1747, made his mark in the next seven years. Jolly Roger, grandson of the Godolphin, was sent over about the same time. Morton's Traveller, a grandson of the Byerley Turk, carried on till 1768. Heber (of *Heber's Calendar*) traded in tobacco and likewise in horses. The first Jockey Club in the world was started at Charlestown in 1734.

Edward Fenwick was founder of the Turf in Carolina, importing eight stallions of Godolphin blood to the Johns Island stud (1750–88) on Stone River. The chief stallions were Brutus, Tarquin, Black-and-all-Black, Pam, Centinel, Fallower, Shadow, and Matchless. He also imported six Godolphin-bred mares in three different batches. His son imported Flimnap.

The first horses in use in Carolina had been the Narragansett pacers, an entirely sorrel breed, imported from Rhode Island in 1682. They were natural pacers. They were evidently descended from the Spanish and Barb "running" pacers so renowned in the seventeenth century as saddle horses, and were described as of "lofty carriage" and very easy to the rider. "Pace easie and wonderful swift," as described by an English writer. Very likely they were of the same breed now called Palominos as the solely chestnut colour suggests.

In Carolina there were the Chicksaw and Choctaw horses, which were also of Spanish foundation from Florida, a small breed, active and handsome and giving very beautiful and fast stock when crossed with English horses. The longest Carolina racehorse pedigrees all go back to Chicksaw horses.

The Seminole horses are described by W. Bartram as the most beautiful and sprightly horses anywhere to be seen, small and as delicately formed as the American roebuck. They, too, came from the Andalusian importations.

Lewes and Clark, 1804, said that the horses of the plains were a splendid race, active and hardy and like English thoroughbreds; some pied with large spots of white irregularly scattered and intermixed with white feet and stars. The differences of confirmation being probably due to different types of foundation stock in the feral horses of mixed Spanish extraction.

A word must be said for the tough little Argentine Criollo descended from Spanish-Arab-Barb ancestry and developed over centuries of feral life to a stout hardy type. In the wars of liberation the expeditions were of 100 to 200 leagues with little food and no shelter. Criollos were dun, khaki, pied or skewbald of medium size, 13.3 to 14.3, skull broad at the base and face narrow. A cobby, thick-set horse with lots of bone and endurance. The dun colour suggests Scandinavian and Northern blood somewhere. Mancha and Gato went in 1928 from Buenos Ayres to New York, 13,350 miles in 504 stages, averaging twenty-six miles a day. Their ages were eighteen and nineteen years.

One of the stages of ninety-three miles across the desert of Ecuador was done in a day with a temperature of 120 Fahrenheit without food or water. These horses died in 1945 aged thirty-five and thirty-six years.

A thoroughbred horse named Valiant was imported to the Westover stud, Virginia by James River, c. 1755. Crawford was at stud (1762) in Virginia at a fee of £20 currency. He was a grey 15.2 by Lord Crawford's Arabian. Traveller, another half Arab by the same sire, was at stud at £10 in 1767. The Crawford or Stamford Turk will be found in *Pond's Calendar*, 1751, p. 224. In 1762, Cade was imported from England. He was inbred to the Godolphin Arabian, being by Old Cade (by Godolphin Arabian) his grand-dam also by the Godolphin. Other horses of Arabian origin continued to be imported as "English" horses, including Pharaoh, another grandson of the Godolphin Arabian, and a "fine Arabian mare."

The same year a Barb called Abdulla and a "leopard-coloured" Arabian mare are noted. The Barb seems to have been by an Arabian belonging to the Emperor of Morocco out of a grey mare belonging to the King of Arzela in West Barbary.

The first Carolina Jockey Club was started in 1758. Doubt has been thrown on Bruce's statement that Old Tarquin was out of an Arabian mare because no Arabian *mare* was likely to be in England in the seventeen-fifties. This, of course, is incorrect as Arabian mares were often found there, bred from the numberless Arabians then in England.

Shadow was very successful in Carolina. He began racing at nine years old and was unbeaten, retiring at the age of eleven. In 1795, William Randolph of Turkey Island founded a Thoroughbred breeding stud. Everard Mead also bred eight good colts (1774 to 1784) which sold for £14,000.

The Roanoke stud was founded on Celer's blood—Celer was by Janus (1776) by the Godolphin Arabian, exported to Virginia. Janus ran in England 1751–53, as Little Janus. He was exported before 1761 and lived to be thirty-four. Celer lived to be thirty. About 1760, a number of breeders imported English stallions. Amongst them John Hoomer was a large speculative importer. Randolph's first mare was of doubtful stock. She bred Quasha by a grandson of Flag of Truce. Medley, a grey colt (1776), was imported 1784. Descendants of the Darley Arabian, Mosco Grey Arabian and the Godolphin Arabian, were imported into Maryland. The Belair stud was started in 1746, and is now the property of Mr. W. Woodward. A cup was won in 1751 by a horse belonging to the Lewis family, still prominent on the Turf.

James De Lacey was termed the Father of the New York Turf. He imported Wildair, Lath by Shepherd's Crab, and the Cub mare, reckoned the best mare ever imported, better even than Selima as a foundation mare. The famous Godolphin mare Selima, "Queen of Maryland," won against the imported Tryall in four-mile heats in 1752 at Gloucester, Virginia, for $10,000.

Edward Leedes repurchased Wildair for £500 in 1773 and he went back to England. In 1775, owing to the Revolution, the stud was sold and De Lacey emigrated to England.

In 1780 a continental lieutenant stole True Briton from a cousin of his and took him to Connecticut, where he sired the famous Justin Morgan.

Magnolia, foaled 1780, was a son of Lindsay, his great grand-dam being Selima by the Godolphin Arabian. He belonged to George Washington, who sold him for 5,000 acres of land in 1788 to the revolutionary Harry Lee.

Diomed, by J. Wootton. This is the genuine original picture

Fearnought, a son of the Godolphin Arabian, about fifteen hands, was imported in 1764, and is considered to have surpassed all other horses of the Colonial period as a sire. He succeeded Janus, 14.0¾, also a son of the Godolphin Arabian, as an important sire. Fearnought was a stayer; Janus, himself a stayer and bred to stay, lived to be thirty-four, so Fearnought was doubling a stayer! Breeders may, however, take note of the curious fact that the pre-eminence of all his stock was as brilliant *sprinters* of thrilling speed and not as stayers. Their combined blood had incalculable influence on American bloodstock. From 1774 the Revolution put a stop to racing, and studs were scattered wholesale.

Most of the horses imported after the crisis were cheap lots, but four were outstanding sires: Medley, Shark and Messenger (imported 1786), and Diomed. The pictures of Diomed in America are clearly not the same horse as that in the Wootton picture owned by his breeder's family in England. The markings are quite different. Most of the American pictures are not Diomed, as they show a bob-tailed, heavy-headed horse with no white feet visible in the picture. In the alleged Stubbs picture in U.S.A. he is shown bob-tailed with only a white hind foot. The Wootton picture has a narrow blaze with small spot on nose and a long near hind stocking and a long tail. This is an undoubtedly genuine portrait done from life.

The famous sculptor, Herbert Haseltine, modelling the equally famous Man o' War

Shark by Marske (reputed sire of the great English Eclipse) and winner of 16,097 gns. and eleven hogsheads of wine, was sold for £120 at the age of seventeen. His success was as great in America as his failure had been in England, as he sired a number of important brood mares.

The grey Messenger was twenty years at stud. He was the grand-sire of American Eclipse and was the progenitor of the standard trotters. (See p. 178.)

American Eclipse, by Diomed—Damsel, a brilliant daughter of Messenger, had a sensational career. Bred by General N. Coles, he did not run till he was five, when he won twice at two- and four-mile heats. He was sent to stud for two years and in the autumn of 1821 was put hastily into training and defeated the famous Lady Lightfoot, Heart of Oak and Flag of Truce. In 1822 he twice beat a dangerous rival, Sir Walter, at four-mile heats. He then ran what is amusingly referred to as a "four-mile dash" against Sir Charles (by Sir Archy) for $1,500 a side, and Sir Charles broke down, the "dash" having been too much for him. Eclipse, then carrying 126 lb., ran a tremendous race in 1823 against Henry (Sir Archy—Diomed mare) carrying 198 lb. (17 stone) for $20,000 a side, which magnified itself into a North v. South contest which brought sixty thousand American enthusiasts to the course. Henry won the first heat by a length. William Crafts, the jockey on Eclipse, was summarily removed from the saddle and replaced by a boy, Sam Purdy, and Eclipse won the second heat by two lengths. In the third heat he won by a large margin. He was then nine years old.

He sired Ariel, a mare which ran fifty-seven races in five years, and won forty-two (seventeen of them at four-mile heats); she was second in every race which she lost, and was ridden three thousand miles from place to place. She began as a sprinter but must have been a stayer.

Black Maria, by American Eclipse out of Lady Lightfoot (thirty races and unbeaten till she was eleven years old) ran twenty-five races, being first thirteen times, second ten times and once third. Her greatest performance was on October 13th, 1832, carrying 8 st. 6 lbs. at four-mile heats. She won the first, dead-heated with Trifle in the second, lost the third to Trifle and the fourth to Lady Relief by a neck and won the fifth by beating them both. Lady Relief died after the race and Trifle was laid up with a game leg for nearly a year. She distanced Black Maria in a return match owing to an error of her rival's jockey. Trifle had previously done prodigies of endurance and speed.

A quantity of importations were made by Messrs. Hoomes and Taylor. William Lightfoot imported Saltram (Derby, 1783) at the age of twenty. Another company imported Sarpedon, Tranby, the lovely Zinganee, Margrave (St. Leger, 1832), and Trustee, and the mares Delphone and the dam of Beeswing. James Jackson imported Leviathan and Glencoe, for which latter horse he paid 2,000 gns.

A number of memorable matches were run. American Eclipse v. Henry, 1823; Wagner v. Grey Eagle, 1839; and Boston v. Fashion in 1842. (At nine years Boston had already won thirty-seven matches of four-mile and three-mile heats, and the mare, Fashion, seven races at less distances.) Boston carried 126 lb. and Fashion 111 lb. Fashion won, but Boston ran again three days later against Marnier at four-mile heats which he won and again won later in the season. He retired with a total of forty wins out of forty-five starts and twenty-eight out of thirty races at four-mile heats.

Fashion had won twenty-three races out of twenty-four when she met the unbeaten Peytona in 1845. Peytona was a gigantic mare nearly seventeen hands, and she won again, but was badly defeated in a return match with Fashion. Peytona won altogether $66,000. Fashion bred good stock, but Peytona was no good at stud.

Boston's sons, Lexington and Lecomte, were the next most famous runners, and after some brilliant racing Lecomte's owner challenged the world. Lexington beat Lecomte's record for four miles, doing it in 7 mins. $19\frac{1}{2}$ secs., and beat Lecomte right out of the field, and out of life itself, for he never fully recovered and died early.

Planet, grandson of Trustee out of Nina by Boston, winner of twenty-seven out of thirty-one starts, was the last horse of note before the Civil War. Racing was abandoned till 1864.

Lexington's descendants completely monopolized the succeeding ten years. He himself died at twenty-five in 1875, and was bewailed as a national hero. He was only $15.2\frac{1}{2}$, and was a bright chestnut with white feet. Many of his stock were never defeated, and he got both the fastest sprinters and the best stayers. He is said to have sired a world's record number of first-class racers. Curiously enough his male line is now nearly extinct, but his blood is predominant.

Racing now had a revival but it was not universal. Kentucky was a leading stallion at Mr. Belmont's stud, but died early. The Kentucky Derby and Oaks were started in 1875, and the former is worth $50,000.

Leamington, foaled in 1853, son of Faugh a Ballagh and a Pantaloon mare, was a failure for six seasons in England but proved a dazzling success in America. He sired Iroquois (Derby and St. Leger), imported to England by Mr. P. Lorillard.

Longfellow was his most popular son and won fourteen of his seventeen starts. This horse's dam, Nantura, was grand-dam of Ten Broeck, winner of twenty-two out of twenty-eight races and holder of almost every major record. We hear of him, as of many others, that he was the fastest horse that ever lived. As a sire he was mediocre.

From 1880 to 1890 was a golden era. General Hardy's Bonnie Scotland was wasted for fifteen years. He began his real stud career at the age of nineteen in 1872. In his first season he got winners of 137 races. In 1874, when he was twenty-one years old, his progeny won 169 races. He died at twenty-seven. He was by Iago and the great Queen Mary. With him died the system of four-mile heats, the last of which was the Great Long Island Stables run at Sheepshead Bay, which soon became a popular course. Glenmore was the last of the really famous four-milers.

Luke Blackburn by Bonnie Scotland was the next great star, winning twenty-two out of twenty-four races up to two miles. He might indeed be called a constellation! He was indifferent to hard or soft ground and to good or bad conditions, and at three years old ran right away from all opposition. He pulled his jockey's arms out and went ahead like a racing steam tug. He made havoc of horses old and horses young, and of all weights and distances. This horse again is spoken of as one the like of which has never been seen before or since.

Bramble, also by Bonnie Scotland, followed, winning fifteen out of twenty races. He failed at stud, his only success being the almost accidental mating with Roseville from which Ben Brush was produced.

Miss Woodford, a big mare (1880) by Billet (Voltigeur) again said to be "the best mare ever bred" in America, winning thirty-seven out of forty-eight races, and she held the record for money won till 1925, with $118,270. Billet's son Raceland won seventy high-class races and $116,391.

Glenelg by Stockwell, was the sire of Little Minch, a sprinter that won eighty-five races, and Gleaner that won fifty. His daughter, Firenze (1884) succeeded Miss Woodford in the title of best mare that ever lived. She was small and a weight carrier and won forty-eight races, being second in twenty others between 1886–90. She lowered the $1\frac{1}{2}$ mile record to 2.33, on which she was publicly kissed by an enthusiastic crowd. She won $112,586.

Virgil by Vandal became leading sire in 1885. He sired two meteors in Vigil and Vera Cruz. His son, Hindoo, won, up to three years old, twenty-five out of twenty-nine races and went on to even greater triumphs at four.

At stud, Hindoo got Tremont, the fastest American two-year-old, winner in 1886 of thirteen consecutive races. Even his half brother Hanover, could not touch him on the Turf. Hindoo, Luke Blackburn, and Hanover, were the property of the famous Dwyer brothers. Hanover is said to have been a magnificently beautiful, indeed "glorious" chestnut horse, faultless, and with a lovely head. He won in succession fourteen of the most valuable stakes of the Metropolitan season. He won twenty out of twenty-seven starts, but was raced nearly to death, was nerved and raced again, ending with thirty-two wins out of fifty starts. He was a splendid sire but died of gangrene in his nerved leg. His daughter, Rhoda B, produced Orby (Derby) and Rhodora (One Thousand Guineas). Another daughter, Urania, was grand-dam of Durbar II (Epsom Derby, 1914).

The owner of Firenze was Francis Ben Ali Haggin, who bought Salvator by Prince Charlie as a yearling in 1887. One of the fastest colts in training was Tenny, and as he had a "saddle back" it is interesting to note that he won a great number of races. He and Salvator had several prodigious matches but Salvator beat him often by the merest hairsbreadth. In the last years of the nineteenth century races were further shortened.

The American Derby of 1893 was the first race in America which was worth $60,000. It was won by Boundless. In 1890 it increased to $67,675 and was won by Potomac from Mr. Belmont's Nursery stud where St. Blaise had been a leading sire in 1883. His Highness, also from this stud, won the Futurity and eight other races, and netted $106,900 in one year alone. Morello was the next meteor in 1892. A grandson of Leamington, he was cast out and sold for $100, afterwards winning twenty-four races out of thirty-two.

Domino, a speed marvel, surpassed them all, winning the Futurity Stakes of 1893. He was the grandson of Alarm, the Champion miler of his time. He was purchased by James R. Keene, of New York, who had won big stakes in England with Foxhall. As a two-year-old he was unbeaten, winning $170,890, a record for a two-year-old anywhere up to a few years ago, but he could not race more than one mile. His total wins were $193,550 (nineteen wins out of twenty-five starts). He died suddenly at the age of six. His son Commando also died at seven years old. Domino's quickness from the start was said to be incredible. He met his fate in Henry of Navarre, descended from Leamington. This brilliant horse won some sensational victories, but failed as a sire.

Lexington's son, Norfolk, was never beaten, and established record times for three-mile heats. A great mare was Marion, grand-daughter of Bonnie Scotland. She was

142

bought for $500 by Mr. Winters and Bruce Lowe called her the best American brood mare. Two of her best sons were Emperor of Norfolk (twenty-one out of twenty-nine races) and El Rio Rey, never beaten.

Emperor became leading sire at the Santa Anita Stud near Los Angeles, owned by Mr. E. J. Baldwin. His son went back to Ireland with his owner, Richard Crokes, who emigrated to that country. His name was changed to Americus and he sired the flyer Americus Girl. She ran five furlongs at Epsom in $56\frac{4}{5}$ secs. and was the dam of Lady Josephine, dam in turn of the dazzling Mumtaz Mahal. California was the home of many good horses. Joe Hooker bred to Marion, 1889, a chestnut filly Yo Tamblen, winner of forty-four races. She unfortunately was the property of a gambler and was grossly over-raced and died foalless.

The final substitution of short for long distance racing completely revolutionized racing at the beginning of this century. A man called "Snapper" Garrison had originated a new seat and James Todhunter (Tod) Sloane introduced it with electrifying results. He rode crouched on his horse's neck "like a monkey on a stick," and being an admirable judge of pace won races wholesale, and every jockey in the world imitated him.

From that time races were "all out" from start to finish. It was "hell for leather and Devil take the hindmost." Horsemanship as a fine art died a violent death and horses were recklessly spoilt, frightened, and ruined by the mad rush for speed. The four-mile system ended with the Kentucky Endurance Stakes in 1912, Sotema establishing a world's record of 7 mins. $10\frac{4}{5}$ secs. in 1912. In 1913 Flora Finn fell dead after finishing second, and the race was abandoned.

The Board of Control had been instituted as a governing body and in 1894 was succeeded by the Jockey Club. It purchased the American Stud Book from Colonel Bruce, the original author. It also instituted a Racing Calendar. The first chairman was Major August Belmont, succeeded by Mr. William Woodward with Mr. Widener as the vice-chairman.

Spendthrift, property of James R. Keene, was a grandson of West Australian, foaled in 1876, and he founded a family. His son Kingston won eighty-nine races and was only four times unplaced in 139 starts. Fairplay, a grandson of Spendthrift, proved an outstanding sire. The colossal winnings of his progeny are said to be a record for all countries. He sired Man-o'-War $249,465 and Display $255,176, and many other heavy money winners. America is the land of records.

Major Belmont purchased Rock Sand for $125,000, but re-sold him to Europe. His son, Tracery, was foaled at the Nursery stud and sent to England. The three dominant lines trace back to Bonnie Scotland (1857), Australian (1858), and American Eclipse (1859).

The St. Simon, Bend Or and Hampton families failed in the male line. Ormonde was imported, but was an almost incapable foal getter. St. Simon horses, in fact, were no use at all. Prince Palatine, sold at an enormous price, was another incapable breeder.

The Finn (1912) was out of a daughter of Star Shoot, a horse whose daughters are highly valued as brood mares. The Finn sired the renowned Zev, whose winnings reached $313,639, which is in America considered a world's record. He was bred by John E.

143

Madden of Lexington, Kentucky, who from 1917 to 1928 stood at the head of winning breeders, the horses he bred winning 4,130 races. Star Shoot belonged to him. It is interesting to me to know that after this successful career he stated that he had no principles whatever of line breeding, or any mathematical theories, or any theories of crossing for speed, or stamina, his sole principle being "Breed a good mare to a good horse." This has always been my personal view, and it has certainly been successful in my own line of breeding, as I have bred two World's Champion show winners and four long-distance world's record racing champions as well as Civil Code which beat the world's sprinting record over three furlongs in 1945, and a record track breaker over a mile in Brazil, and innumerable other champions.

Omar Khayyam, a son of Marco and therefore half brother to Hurry On by the sire, imported by Mr. Billings, was a horse of reputed extraordinary beauty which won the Kentucky Derby. In contrast, Imp, a very ugly, rakish, black mare became a popular idol that started 171 times, winning sixty-two races, an astounding performance, but not a good average. After such a racket it is no wonder she failed at stud.

Ethelbert and Eothen accomplished good work, but were exported to France with a host of other racers during the collapse of 1908–12. Hanover's best son was Hamburg, both sprinter and stayer, whose daughters Artful and Hamburg Belle were among the fastest speed marvels of modern times. The handsome Artful was the best, and is spoken of in the usual "best ever seen bar none" style. She carried 130 lb. six furlongs in 1 min. 8 secs. as a two-year-old. Neither have succeeded at stud.

A number of fine performers preceded the great debacle, among which Broomstick by Ben Brush is singled out as a good sire, and won fourteen races. Commando, a son of Domino, sired the two wonders, Colin, a horse of much quality, and Peter Pan. The former was never beaten. He won twelve consecutive races at two, at three he won three more, but was exported to England with winnings of $180,912. Ben Strome (1903) sired Roseben, the greatest sprinter of America, seventeen hands, he was called the "Big Train," and performed prodigies over short distances and could not be approached at all till 10 st. 10 lb. had been heaped on him.

Legislation put a stop to enterprise, and disaster overtook the race breeders and racing industry. It annihilated the great western counties, St. Louis and Chicago, and soon New York followed. The whole system was swept to extinction—breeders were ruined, with no market for their stock, the horses were scattered all over the country to working farms or sold abroad for a song. One breeder survived, with eight hundred mares and forty stallions, Mr. J. B. Haggin, of Kentucky and California. In 1913 a flicker of revival was seen, but the racehorses were mostly geldings. The best of these was Roamer (1911) winner of thirty-nine races and beater of the mile record.

Exterminator by McGee, won fifty races in seven years. About ten years later the bay mare Princess Doreen (1921) won thirty-four races and $174,745. Anita Peabody, bay filly (seven out of eight races), $113,105. Rose of Sharon in 1929 was the best since Regret which won the Kentucky Derby in 1915.

In 1918 a colt by Fairplay—Mahuba (by Rock Sand) was purchased for $5,000 by Mr. S. D. Riddle, of Pennsylvania. On his first season he captured public approval. This was Man o' War. So invincible was he, that at the last few owners ventured to start against him. He won the Belmont Stakes by twenty lengths in record time, and the Realization by 100 lengths also in record time. Opposition was paralysed and his owner reduced to challenge for a match which he won by six lengths against a four-year-old Sir Barton for $80,000 and a gold cup. He retired with a score of twenty wins out of twenty-one starts and record stakes. He was barred from the English Stud Book. His son Battleship at eleven years old won the English Grand National.[1] Crusader followed his sire as a champion with eighteen races.

Mr. W. S. Kilmer, owner of Sunbriar and his son Sunbeam, the best long and middle distancer in 1929, also bred Reigh Count from the latter, but sold him to Mrs. J. D. Hertz, of Chicago, owner of Anita Peabody, whose success with him was very notable as in addition to brilliant running at home, especially some dazzling races in 1928, he won the Coronation Cup in England, 1929. Blue Larkspur was the champion three-year-old of 1929, and won ten of sixteen races, $272,070.

Dirt tracks are now universal in America, the theory being that better time can be made on them than on turf. Be that as it may, the records seem still to belong to our turf courses. America being a big place, the racing season covers the whole year, moving from winter conditions to the south in Florida and Louisiana and Havana.

Harry Payne Whitney, of the Rancocas Stables, became the leading breeder in 1929 at the death of John Madden. His trainer, James Rowe, had previously trained for the Dwyer Brothers and for R. Keene during the best periods of their success, and was generally accepted as America's greatest trainer and manager. Mr. Whitney was a breeder on the grand scale for twenty-five years. Mrs. Whitney carried on the great stables at his death in 1930, and Mrs. John Hay Whitney is the lucky owner of Royal Minstrel, who stood at stud in England.

Other prominent women owners are Mrs. Vanderbilt (Fairstable), Mrs. John D. Hertz (Liona Farm, Chicago), Mrs. H. Phipps (Wheatly Stable), owner of Diavolo, the champion distance racer of 1926. The outstanding name of late years is that of Mrs. Elizabeth Dangerfield, sister of the secretary of the Jockey Club, who managed Man o' War during his whole career. In 1927 Banquet b.g. (1887) by Raymond'O won sixty-two races, and Boniface b.h. (1915) won thirty-four races and $119,950.

BELAIR STUD

Mr. Woodward's stud sent its first representatives to the races in 1918, and down to July 1935 the stock bred by the stud had won $3,145,000 and 164 important races. Its leading stallion was Sir Galahad III and his son Gallant Fox, 1927, fourth on the list of largest money winners in the world in 1937, having won $341,365, representing at that

[1] Probably they are now included at Weatherby's.

145

time some £68,273. Gallant Fox was descended from St. Marguerite in tail-female and Sir Galahad III was by Teddy, his dam combining St. Simon, Petrarch and Carbine blood.

SWARTZ STUD

Paulfred Farms, 1735 Norfolk, Tulse, Oklahoma. Founded in 1929. The mares are of the best blood bought during the depression. The stallion, Sweeping Light by Manna—Sweeping Glance, goes back to Jenny Diver on the dam's side, and won twenty-one races. Pair by Pair won nineteen races.

COURT MANOR STUD

Willis Sharpe Kilmer bred, owned and raced Sun Beau, since 1931 the world's greatest money-winner with $376,744; owned and raced Exterminator, one of America's greatest cup-winners and usually regarded as the best gelding to race on this continent, with winnings of $252,596; bred, owned and raced the double Futurity winner, Sally's Alley, a leading money-winning filly with winnings of $104,362; and since 1917, he has bred and raced the winners of over $4,406,000. But it is probably in his record as a breeder that Mr. Kilmer takes the greatest pride, for since the inception of his stud he has maintained a standard that has never been lowered. His stud had a pre-war average of over $200,000 a year.

Some big racing records are as follows:—

Colin (1905)	won 15 races and		$180,912
Zev (1920)	,, 23	,,	$313,639
Blue Larkspur (1926)	,, 23	,,	$272,070
Exterminator (1915)	,, 50	,,	$252,596
Sarazen (1921)	,, 28	,,	$225,000
Man o' War (1917)	,, 20	,,	$249,465
Lamplighter	,, 29	,,	$88,545
Princess Doreen (1921)	,, 34	,,	$174,745
Golden Prince (1924)	,, 23	,,	$147,075
Mad Hatter (1916)	,, 32	,,	$194,525
Kingston (1884)	,, 89	,,	$138,917
Sun Beau (1925)	,, 21	,,	$376,744
Boniface (1915)	,, 34	,,	$119,950
Hanover (1884)	,, 32	,,	$118,872
Banquet (1887)	,, 62	,,	$118,535
Miss Woodford (1880)	,, 37	,,	$118,270
Raceland (1885)	,, 70	,,	$116,391
Strathmeath (1888)	,, 59	,,	$114,958
Firenze (m) (1884)	,, 48	,,	$112,586
Billy Kelly (1916)	,, 39	,,	$99,782
Dr. Clark (1917)	,, 39	,,	$99,004

Roamer (1911)	won 39 races and $99,000	(second 26 times)
Los Angeles (m) (1885)	,, 48 ,, $97,786	
Sir Walter (1890)	,, 33 ,, $908,840	
Yo Tamblen (m)	,, 44 ,, $894,270	

Many others have won between twenty and twenty-five races apiece and the number of races indicates the recklessness with which horses are forced along. The large prizes given seem no guarantee that horses will be raced reasonably and over-racing is getting ever worse and worse.

The American Turf has to contend with the lack of discipline which usually follows on a war, but it is to be hoped that Press reports of rough riding and doping are exaggerated. Two-year-old racing is supreme, and high prices are paid in the sale ring at Saratoga. In 1928 Mrs. T. J. Ryan paid $75,000 (£15,000) for a colt by Whisk Broom II out of an appropriately named mare, Payment.

MORGANS

The Morgan horses were a branch of the mixed blood with an Arab foundation. We are told that they have five lumbar vertebrae instead of six, and are very good looking saddle horses.

Rodeo Champions dissolve partnership

147

Champion Peavine King   [*Copyright Rounds*

World's champion saddle stallion, Chief of Longven

148

[*Reproduced from "Riding for Children" by Wynmaler & Lyne, by kind permission of Penguin Books, Ltd.*

AT FULL STRETCH

THE AMERICAN SADDLE HORSE

This has much Hackney and Spanish blood as well as Arab and is noted for its artificial high carriage of the tail and high stepping action.

It is the most exaggerated type of horse in existence and extremely spectacular. It is a very fashionable show horse but has never to my knowledge been seen anywhere except in America.

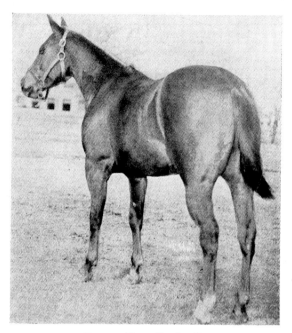

Quarter Horse Border Sis

The Tennessee *Walking Horse* is another American type; the Quarter Horse already mentioned (p. 134) is reckoned the world's fastest sprinter over $\frac{1}{4}$ of a mile or less.

He is always photographed stern first which once led me to suppose that his name was a personal adjective and not a measure of distance.

THE ARGENTINE AND BRAZIL

The history of horses dates from the spreading of the foundation herds of South America.

Thoroughbreds of the highest class are now being bred from English imported stock and there is a stud of some three hundred high-class Arabians, the property of Señor Rafael Ayerza which was founded by Herman Ayerza some half a century ago.

CHAPTER XII

GOLDEN PALOMINOS AND PARTI-COLOURS

ORIGIN OF SPECKLED AND OTHER RARE COLOURED HORSES: PALOMINOS, COLORADO
RANGERS, APPALOOSAS, KATHIAWARIS, ALBINO, CAMARILLOS AND PINTOS

AMERICAN breeders are centralizing and encouraging what till a short time ago
were almost lost breeds. The British Spotted Horse Society and the Golden
Horse Society have followed suit.

There are three outstanding breeds in America with their offshoots, which were in
danger of dying out and have only survived by the tenacity and prepotency of the foundation blood. They all come from an original Oriental stock which is of immense antiquity
and were all imported to America from N. Africa and Spain with the Spanish expeditions
and, being abandoned there with the other Spanish cargo, have multiplied into immense
mixed herds. They have now been rescued from oblivion and specialized to preserve the
various colours. The main varieties are the Golden Palomino, the speckle-spotted
Appaloosa (preserved by the Indians of the Palouse river) and the skewbald and piebald
Pintos. The offshoots are parti-colours, loosely referred to as Colorado Rangers, the
White Albino and the Camarillos. Specialized for the last twenty-five years, the Palomino
with its spectacular gold colouring is already recognized as a definite breed in America,
where there are two rival societies, and the Appaloosas and Leopard spotted horses,
though specialized, are not yet recognized but deserve to be so as the speckle-coated
horses, together with the parti-colours are the only prehistoric colourings of which we
have positive pictorial proof dating back some fifty thousand years to the cave drawings
of Southern France and Spain. At Teyjat there is a cave drawing of a speckled mare and
foal and a parti-coloured pony.

Taking the Palomino first: The American societies are like our own—a colour register,
for Palominos are a colour, not a breed, but where the colour appears the original type
belonging to it will follow. They are having a tremendous vogue now—prices are fetching
from $1,000 for yearlings, $3,000, $5,000, $7,000, and up to $12,500 reported
paid for the two-year-old Gold Alla.

The Palomino Society of California registers both the black-skinned and the golden-
skinned varieties. The Texas one registers only the black skins.

Lord Wentworth, afterwards
Earl of Lovelace, riding a Palomino coloured Barb, Yellow Boy

Colorado Ranger colour

Palomino Welsh pony, property of Miss de Beaumont

Palomino stallion with abnormal mane and tail

[*Photograph : Lady Wentworth*

Skewbald Shetland pony, Bobolink

Mr. Turner's Palominos. $\frac{3}{4}$ Arabian mare, $\frac{7}{8}$ Arabian foal
Turner Ranch, U.S.A.

153

Champion Gold Alla. Arab bred Palomino colt, two years old

This colour is of Arab origin and something approaching it is seen in Arabians of to-day. That it should have persisted shows a prepotency which can only exist in a foundation breed. It should be as nearly as possible like plated gold, a gorgeous iridescence like golden shot silk with a white or silver mane and tail and white blaze and stockings.

Tiger Horse
As this horse is spotted and not striped, the title is curious

The Arabian mare, Rose of Sharon, was a flaming example of this colour, but most of the Arabians I have bred with white manes have later on turned to a deep maroon chestnut almost plum coloured, and their manes darkened slightly to red with age though Rose of Sharon remained white-maned to the end. The Spanish Palominos originated in the Barbary States which in turn got them from the Saracen Arabian invaders. They spread from Arabia to Greece, and the preservation of colour is almost miraculous considering the amount of crossing with other colours which must have taken place in America during the three hundred years before the breed was specialized some twenty-five years ago. It is greatly prized in Algeria and Morocco, and very rare. The re-infusion of Arab blood is most successful, as might be expected for it is returning to its pure source of origin, and in North Africa the more Arab blood the more highly it is valued. The finest stallion now living is Gold Alla, bred by the Arabian Alla Amarward, tracing back to the Crabbet Arab Mahruss II.

The distinguishing feature is, perhaps, that the foals do not follow the usual rule, but are born white or cream and only change to gold with age. In this connection it will be remembered that Lady Anne Blunt once saw a white Arabian foal which belonged to a Bedouin who travelled for a day or two with their caravan. She described how friendly it was, and that one night she woke in her tent to find it lying asleep beside her with its head on her pillow, but she unfortunately did not record the colour of the dam.

The following account was sent to the American Palomino Society by His Highness El Sherif Sidi Hassan Raissuli in answer to a query.

"The Golden Horses of Morocco"

"Yes, there are Golden Horses in Morocco, but we do not know them as Ysabellas or Palominos. When speaking amongst ourselves we call them the 'Sefer el Judi,' for this means the colour of the Jews.

"Our Moorish horses are Barbs, and so, of course, the Golden (Yellow) Horses with white manes and tails are Barbs too, and they are bred and owned by our Caidchiefs.

"They tell me that in the United States of America you want to know about our Barbs. They are the horses of the mountains of North Africa. About two hundred years after the time of the Christian Christ, warriors from the north came here with their horses, but of what race those horses were I do not know. But those horses, when crossed with our native ones, resulted in animals of larger size than our own; at that time our own horses were very small ones, scarcely large enough to ride.

"Then, five hundred years later,[1] the Arbicos (Arabians) came here on their desert steeds. These Arab horses were crossed with our Barbs. And from this crossing come the Barbs of the present day. They are somewhat larger than the Arab horse,[2] we think they have a stronger constitution, they are used to scanty rations and have much endurance. In fact, you cannot tire them out. We prize them very highly, and as we find that the best of them are those which have at least five-eighths of Arab blood in their veins, we must at the very least give credit to the horses of Arabia. This is the history of the Moorish Barbs as far as I know it.

"And now for the Golden ones you want to tell me of. I cannot say of what origin they are, for you see the Arabs have them in their own country and we also have them here. Your Golden ones in the Americas are Barbs, horses taken by the Moors to Spain, and the Spanish in turn took them to Mexico.

"Their beautiful colouring—ah, from what and how does it come? Indeed a difficult question to answer for me. This strain of golden colour may have existed

[1] And also much earlier.
[2] When they are larger this comes from the modern cross of thoroughbred.

156

as long as the desert horses themselves. It may be possible that they may have originated from crossing a pure white stallion with a bay mare,[1] for it happens sometimes, even to-day, that white and bay colts are born outside the Golden strain. This I have heard of from my relatives who breed them, but I have never seen it happen myself. Also I am speaking only of our Barbs, as I myself know nothing about the breeding of the pure Arab horses.

"The Golden ones are our best horses, and they are much desired. But only the Caids own them, and it is impossible for a Christian to buy one or even to come near them. Sometimes in the hands of those who buy and sell for barter, we see horses that are black and white or brown and white. We call such horses 'El Begaa' —the brother of cow. This is, amongst both Moors and Arabs, the most despised horse of all, and to us rated of no value at all.

"Amongst ourselves we do not buy or exchange horses bred between 1930 and 1936 without the most careful examination of their breeding. Horses born between those dates may have base blood from the Bretons and Percherons imported by the French Government to use for cross breeding to get work horses. This was a bad mistake, as horses with this cross are large, coarse, clumsy, and have nothing in them. Our best stock are those with much Arab blood in them; you can know them by their clean-cut heads, round croups, and high-carried tails. These are the best we have.

"There is a story that a strain of Golden ones exists amongst the pure Arabs, but they are rare and only owned by the highest chieftains far to the east of here. It is doubtful if one was ever seen in Morocco."

"THE ARAB-BARB GOLDEN BREED"
The Ideal Colouring of a Palomino
(By "Nemo," a Spanish writer)

"We do not call them Palominos in Spain. To us they are Ysabellas, so named after Her Most Catholic Majesty, Ysabella de Bourbon, that dearly loved Queen and most gracious lady who, in the kindness of her heart, pawned her jewels that the expenses of the expedition which discovered the New World might be paid. In the Remuda Real of Spain, Queen Ysabella kept a full hundred of these splendid animals, and as the chosen favourites of the Crown only the members of the Royal Family and the nobles of the Household were permitted to ride them. A commoner might not own one.

"The Moors first brought them to Spain, and when the Cross of Christ triumphed over the Crescent of Islam the Golden Horses became our own, spoils of the battle-field. From captive Moors we learned that they, in turn had first taken these splendid horses from the desert tribes who bred them for captains of their fighting men to

---

[1] White and Bay could not produce Gold. Nor can white appear as a reversion.

157

ride. And thus and so, to us, the cabello de oro became the Horse of the Hidalgo—the chosen mount of our leaders in Peace and War.

"But they are hard to breed. Their beautiful golden colouring, their white manes and tails, pure white markings, come only as the result of careful mating and close study of family colour inheritance. And they can only be bred in all their matchless beauty from the best of Arabian and Moorish strains. And so this careful breeding finally produced not only a picturesque horse but also an animal of exceptional courage and intelligence, of stamina far beyond the ordinary, with all the traditional docility and teachableness of the desert horses of Arabia, who are the companions of their masters from the day of their birth. . . . The colour of an Ysabella changes with the seasons. In full coat the body is of burnished gold, which often, in full sunlight, glints into shimmering satin, then shifts into dazzling, amber gold. As to the markings, a clean-cut, intelligent head should carry a full-length blaze down the face. White stockings half-way between knee and hoof on the front legs, and on the hind legs white stockings, again half-way to the hocks."

The real Ysabella, however, is not golden, but pale primrose cream with black mane, tail, and legs.

It will be noted that in North Africa they have been preserved only in Morocco, which is the district where pure Arab tribes settled and though their horses have been confused with the ordinary Barbs their pedigrees and strains were carefully preserved, and from them come the Morocco "Barbs" of the English Stud Book, and there is a painting of one in the Milbanke Collection.

In confirmation of the story of the Golden ones of Arabia we find mention of them by early oriental writers.

King Omar of Yemen owned a big racing stable and had a celebrated racehorse El Mouji. He was a high-bred kehilan Arabian of golden Palomino colour.

El Munkar was another golden coloured horse with white mane and tail, who three times defeated a famous runner belonging to Meslaweh in three successive heats, Meslaweh increasing the stakes each time, unable to believe that the horse could stay the test.

Of another golden horse the writer swore by the daughters of the wind that nothing could out-pace him.

Caliph Malek el Mansour was very partial to this colour and the author of the Kitab el Akhwal called his Palomino coloured "Taf" the diadem of all horses and Safaraneh, a mare belonging to Moayad, is recorded by Abu Bekr as "Extraordinary for perfect type beauty and pedigree and for her remarkable height; qualities most admired in pure bred Arabians."

The existence of racing stables in Arabia is therefore well established, and the value of the "Palomino" colour is also demonstrated.

In the legend of Ishmael "God said to the wind, 'Be thou gathered together.' And the wind was gathered together. And the Angel Gabriel took of it a handful and said to the

King Tut II, Pinto Skewbald

Starbruck Leopard from Barbary States

[*Photograph : Thomas Fall, London*

Sugar Plum, a Skewbald mare with chestnut spots

Lord: 'Behold my hand is full.' And God created of the handful of wind a horse of chestnut colour, like gold, and said to the horse: 'Behold I have created thee and made thee Arabian, and thou shalt have station and power above all things of the beasts that are subject to man. And I have bound all fortune and a treasure to thy loins, and on thy back a rich spoil, and to thy forelock a fair issue.' And God set loose the swift runner and he went on his way neighing."

The value of the above poetic fantasy lies in its unconscious record of the fact that the Arabian was the origin of speed.

The Greek "fair maned" horses have puzzled historians. They are seen on Greek painted vases and it is obvious to anyone who knows the type that they were Arabians and evidently were much admired and sought after. There should be no further arguments as to what colour was meant by the word Xanthos for the fair mane stamps its identity. The strong tendency in chestnut Arabians to produce big blazes and stockings is traditional and quite correct.

The word is sometimes translated "dun," but dun is a northern non-racing dull colour which could by no possibility be described as "shining like the rays of the sun."

From information up to date, the inheritance of Palomino colouring is not at present true, but when mated to each other about 50 per cent of the progeny will be Palominos and the other half about equally divided between chestnuts and what are called albinos. A pure gold may appear when one parent is of another colour.

The American Society does not register the chestnuts or albinos bred in this way but continues with the pure colouring.

Abder Rahman Minni told the Blunts when they were in India that there was a special breed of chestnut Arabians called "Kumeyt" indicating a palomino colouring of either gold or deep maroon chestnut with silver or white mane and tail and the Emir who bred them said to the Blunts that they were never sold as being too precious, but that if they would come to his stud in Persia he would possibly present them with a pair. Unfortunately, they were unable to go, but the term Kumeyt remained on their minds, and the appearance of Rose of Sharon and of several maroon chestnuts confirmed the existence of such a colour.

APPALOOSAS

This is another prehistoric breed seen in the European cave drawings. It is white with myriads of small black velvet spots. Its origin is the same as that of the Palominos except that we find more traces of them in history. Small varieties are also mentioned south of the Himalayas and in India and large ones appear still as agricultural horses in the low countries and Germany.

Among the drawings of Teyjat there is a speckled mare and foal.

In his vision of the four breeds, Zacharias describes the horses which went south and all over the world as leopard-spotted (see Arabic version). Again he says: "And I saw by

161

night and beheld a man riding on a red horse and he stood among the myrtle trees. . . and behind him were horses red, speckled and white."

The Musjid breed on the Persian Gulf was white with deep brown or black speckles.

Spotted Appaloosa foal

It was considered the best of all parade horses and called Tazi in India. They originated in the Isles of the Red Sea, called the Erythrean sea, and Bahreyn on the Arabian coast.

The Appaloosa of America was described by Mr. Parsons as American bred Morocco Barbs (Arabs), strikingly beautiful, pink-skinned and covered with a milk white coat of silky hairs, with myriads of jet black velvet spots like a leopard varying in size from a sixpence to a dollar. These are embossed on the coat and can be felt as well as seen. They are covered with them from muzzle to tail, the spots being most numerous on the quarters. Some advocate that they should be confined to the rump, but prehistorically they are seen all over, and their absence would seem to denote a partial loss of spots through crossing. They have black nostrils and black eyes. Variations are said to be dark bodies, heads and necks, and spotted quarters, roan-bay or chestnuts with white spots, or white with chestnut or brown spots, or white body with roan rump and white spots, but I believe these are mostly now classed as Colorado Rangers. In a Welsh pony of Arab descent called Lillywen of Tycanol the colour of the skin under the spots was black, the rest of the skin being pinkish white. She was a beautiful Arab-like pony and the spots were quite tangible. Leopard colour is said to be seen in ancient Chinese paintings. The colour has been known in England as Blagden, and occurs in some strains of Welsh mountain ponies. Arab blood nicks well with it, just as it does with the Golden breed, indicating a probable return to the foundation breed. Judging from photographs it would seem that some of the speckled foals have black manes and tails which grow lighter later on. The American Leopard horses have larger and rounder black spots, which continue all down the legs on a white ground. The horses of the Barbary States were famous for every variety of variegated markings, but the Leopard horses are a most distinct variety. In the *Apocalipse de Beato Cavalieros a gineta* there is a speckled horse, and in a Spanish MS. of the eleventh century two soldiers in armour are mounted on profusely speckled horses.

The Appaloosa Club says it is a variant of the name of a breed developed for war by the Nez Perce Indians in the Palouse country of Central Idaho and East Washington, and Dr. Francis Haines describes its markings as colour spots on the rump, a good deal of white in the eye and pink skin on the nose, the varieties being roan, bay or chestnut, with white spots or white body, with bay, sorrel or brown spots or white body and roan rump with white spots. Weight much that of an Arab, 800 to 1,050 lb. and height 14.2 to the limit of 15.2. The aboriginal colour was, however, speckled all over. Some are black or chocolate with white spots.

Appaloosas recrossed with Arab have lots of quality with white blazes and hind stockings. The Rangers are parti-coloured, half the body being one colour and the other of a lighter shade with spots on the hind quarters.

Ridinger's Appaloosa, or Ranger horses, are entitled Russian, Transylvanian, and Turkish. So they were evidently widely distributed and the largest of the present speckled breeds are the Agricultural Pinzgauers of Austria and there are varieties in Denmark and other parts of Europe; the smaller ones are found in India.

When grey Arabian mares turn very strongly fleabitten they become very much like profusely speckled Appaloosas, and I strongly suspect this pronounced fleabitten coat is a throwback to the Musjid Arabian breed of Bahreyn, but this is conjecture.

Great interest is now shown in England in this ancient breed, and Sir Rhys Llewellyn has founded the British Spotted Horse Society, of which I have been elected President, and he registered St. Fagans Spotlight and Lady Gay in the American Stud Book of Moro, Oregon. The American Society favours horses from fourteen hands upwards, but the

Trabag. Champion Arabian mare bred by
Señor Rafael Ayerza in the famous Argentine stud

164

British Society will also encourage the smaller ones which are all of Indian product and traditionally correct.

The heavily speckled mare Freckles is a wonderful specimen of the larger size and another big mare is 16.1 and extremely handsome, though on the coarse side, and had alternate black and white teeth. Sir Rhys has sold St. Fagans Spotlight and some others owing to fodder and labour shortage, but still retains Ermine and Painted Lady.

Trabag, parti-coloured Arabian mare

The British Spotted Horse Society has divided the colours into three sections: all spotted, semi-spotted, and with white spotted rump. I consider the all spotted is the direct reversion to primitive marking, the others being a stage when the markings have been partially lost.

Though the Americans have height rules we shall try and establish markings first. Our Stud Book will register any horse of any size with the typical markings irrespective of pedigree, as the object is to secure the perpetuation of colour which is in itself positive evidence of ancestral reversion, and Sir Rhys also considers that the demand for under 14.2 will be greater than for hunting size. It should be possible to breed any size by selection, and small Appaloosa ponies would be an attractive addition to our shows.

Mr. R. Sotheby borrowed Lady Apsley's stallion, Buckingham—heavily spotted— for some seasons, and bred Sir Rhys Llewellyn's all-spotted stallion Ermine, which he exchanged with a yearling colt Harlequin for St. Fagans Spotlight. Buckingham (unfortunately since gelded) was by Young Buchan (Thoroughbred by Buchan) out of a spotted Welsh cob mare Princess Roma. He also sired Blue Moon, who inherited his colour, and was in turn the sire of Harlequin out of a cream pony mare. Sir Rhys Llewellyn's Painted

Lady was out of Freckles, who originated in a circus, and her sire Gay Lord (out of Lady Gay), bred in France by a French Trotter called Indian out of a spotted Argentine pony mare, thus returning in all probability to the Columbus exports. She is 14.2 roan, with a white rump covered in speckles and has less distinct stripes on her sides.

When markings are well established, or sooner if type deteriorates, a cross of Arab or Starlight would re-infuse quality. The Arab type is strongly desirable, and still evident in spite of three centuries of promiscuous crossing. The mustangs developed from the same origins, but are degenerate in appearance, though of indomitable endurance and usefulness. The Appaloosa has a charming disposition, tractable, full of life, yet easily managed, and is rightly coming to the front in popularity. It stands out as a beautiful as well as useful type and should be carefully preserved as an inheritance from prehistoric times older than anything else in the equine line except the other parti-colours which we can trace to such a colossal age.

VARIATION OF APPALOOSAS

1. White foundation with round or oval spots. Small in front and bigger behind.
2. Dark front with dark round or oval spots on pure white loins and hips.
3. Pointed spots.
4. Small diamond spots.
5. Whole colour in front and white behind, no spots.
6. Mottled dark and white all over.
7. Dark foundation colour with any sort of white spots, speckles and splashes.
8. Pure white with large black round spots all over, including legs (Leopard).
9. White speckled all over with brown or black speckles like a cuckoo's egg.

5, 6, and 7 mixtures are called snowstorm horses.

The quarters of an Appaloosa foaled solid colour may shed off white as he grows up. Head straight, eyes large and showing white at the corners. This is a very typical point.

PINTOS

"The painted horses," piebald and skewbald, are a third prehistoric breed, and are common in India, Russia, Tibet, and all over Europe in all sizes.

Skewbalds were prominent in Spanish horses in the Middle Ages, and parti-colours of every conceivable pattern and shade are traditional in North Africa, and even in Arabian history. The Tanghans of Tibet had magnificent rainbow coloration, from which the Kathiawar got every variety of spots, speckles, splashes, and the oddest streaks, stripes, and patches, including blue and green edgings. In the Himalayas a tiny breed of ten-hand skewbald ponies were observed by d'Hobsonville, wiry, active, fiery, and covered with regular coloured spots. The domesticated ones grow to thirteen hands. They are strong, symmetrical, bold and surefooted, and I feel convinced that they are

Lady Estella Hope's Shetland stallion, Electric Light

Hackney mare, Magpie

167

the ancestors of the Shetland, a multi-variegated breed like the old Indian Kathiawari, and described as follows in the American General Stud Book:

Alboni, a parti-coloured horse, one half of him was sorrel edged handsomely with *blue*, and the other milk white.

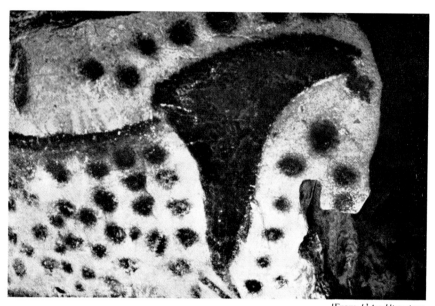

[From *L'Art Historique*
Detail of spotted prehistoric red and black horse from cave Pech-Merle Lot, France (*c.* 10,000 years ago)

Apalusia, a milk white horse with blue ears.

Coslamian, a spotted horse, fourteen hands, with glass eyes, black or rather deep blue body and all four feet white, foaled in 1826 of Andalusian breed.

Spottee. Taken in Africa in a wild state, brought to Spain, and from there to the United States. He was very highly formed and richly variegated with four distinct colours.

VARIOUS ORIENTAL PARTI-COLOURS

The early existence of parti-colours and the value attached to them is also recorded in an Arab horse of unsurpassed beauty, for whose picture the artist had to use seven different colours. The celebrated skewbald Arabians in the Royal stables of the Kings of Persia after the Arab conquest are described in a wealth of poetic rhapsody by El Arifi, A.D. 1530. They are seen in Persian miniatures as such perfectly typical Arabians that the pin-point muzzle, large eyes, crested neck and high tail carriage seem almost fanciful to those who do not know the breed.

El Arifi describes the King's skewbald Arabian playing a ball game: "When he spurs his wind-footed skewbald thou mightest say he mingles fire with wind."

168

"The horse of the King in galloping bore away the ball; he sprang from plain to plain like a ball.

"Fire ran from his hoofs and Tempest hung from his tail.

"If he had not been restrained in his leaping he would have outrun the ball.

"He passed down from the mountain like a torrent.

"He passed over the sea like a wind.

"That mountain (desert) one strained not wherever he put his fore and hind feet.

"The field in which the King plays ball or rides the Arab horses swift of pace might be called the ground of beatitude.

"Going forth to ball play galloping his Arab horse—Water could not keep pace with him nor the wind catch up with the dust he raised."

Abbas Pasha had a parti-coloured Wadneh Hursanieh mare by a Shueyman Sbah sire called Tabbukh belonging to Mohammed Ibn Khubeysan. She originated with Hamoud Ibn Saadūn Sheikh of the Muntaghaj, and was great-granddam of Mahruss I. It is from her that the white patches seen in some of our horses such as Nezma Shareer, Astrella, and Sharfina are probably inherited. I have just received photographs of a pure Arab mare, Trabag, first prize Palermo Show, 1949, lavishly skewbald in irregular patterns, chestnut and white, and tracing back to the Crabbet horse Ajman. She has a white mane and tail.

Abbas also had a white-spotted Rabdeh mare by the Hadban el Nazah of the Mafdūl.

The following colours are listed by Abu Bekr, c. A.D. 750, as Arabian varieties:

Golden Bronze, shaded black, white mane and tail, slightly tinged with gold.

Black and gold hairs (mixed) red mane and tail russet.

Stoat colour or rose colour.

Kohl Sulphur Yellow, mane and tail "ostrich brown," whatever that may be.

⎫
⎬ Probably early stages of grey.
⎭

Cream Yellow, with golden spots and white mane and tail called in Persian "Zarah."

Golden Chestnut, with black points.

Pale Cream Yellow, with lighter cream mane and tail.

Creamy russet, with black mane and tail (Ysabella) and black list down the back.

Black Chestnut with black points and *blue* eyes.

Abu Obeyda gives three others:—

1. Very light chestnut with black mane and tail.
2. Black chestnut with white mane and tail.
3. Pure gold with red line on the back, greyish mane and tail and red legs.

Parti-colours.

1. White body with coloured head and neck or vice versa.
2. Both ends white with piebald body.
3. Speckled with spots of the same size all over.
4. "*Adjnaf*," bay or black stomach, and the rest any other colour.

169

5. "*Mulemma*," spotted.
6. Ears and forelock bay, rest skewbald or piebald.
7. "*Anbat*," white legs right up to the body and sometimes including the belly.
8. "*Tan*," croup covered with black or white chestnut or bay even spots. They sometimes extend all over the body, but must be of even size.
9. "*Sis*," muzzle, round eyes, and croup spattered with spots.
10. "*Ashal*," white back. Ash-coloured body.
11. "*Sinabi*," multi-coloured. For example: Red, black, gold, and white mixed ground with superimposed gold spots, specks and flecks of white and odd designs.
12. Chestnut or bay, with large white patches.
13. "*Abrash*," Appaloosa either in black or white or vice versa, or with white spots "like a leopard," or a variety of coloured spots or stripes.

Lapis Lazuli blue and Olive green are also specially mentioned.

Imagine the sensation that would be created at Richmond Show by a pure lapis lazuli blue coaching team, or an emerald green tandem!

The insistence placed by the Oriental writer on the colour being really blue is verified by Ross Cox, a trader with the Nez Perce American Indians who worked for a time at Spokane Falls at the beginning of the nineteenth century, and greatly admired their spotted horses and described one horse as "*Sky blue* with a white rump." His name was "Le Blu" and he won every race for which he was entered. His most famous performance was racing against time two miles across mountain and forest country carrying Cox and a load of tobacco between noon and midnight to beat some rival traders. A recent writer mentions having seen a blue horse there in 1948.

The Khan of Tartary kept 10,000 white horses and there was an original breed in Eastern Tartary called Karabolo, jet black with white tail, mane and legs. This seems to have been allied to the Dongola Arab of later days and is mentioned in Greek history.

The indigenous horses in Turkey are termed Kurdestan ponies, about fourteen hands with coarse heads, thick necks, short bodies and much bone.

East India, 1615.—An attendant of Sir T. Roe writes: "This Empire further affords excellent good horses curiously (beautifully) made, high met'ld and well managed by the natives. Besides their own they have many of the Persian, Tartarian and Arabian breed which have the name to be the choice ones of the world."

He again praises the riders and their choice high-mettled horses "excellent good at mounting up, bounding and curvetting and when they run them at their full swiftest speed will stop them at a foots breadth. For the scantling of these creatures they are in proportion like ours but excellent well-eyed and headed, limned for their colours raven black but many more white curiously dappled and a very great number pied and spotted all over, and there are some of other bright colours. But it is a usual custom there amongst gallants who ride upon the bright-coloured horses, to have their legs and lower parts of their bellies and breasts dyed into a saffron colour (of which they have much there) which makes them look as if they had stood in some dyer's vat, just to such an height of their bodies.

"The hair upon their horses (whom they keep plump and fat) is very short, soft, and lyes sleek upon them: and I wonder not at it, they are kept so daintily, every horse being allowed a man to dress and feed him, and to run by him when he is rode forth, and this is all his work.

"They tye not down their horse-heads when they stand still (as we do) with halters, but secure each horse by two ropes, fastened to their hind-feet, which ropes are somewhat long, to be staked down behind them in tents, or other places where they are kept.

"They cut grass for them green or withered on the earth as they have occasion to use it, never mowing their ground and making hay as we do. But that which keeps their horses in heart, and in flesh, is the Provender they eat, which is a kind of round grain they call Donna, somewhat bigger than our Tares; which they give not unto them dry, but boil'd, and mingled with some coarse sugar amongst it, and when it is cold give it to them, made up in round balls, which they put into their mouths, as if they cramb'd them; and sometimes they put a little butter into these balls to scour their bodies.

"Their choice good horses are valued there at as dear if not an higher rate, than those we esteem most of in England are prized by us. They make excellent saddles, and some of them are of great value, adorned with handsome and rich trappings, all of them very easie both for the horse and his rider. They manage their horses with strong snaffles, whose reins and head-stalls are made suitable to their saddles and trappings."

Skewbalds are seen in the Duke of Newcastle's stud at Welbeck, and in his pictures of Barbs and Spaniards. The Borghese breed of pied horses still bred in 1841, near Rome, is alluded to by Virgil in the same locality and it appeared in the Trojan games.

The Arab hero Zohara, prisoner of the Persians, escaped on a piebald Arabian horse.

Parthian cavalry horses, pure white with large deep bay spots, piebald, or more technically skewbald mentioned by Homer with good feet and a gentle nature.

In England there used to be teams of piebald agricultural horses, and one of the most famous Hackney mares bred a line of skewbald Hackneys of great beauty.

It is a pity that in England there is such a craze for whole coloured horses; one would think from its avoidance of bright markings that the whole nation was obsessed by a fear of the Evil Eye. It arose, I think, in a military prejudice of avoiding the conspicuous but in these days of camouflage a Tanghan of Tibet might be quite a regimental asset if any cavalry are ever again used. During the war our buildings were painted in quite a presentable imitation of that ancient breed!

ALBINOS

There is an Albino Horse Club in America. Mr. Fachiri writes that he used to think albinism was an accident of birth, but that all his preconceived notions had been swept to the winds. These horses are foaled white and the colour is hereditary. Where it occurs in the Norwegian dun and some other breeds it is doubtless a reversion. A chestnut mare descended from the pacing wild albino stallion which, says Mr. Fachiri, became known as the phantom horse of the Plains, was seen by him at the age of forty with a white-born albino foal at foot.

CAMARILLOS

Another very rare and remarkable variety owned by Mr. Camarillo of California, is white born with pink skin but *black* eyes. The colour persists even when mated to bay but it never reappears when the bays with white progenitors are mated together and in this they resemble ordinary grey horses—one parent *must* be white to produce white.

Though neither the Golden Palomino, Appaloosa or other of these breeds are actually recognized as such by the Horse and Mule Association of America they have their societies and there is no doubt whatever that they are distinct varieties and the Appaloosas and Pintos are both prehistoric and can be traced in Spain, Arabia, Greece and North Africa from long B.C. They have every claim to be classed as definite breeds to be preserved as descendants of the oldest recorded colours dating back to 50,000 B.C.

Lady Wentworth's Welsh trotting champion, Springlight

CHAPTER XIII

SHOW TROTTERS

HACKNEYS

"Prince of Palfreys who trots the air and makes the earth sing
as he touches it with his elastic tread."—Richard III.

THE high-actioned Hackney has a far older history than is usually supposed. We see horses in Chinese art over two thousand years ago, stepping as extravagantly as any modern show champion both under saddle and in harness. They were not native to China but are shown arriving with a foreign deputation—the actual position of the legs is that of a pacer and they are of the proud, crested, Andalusian type which suggests a trade connection with Spain whose parade horses were the finest in the world, the Spanish trot being one of the high school displays. The common native Chinese breeds were of Mongolian coarseness with positively grotesque heads, not the fat but elegant high stepper.

Whatever may be the connection, high action is no new thing; though it is now supplemented and developed by artificial means, weights and elastics, there is always the foundation of natural action without which no horse can be trained.

In England hackneys have been recorded as hacks and riding horses from the earliest days. They appear soon after the Norman Conquest and in a list of horses at the battle of Falkirk, 1298, there were seventeen hackneys of which eight were greys, one "liard" and one fawn with a star and three white feet. They ranged in value from five to twenty marks.

In the sixteenth century the Duchess of Suffolk's stud was full of trotting horses. The modern breed is descended from the famous trotting roadsters of the eighteenth century which were of the same root stock as hunters with a stronger foundation of Spanish blood on which much Arab was superimposed by the Godolphin and Darley Arabians and Flying Childers which figure prominently in their pedigrees. Trotting Jalap was a grandson of the Godolphin. There was a constant influx of Spanish harness horses in this country for centuries, as many as fifty in one consignment under Edward III and many more under James I.

In the sixteenth century land-owners were compelled to keep trotting horses, the

173

number being regulated according to whether their wives wore velvet bonnets or not. All these trotters were allied to the hackney, but the hackney has always had more oriental and Spanish jennet blood—the original "Genetors" in England being semi-light cavalry.

In the nineteenth century the trotters were crossed with the blood of Marshland Shales

Chinese inscription, Hackney prototypes. Earliest representation of high action (126 B.C.)

or Old Shields, a one-eyed trotting horse able to do twenty miles an hour on the road, and there were two offshoots from the same original blood—he was a grandson of Flying Childers, ex a hunter mare, probably Spanish like most of the hunters at that time. The Yorkshire and Norfolk trotters were influenced by the Dutch Hartdraver fast pacing breed, and amalgamated and crossed with thoroughbred later to form the Cleveland Bay. The Hartdraver is described as "swift at running pace, of medium size and able to curvet as well as any Spanish Jennet."

At Beverley an American-bred sire of wonderful trotting action beat all the English roadsters which could not touch him for pace. He was an Anglo-Arab and got a strong Arab type with crossbred mares.

174

Champion Black Magic of Nork

Mrs. Haydon driving Bossy, winner of the Champion Harness Pony Challenge Cup at the International
Horse Show at the White City

All our roadsters date back to the galloping Post Coach horses of the eighteenth century and have only diverged through heavier crosses at periods which it is impossible to verify exactly. The types have coarsened considerably from the horses in the old aquatints of the period which had small beautiful heads and high tail carriage. Roadsters also date back to Theobalds Champion purchased for £1,000 from the French Imperial stud (which was mainly if not entirely Arabian) and from Bonds Phenomenon. In Ireland the breed

Hackney team

was marred by Lord Charlemont's pedigreeless horse Broadshanks. The piebald hackney pony Maggie foaled in 1878 appears to have been the most popular winner ever in the show ring—she won 400 first prizes and was as pre-eminent in saddle as in harness.

It must be remembered that classic strains of Arabians have spectacular natural action when fresh and excited resembling that of deer trotting through fern. The Arab stallion Naufal won the £20 trotting prize at Richmond Royal Show some years ago, so the Arab cross would nick well with the Spaniard of already oriental descent.

In 1729 an Arab stallion 15.3 and a Yorkshire stallion were sent to cover in Norfolk and the breeds much intermingled. One of the best sires, Bellfounder, was exported to U.S.A.

Mrs. Black's Florette, Grand Champion Hackney mare, 1950, 1951, 1952 and 1953

Early Trotting Records in England

Marshland Shales	.. ..	17 miles carrying 12 st. in 58 mins.
Wroots Pretender	.. ..	16 miles carrying 16 st. in 60 mins.
Phenomena ..	.. ..	19 miles in harness under the hour and returned in 52 mins. 55 secs. for £2,000 stakes.
Phenomena ..	.. ..	17 miles carrying 12 st. in 53 mins.
Reads Fireaway (1801)	..	16 miles carrying 16 st. in 58 mins.
1820 A "Roadster" ..	..	100 miles carrying 12 st. in 11 consecutive hours on the Ipswich road carrying 12 st. for the first 50 miles and 11 st. for the second.
1822 Woodcocks Blind Mare		40 miles on the London Road 3 hrs. 40 mins.
Dysons Wonder	.. ..	3 miles carrying 15 st. 4 lb. 8 mins.
1832 Non Pareil	.. ..	100 miles driven 9 hrs. 56 mins. 57 secs.
Driver ..	.. ..	17 miles under the hour.
Wests Driver	.. ..	17½ miles carrying 15 st. under the hour.

177

Norfolk Cob (Master of 20 St.)	2 miles		5 mins. 4 secs.
Norfolk Phenomenon was still road racing at 30 years old.			
Crocketts Grey Mare ..	100 miles		11 hrs. 40 mins.

(She was not tired but her jockey nearly faded out.)

1830 Lady 14.2	17 miles carrying 12 st. in 55 mins.		
1836 Lady 14.2	2 miles carrying 12 st. in 5 mins. 58 secs.		
1836 Lady 14.2	5 miles		14 mins.
1836 Lady 14.2	17 miles		58 mins. 40 secs.

Phenomena won similar matches when over 20.

Our present Hackneys are magnificent. Mr. Black's Florette, supreme champion at Olympia 1949, has to be seen to be believed and is perhaps even more perfect than the spectacular Black Magic of Nork, but both are superb.

TROTTERS

RACING TROTTERS AND PACERS

The great centre of trotting races is in the U.S.A. It originated in Spanish and thorough-bred blood (which includes Arab) and the star foundation sire being Hambletonian (1849) descended from imported grey Messenger. This amazing sire founded the trotting breed which has developed to a speed as remarkable in its line as our racehorse is in galloping and the prices commanded by winners run into thousands of pounds. Two yearlings, Victory Song and Bombs Away, were sold in 1944 for over £9,000 each and a yearling pacer, Ladymite, fetched £4,000. The stakes are the incentive, the highest prize, the Hambletonian, being worth £10,000—£15,000 divided between the first six, winner taking fifty per cent.

The pacers appear allied to the Hartdraver Dutch pacing breed described on p. 174. Both were probably from the same original Spanish blood. Orloff trotters were produced from much the same mixture of blood with less actual thoroughbred and cannot compete with the American-bred stock.

As much as $60,000 (£12,000) has been paid for an American Trotter for export and £15,000 was refused for Harvester whose record was 2.01 in 1912. Guy Axworth (2.08¾) was a magnificent looking horse and Belwin (2.06¾) was one of the fastest modern horses, though Peter Manning held records down to 1.56¾. The standard records comprise 40,000 trotters at 2.30 to 1.56¼ and 35,000 pacers from 2.25 to 1.55¼. The record is held by Greyhound, 1.55¼. Of these at least 50,000 are descended in direct tail-male from Hambletonian and the rest collaterally. The astonishing records of Goldsmith Maid are never likely to be beaten under similar conditions for the trotting races are now run with artificial aids, such as wind screens and comparison with the unaided records is impossible. Goldsmith Maid (1859) began as a rank outlaw. She had much Arab blood through the

LADY SUFFOLK

179

The Arab-bred Goldsmith Maid breaking four world records at the age of nineteen

usual foundation racing sires and some think her actual sire was an Arab to which her astounding stamina would lend some confirmation. She won 116 races out of 128 and aged nineteen held four world's champion records. She was sold for £8,000 and went on racing till she was twenty-one when she retired with £72,800 and became a brood mare, having her first foal at the age of twenty-two with two more to follow. Her record was 2.14 for the mile and she could trot five or six heats in one afternoon at about this average speed. She was highly temperamental and would not race unless her stable mate, a yellow curdog, was somewhere on the course. She could eat half as much again as a horse of sixteen hands and would consume enormous quantities of hay the day before a race. Nothing could make her race if she did not choose, and nothing could live with her when she meant business. She knew perfectly well when a race was to be run and showed such violent excitement that her hoofs would shake and clatter on the ground like a man's teeth with cold, but the moment she was harnessed and her driver took up the reins she became quite calm. She ran her own races, gauging the pace and making her spurts as she calculated the chances, and woe betide anyone who tried to interfere with her.

Serious racing began in the Southern States towards 1835 by inter-state matches. Now anything from twelve thousand horses start every year for public races.

Veter Bouring, Orloff trotter at the International Paris Show, 1900

CHAPTER XIV

THE DOMINIONS AND INDIA

SOUTH AFRICA

SOUTH AFRICA, like America, had no indigenous horse stock but it had enormous herds of Zebras which were at first mistaken for horses. The climate and conditions were unfavourable and it was not till the Dutch occupation that Johann van Riebeck shipped the first consignments from Java in A.D. 1655. The herds had rapidly deteriorated by 1689 so that further Persian Arab stallions were imported and nine years later South American stallions were brought over. Over 150 years afterwards thoroughbreds began to be imported and serious racing started in 1802. Though the African Turf Club had already been founded in 1797 and race meetings had been held, the Dutch farmers had no idea of the laws of breeding—they disregarded the female side altogether, considering that any mare would do, so long as the stallion was good. They said "the mare is a sack, if you put in gold you take out gold, whatever the sack is like." The Governor of the Colony, Lord Charles Somerset, encouraged horse breeding and racing in 1814, and incurred severe reproof from the anti-gambling element which talked virtuously of ruinous amusements and of the scandal of importing animals useless for trade or agriculture. Indeed the leader of the Opposition spoke with horror of a single horse having been sold for the outrageous sum of £600 and a two-year-old for £200! His attitude recalls the indignation of General Lord Fairfax against the importation to England of "over-valued Pigmy Baubles" for the despicable pleasure of racing. Lord Charles, however, persevered in spite of bad luck by which he lost half his importations at sea, but a pro-portion of the forty-eight imported by Mr. Wallace between 1809–1820 arrived alive, including a mare by Walton which left good produce and Rhoderick Dhu, a stallion by Sir Peter, sold for £350 to Mr. Porter who started a stud in the Koeberg in 1817. A Captain Christopher traded in horses to the Cape and to India and the Mauritius.

One of the foundation mares was The-Hen-that-lays-the-Golden-Eggs. Her sire was the Watney Arabian called Sultan which won the Silver Cup in 1799 and the Ladies Purse in 1800.

Mr. Duckitt's horse Loyalist was inbred for many years successfully to his own daughters and other descendants. Mr. Pringle of the British East India Co. imported a mare said to be thoroughbred which bred South African Eclipse. The Van Rennen Bros. imported Nestler, the sire of South African Eclipse, The-Hen-that-lays-the-Golden-Eggs and Loyalist.

The early pedigrees were all most unreliable and kept in a hopelessly haphazard way, and in 1840, Mr. Bayley who had set out to unravel their mysteries gave it up saying that the elasticity of the stud grooms' imaginations defeated him completely. Walton (Sir Peter—Arethusa) was imported in 1825. In 1828 the Cape Derby was founded and racing proceeded apace for a while. The racecourse at Cape Town was however hardly an ideal spot, being a grazing ground for cattle and so exposed to gales that racing was sometimes impossible. It was heavy stony ground and so thick with dust that horses often became invisible and racecourse dogs were so numerous that they caused serious accidents, in fact it was a happy-go-unlucky sort of business.

Horse breeding was a continual struggle with adversity and mismanagement. Mares were allowed to die to save feeding expenses, scrub stallions and donkeys ruined the herds and an immense amount of damage was done by the use of Holstein and dray stallions for thoroughbred mares. Breeders were faddy about white markings and would not have them at any price. Everything was kept in shocking condition and many mares died and slipped foals from being made to slave day and night at the heavy work of treading out the corn—the proportion of foals born alive being in one instance three foals to sixty-one mares.

What wonder that horse sickness raged every twenty years. One hundred and eighteen thousand horses died of it in 1839. Wars also raged perpetually and racing only settled down again in 1867. Meanwhile one of the leading winners in 1861 was Express bred by Mr. A. van der Byl, but having been sent on a long rough voyage in a sailing ship which took three months to reach England he was unable to do himself justice when he got on to the English Turf. About the same time Gazelle, whose dam was by Rob Roy (Arab), was a brilliant winner. Marmotte, Masher and the Marquis all won the Trial Stakes and every other big race including the Natal Derby and the South African Derby at Port Elizabeth. The Queen's Plate open to all breeds was won four times by Riley, and when aged he could give two stone to the best three-year-olds over 1½ miles. Here-I-go-with-my-Eye-Out was another well-known horse, and one of the leading sires and racers was the Madras Arab Dreadnought, purchased in Egypt by General Pigot and evidently of the Mohammed Ali racing stock. He was pure white and though only 14.2 had every attribute of a large horse, and was obviously one of the old high caste Arabs now so seldom seen even in India. His son Grey Momus was exported to England and some of his stock won many races, and many half-Arab mares produced winners. Firetail, daughter of the Damascus Arab, was the dam of two big winners, Grey Dayrell and Kate Dayrell. Blackrock (Arab) by Damascus ex an unknown mare was the best racehorse of the Western Province in 1878.

Natal followed the Cape in becoming a racing centre, where Naughty Boy won the Breeders Plate three times. The chief race was the Maritzburg Railway Stakes. Durban began racing systematically in 1881.

In 1886 the beautiful Marquis won the South African Derby. A black filly, Marmotte was considered the best in training and was sent all over the country thousands of miles in search of victory. Le Faineante by Vedette was one of the great brood mares at the time. Considering the various horse sicknesses to be faced, breeders did wonderfully well.

Brian Boru, a horse sold in England as a bad roarer, recovered out in South Africa and had a brilliant career. He won the welter weights in consecutive events, and in record time, and was reckoned two stone better than any colonial bred horse. His roaring, we are told, was not inherited.

Over three hundred mares were included in the first volume of the stud book and stakes were quickly increased. Plum, purchased for £20 with his dam, at Kimberley, won over £30,000. He was bred in Cape Province. He won everything all over the country. His dam's breeding is in dispute. Thirty races are recorded as won by him, but there were many unrecorded ones. He was killed, being stung to death by bees. Forest King was claimed as a star of South African thoroughbred breeding.

After 1896 British and Argentine importations were supreme until 1909–10 when dead heats were run with Colonial-breds against English importations. Abelard broke the sequence in 1911, but Argentine horses proved far superior racers and competition was of mixed nationality. In 1913 the local horses were improving, several proving themselves equal to all opposition, but, taking them all round, they seem to have been of average welter weight plater class.

Flush of Dawn deserves mention as, like Helleniqua (winner of the Cambridgeshire), she was a diminutive mare of marvellous speed. She gave away weight, stayed a severe ten furlongs, and won the Champion Stakes a week later easily. Pindi was a mare whose produce won over £10,000, yet she only won one small race herself. Bonnet Box and Miss Rose, Argentine bred, were both outstanding brood mares. At the three principal racing centres large sums can be won. Hussein won two races total £9,000, and Roamer won £11,000 with three races.

The Colonial times are not much behind the average and Flush of Dawn holds the South African record for 1¼ miles in spite of her miscroscopic size. Sir Abe Bailey has been the principal owner many times and bred four winners of the South African Derby. Charles Southey bred eight winners of the same race between 1889 and 1908. Hilton Barber and Alex Robertson each bred four winners; H. Nourse five winners of the Oaks and two of the St. Leger. Sir Abe Bailey also bred the winner of the South African Oaks three times and of the St. Leger five times.

A number of Crabbet Arabs have been imported—Cecil Rhodes purchased Azrek and Merzuk, and of late years a number have gone to Mr. Kock of Orange Colony. A stallion of almost pure Crabbet ancestry descended from the Crabbet race winner Belka was recently grand champion of all breeds at the S.A. Richmond Show. The most recent Arab importations are Grand Champion Raktha sold at the age of seventeen for a record price and several mares from £2,800 apiece. Mr. Botha should be the leading owner of the future.

CANADA

The Dominion of Canada extending over vast territories comprises every extreme of climate and is not favourable to racehorse breeding as a whole. Horses were introduced by the French in the eighteenth century and were mostly cavalry and agricultural.

Later the bulk of horse stock imported from America was used for harness and the first typical Canadian horse evolved was the pacer which originated in Quebec and spread through the United States. It is described as small, rugged, closely knit, hard and long lived and a speedy pacer—the prices fetched in the nineteenth century were about equal to those of racehorses.

There is practically no original source of Thoroughbreds in Canada—the first recorded horses were noted in the American Turf register of 1830 as Sir Walter and Cock of the Rock, competing in the Montreal Jockey Club purse, but they were both bred in the States and both traced back to the English bred Diomed, the first English Derby winner. The Montreal race of 1928 was of four-mile heats and the horses were eleven and fourteen years old respectively.

In 1836 King William IV presented a fifty guinea plate to be run for in Lower Canada. Queen Victoria endowed races for horses bred in Upper Canada. King Edward VII patronized the Blue Bonnets course at Montreal in 1907 and the King's Plate run at Toronto was the blue ribbon of the Canadian Turf.

Roxaline was an outstanding brood mare—she was bred at Chicago and own sister to the celebrated mare Marion. Roxaline's produce were as follows:—

1879	Easter B.M.	won 18 races including the Ontario Derby.
1880	Princess	,, 38 ,,
1881	Willie W.	,, 17 ,,
1882	Brait	,, 33 ,,
1883	Fred B.	,, 6 ,,
1887	Roquefort	,, 8 ,, Total 120 races.

Marion produced winners of 138 races.

Advance Guard is considered the greatest of Canadian-owned horses. Foaled 1897 by Great Tom (King Tom out of a Voltigeur mare) he was sold for nothing as a yearling and ran thirteen times unplaced at two years, but in the end he took part in 162 races, won forty-eight, was second in thirty-eight, and third in thirty. Sir Barton won thirteen out of thirty-one races. Hallucination also had a great reputation.

Steeplechasing began at Montreal in 1838, and became an enormously popular sport. Milesian in 1872 won the Grand National at New Jersey and in 1874 covered himself with glory in the Grand Steeplechase Post Stakes, and jumping races generally appeal to a wider public than flat races. Jack the Barber cleared a water jump 28 feet wide, but a Crabbet Arab in England cleared 32 feet over water, so that this is not a record.

The Canadians take a great interest in Percheron horses and have secured them for agriculture, but highly bred light breeds are scarce.

AUSTRALIA

Like America and New Zealand, Australia's possession of horses is comparatively recent, and dates from colonizing explorers. Racing is little more than a century old. The first race meeting was held in 1810 by the officers of the 73rd Regiment stationed in Sydney.

The meetings were irregular, but various clubs were formed and new courses laid down, and in 1840 the Australian Race Committee adopted the Newmarket rules. The use of the name Eclipse for horses in many countries and the constant repetition of the race names Derby, Oaks, St. Leger, etc., which is now spreading to greyhound events shows an astonishing lack of imagination, and is apt at times to be confusing to the man in the street who reads a glowing account of last year's Derby winner and finds it is after all about a dog, not a horse! Australia is no exception, and we find Eclipse winning the St. Leger in 1840, and Quail walking over the Champagne Stakes. Soon the racing fever epidemic spread all over the country, and a now famous course by the salt-water river was selected.

We have the Victoria Derby, Oaks and St. Leger; the New South Wales Derby, St. Leger, Gimcrack and Champagne Stakes, and some races in South Australia, West Australia, and the Queensland Derby and St. Leger in 1878 and 1881. From 1860 the Australian Jockey Club's distribution of stakes rose from £2,327 to £146,458! The discovery of gold was celebrated in West Australia by a great racing boom and the institution of a Derby and St. Leger like the Eastern States. Hurdle races and steeplechases were included in the Jockey Club programmes and attracted even greater crowds.

The big yearling sales are held at Sydney at Easter. The jumping season at Randwick is in June and pony racing is catered for at Kennington, Ascot and Roseberry, with £100,000 annually in stakes. The Melbourne Cup, a two-mile handicap, is the most coveted race in Australia, worth £10,000 of added money and a gold cup. This compares favourably with the value of the Epsom Derby. The Grand National meeting is in July.

The great Flemington course is 1 mile 3 furlongs 111 yards in circumference, with a straight 6 furlongs on the river side and dead flat all the way and, inside it, is the steeplechase course with the stiffest jumps in the country, and it includes training tracks of grass and sand. The amounts paid away by the racing clubs in the Metropolitan area of Melbourne may amount to round about £300,000.

Wallace is said to have been one of the greatest Australian sires. Comedy King is also claimed as outstanding being credited on eight occasions as winning sire, with winners of over £20,000. He died in 1929, having sired 823 winners, and won £288,656. The most beautiful of all Australian sires seems to have been the lovely imported Valais by Cicero—Lily of the Valley. No imported or Australian bred horse ever equalled his short, brilliant stud career. He headed the winning sires list five successive years, 1924–28. He was, like his sire Cicero, a strongly Arabian type, and was sold for 14,400 gns., a record price in Australia. He sired another very good-looking horse, Manfred, claimed as the best of all time. The imported Magpie was also prominent.

Carbine is considered, all in all, the greatest of all horses which are quoted as "the best ever" on the Australian Turf, though the credit of his birth belongs to New Zealand. At the Easter meeting at Randwick he was beaten by Abercorn on the first day. On the second day he defeated Abercorn and Melos over two miles. On the third day he won two races of a mile and two miles, and on the fourth day he defeated Abercorn again over three miles. A wonderful record for one meeting. It seemed quite usual for a horse to run every day for four consecutive days, and he repeated his performance at Victoria Spring Meeting and at Sydney he won the Autumn Stakes ($1\frac{1}{2}$ miles), Sydney Cup (2 miles), the All-Aged Stakes (1 mile), the Cumberland Stakes (2 miles) and the Jockey Club Plate (3 miles)—five races amounting to eight miles in four days. Five more big races in four days. He was purchased for 4,000 gns. and taken to England by the Duke of Portland in April 1895, and died at Welbeck Abbey at the age of twenty-nine. Windbag won £35,891 in stakes.

Manfred had a very uncertain temperament. He would refuse to start, and having lost half a furlong would sprint in pursuit, catch up and win by lengths. He won the Jockey Club Derby after this sort of start—$1\frac{1}{2}$ miles in 2 mins. 28 secs. He won the Victoria Club Derby, $1\frac{1}{2}$ miles by twelve lengths in 2 mins. $31\frac{1}{2}$ secs. Then in two races he refused to start at all, after which he won a few more and retired with £28,830 in stakes. The Barb was held up as equal to Carbine and the best horse of his day. Grand Flaneur was unbeaten in his day and then Trafalgar became a public idol and won £22,111. Up to $1\frac{1}{2}$ miles Gloaming was supreme and went to New Zealand. He won fifty-seven races, nine seconds and was once unplaced. Another brilliant son of Valais was Heroic. He won £38,062.

Among leading mares we find Wakeful winning twenty-five races. La Carabine raced till she was seven and failed at stud. Carlito a great winner failed as a brood mare. Briseis won the Victoria Derby, the Oaks and the Melbourne Cup in one week. Desert Gold was another famous mare.

Numbers of steeplechases are run in the Eastern States and horses are called upon to be tough and lasting.

Australians have had great importations of Arabians. There are several good studs, the largest being Mrs. McLean's at Melbourne. An Arab from Crabbet was champion at Melbourne for many years in succession, and was followed by others of the same blood, each seven or eight times champions. The champions at Sydney have also been of Crabbet blood. The racing performances of Anglo-Arabs have been outstanding, including Melbourne Cup, Victoria and other Derbies and are dealt with in another volume.

INDIA

India has depended for all time on imported stock, the climate being deadly. In fact, at one time it was proverbial that no mares could bring up foals there. The original importations were yearly cargoes of Arabians, which were over-ridden, badly fed and died off, having to be constantly replaced. Hundreds were packed under canvas in open vessels and lost at sea in rough weather.

Racing is divided into several distinct periods. The first was from 1795 till about 1855. The first recorded race was between a fleabitten grey Arab, Lothario, and The Boy in 1791.

There were Persian countrybred and Cabul ponies, but Arabs were scarce. In 1794 the Resident at Basra, Mr. Manesty, began sending numbers of Arab horses until Madras was full of them and they remained supreme on the racecourse for over 100 years. Madras had its first meeting in 1795, starting with a race for *untrained* Arabians in heats over two miles. It was not till 1799 that an English mare, Brown Bess, competed. In 1808 Arabs almost monopolized the programme and in 1830 the Calcutta crack Esterhazy was beaten at Madras by the grey Arab Salonica. Mr. Manesty also sent a brother of the Basley Arabian to England.

Calcutta began racing in 1798 for country breeds. The Pearl, a very fine Arab, is the first mentioned winner. The racing was poor owing to the scarcity of Arabs. Bombay followed and Poona, later to be a great racing centre, began racing in 1819—the shortest race being 1½ miles. Two and three miles races were run in three to five heats to test stamina.

In the Bengal Cup, 1845, the grey Arab Crab and the bay Arab Oranmore ran five heats carrying 8 st. 7 lb. each over two miles—first won by Oranmore, second dead heat, third won by Crab, fourth dead heat and fifth won by Crab. No interval of rest was allowed between heats beyond the half hour for the jockey to get weighed. The saddling bugle went at sunrise and the races were run in early morning or after sunset. Rs. 5,000 to Rs. 10,000 were common prices for Arabs.

In 1850 the class of Arab deteriorated and walers, English and countrybred, ran together. The same thing happened as was happening in England, where interdicts in the East had stopped the flow of high-class stock to foreign countries.

British breeders tried importing Arabs from India, and in 1830 the grey Arab horse Signal went to Scotland, followed by Paragon and Honesty. Buckfoot and Hamdanieh [sic] both 14.2, were sent to England and were said to be the most perfect horses ever seen. The grey Arab Boxkeeper, 1825–29, ran thirty-three times, winning twenty-one races.

Mr. Hilliard writes that of all horses the Arab is the most uncertain racer, never to be relied on, and the tale of Indian backers was one of ruin, mortgage and blasted hopes—but it is possible that gambling jockeys were more responsible for this rather convenient reputation as "two stone change of form in a few months" is hardly credible as an honest occurrence. After 1850, racing declined—Australian horses had been put under embargo and horse sickness stopped the Cape importations, while English horses could not stand the climate.

In 1856, the Viceroy's Cup of Rs. 1,000 was won by Nero, an Arab, against all comers. He started by racing off with a lead of thirty lengths, and over the St. Leger course won by

188

a neck. At Bombay in the same year Lucifer, a grey, 14.3½, imported from Arabia and bought for Rs. 1,000 ran in nine races and won them all, and was never touched with spur or whip.

Heats were now abolished. Arabs were then fetching Rs. 2,000 as a minimum, the Calcutta Derby, two miles, for Maiden Arabs, attracted a record crowd and a field of thirteen. The Indian Mutiny had a disastrous effect on racing and it languished for some years.

The first definite attempt at horse breeding in India was made by the Hindus with horses called Kalthiawars and other foreign varieties. It cost fabulous sums and the stock was imported from countries bordering on the Red Sea and Persian Gulf and vast amounts of money continued to be expended on establishing a breed. In the Luckhee Jungle tazees were bred. In 1818 the British Government took a hand and stallions were located in districts to help local owners of mares. Hurdling, steeplechasing, and flat racing now proceeded apace and by 1870 were in full swing, patronized by viceroys and maharajahs.

One outstandingly fine Arab made history, namely, the grey Grey Leg, reputed to be able to give 10 lb. to any Arab in India at any distance up to four miles. He came from Basra and beat a thoroughbred English mare by Harkaway in Bombay, and established a supremacy which could not be taken from him, winning fifty-one races. A typical Arabian of perfect conformation, with black skin and a silver grey coat, 14.1, with great depth and substance. He was a lazy racer and required rousing, but was never beaten. The Arab Hermit "the Eclipse of his day" was another grey, 15 hands, and also "faultless to the most fastidious eye" and of great bone and substance, won thirty-four races at all distances and weights. He never showed a windgall on any leg during his six years' training. He was purchased at Bombay in 1857.

His first race was in the Calcutta Derby, 1859, in which he ran second to Rocket, and from then onwards he won everything and gave Ellerton, a good Waler, 7 lb. and a beating for the Calcutta Stakes, 2 miles in 3 mins. 51 secs.

In February 1862 he ran a desperate race with the English thoroughbred Votige for the Trades Cup, 2 miles in 3 mins. 46 secs. He was eventually defeated by Grey Leg.

The Arab Opal (an opalescent grey) went to England and won first prize at Islington in 1862.

Mangosteen (afterwards Starlight) was a celebrated Arab racer. He was won in a raffle by Colonel Turnbull from Sheikh Ibrahim, who raffled off three of his horses, grey, bay and chestnut, for Rs. 6,000, three throws with three dice. Colonel Turnbull got third choice. Two Arab merchants got the others, one of which was immediately sold for Rs. 2,000.

The opening of the Suez Canal in 1869, shortening the sea voyage from England, revolutionized Indian racing by opening also the door to an influx of Thoroughbreds. In 1869 the Arab Derby attracted seventeen Arabs and was won by Akhbar—and the Viceroy's Cup was won by Favourite, an Australian mare. The next year Favourite ran again but was disqualified, together with another entry Longden, because Longden crossed and cannoned into Detrimental, who was pressing Favourite hard. Under the Calcutta rules if any horse crossed another all the owner's entries were disqualified and Longden's jockey was fined and suspended and Favourite, being owned by the same man, was also disqualified. This raised a hornet's nest as the owner of Detrimental, not having declared a partnership, his horse was added to the disqualified pair and the owner of the fourth horse claimed the race. The race was then declared void and ordered to be run again next week when Favourite walked over, but the Cup was retained as the other horses did not start. The matter was so hotly disputed that a ruling was asked from Messrs. Weatherby who decided that Favourite should not have been disqualified and the Cup was then awarded to her.

Flat racing at Calcutta then declined in favour of steeplechasing—in 1872 the Bengal steeplechase caused another upheaval—a rider was killed. Delphos, the winner, was objected to for not keeping to the course. Another objection was made to the second horse and the third horse coming in dead lame claimed the race, but meanwhile the judge had disappeared and the race was declared void, whereupon the Lt.-Governor prohibited further steeplechasing. Shortly afterwards Lord Mayo was assassinated.

Poona and Meerut established racing—one of the best riders was Bertie Short of the Indian Police, whose duties as police officer took a very unimportant part in his life. He was a determined man, and when he lost one hand through being savaged by a countrybred he was back in the saddle within two months, doing as well as ever armed with a hook round which he twisted the reins.

Meetings at Calcutta got worse and worse till the advent of Lord William Beresford gave racing a new impetus. Natives began betting heavily, stakes improved and Walers came to West India, and a fine bay Arab Merrylegs, appeared at Bangalore, while the Australian, Satellite, won at Delhi. Kingcraft, a Waler, won forty-six races out of sixty-eight.

Racing improved and spread, and at the Calcutta meeting of 1881 Rex, a diminutive bay Arab marvel, 13.2, made his debut. He was from Nejd and made racing history for five years and is mentioned in Lady Anne Blunt's diaries.

In 1883, at Lucknow, the valuable Civil Service Cup was won by a bay Arab, Rajah, with the Arab Leo second. Until 1927 it remained the pony Derby of India.

In 1884 it was again won by Rajah. General Sir Edward Locke Elliot swept the board about this time with three Arabs, Euclid, Lanercost, and Isonomy, Lord William Beresford bought Euclid and Lanercost and a two-year-old Latchkey for £5,000, after Euclid had easily won the Governor's Cup. It has been stated that Euclid was sold to the Russian Government for £2,000, but he was actually purchased for the Polish stud of Count Joseph Potocki. He proved a failure, turned savage, killed a man, and was destroyed.

The Civil Service Cup was increased in value in 1886. The stakes being Rs. 10,000 and the lotteries Rs. 70,000. It was won by a remarkable grey Arab, Blitz, bought for £70, and the race was easily won by three lengths. He became the champion of his day.

The Turkish authorities, having noted the excessive demand for Arabs overseas, put an embargo now on all export which sounded the death knell of Arab racing in India. English and Australian horses gradually replaced them.

Meanwhile, Blitz won the Civil Service Cup again as easily as before, and in the Autumn won the Pony Derby, a five furlong race in 1 min. 8½ secs. This cup was won in 1893 by an Arab, Pekin, against English and Australians. In December, an open race for Arabs was won by Lanercost. The excessive popularity of the big Arab races causes one to regret that they were eventually discontinued.

In 1889, the wonderful Blitz was just beaten into second place by an English Thoroughbred, Mike, but it was no disgrace, for the *Arab was giving him 2 stone 8 lb.* He was again second giving 1 stone 3 lb. to a Thoroughbred, Silver King, in the Innovation Stakes. In fact, Blitz appears to have been weighted out of all reason when competing with thoroughbreds, but he won the Eclipse Stakes for the Maharajah of Patiala, and the following year a chestnut Arab, The Brat, won it, this being the last year it was won by an Arab. The last Arab to win the Civil Service Cup was Pekin in 1893 and the Maharajah of Mysore's Child of the Islands was the last imported Arab to win the Governor's Cup at Madras the same year.

Maidan had an unbeaten career from 1871 to 1874. He then carried Colonel Brownlow (18 st. with equipment) in campaigns for twelve years, also winning the Ganges Cup and a four-mile chase. At seventeen he was put to racing again and was imported to England, raced and hunted. He won a steeplechase of three miles at the age of twenty-three against thoroughbreds.

Kismet was another remarkable horse. He won £30,000 in stakes, and was imported to England in 1884, where he won two races against Asil at Newmarket. His record in India was unbeaten, but met defeat in previous races at Newmarket and Sandown.

1883	Bangalore	July 12th	Mysore Cup	..	1¼ mile weight		139	lb.
		July 14th	Mysore Purse	..	1½ ,,	,,	134	lb.
		July 19th	Aga Khan Purse	..	1½ ,,	,,	134	lb.
	Poona	Sept. 8th	Aga Khan Plate	..	1¼ ,,	,,	126	lb.
		Sept. 11th	Aga Khan Purse	..	1¾ ,,	,,	131	lb.
	Hyderabad	Nov. 22nd	Deccan Handc'p	..	1½ ,,	,,	119	lb.
1884	Bombay	Feb. 12th	The Derby	..	1½ ,,	,,	136	lb.
		Feb. 14th	Aga Khan Purse	..	1½ ,,	,,	133	lb.

The Aga Khan inherited a stable of seventy horses in training on the death of his father in 1885, when he was eight years old and his Arab Venture, then the best in India, won the Governor's Cup in 1894, carrying 9 st. 6 lb. in almost record time. Everyone knows what the Aga Khan has accomplished on the English Turf, and it is to be regretted that, at the outbreak of the second World War, he broke up his stud and sold his three Derby winners to U.S.A. He has resumed racing but the brightest gems are gone.

In 1895 Red Rube won the Governor's Cup at Poona. He had started as a subaltern's charger, but, having got loose one day, he gave such a spectacular display of speed that he was put into training.

The Indian Grand National was first run in 1895 and won by the Maharajah of Patiala, a grey Arab pony Shannon winning the Army Cup, but the Arabs were gradually being crowded out by the thoroughbreds.

In 1909 the Viceroy's Cup comprised five English, six Walers, one American and one countrybred, but no Arabs. Some of the last winning Arabs were Bay Middleton, 13.3, winner of three successive races in 1903, six in 1904, including the Poona Derby, and went on racing till 1912, winning a large number of races of anything up to seven furlongs, but he won also over $1\frac{1}{4}$ miles. His times were half mile in $52\frac{1}{5}$ secs., carrying 9 stone 8 lb.; five furlongs in 1 min. $6\frac{1}{5}$ secs.; and seven furlongs in 1 min. 36 secs.

One of the most beautiful Arabs, and also perhaps the best, was a famous grey named Precious, who was over the pony standard. He won his first three races and ended up in 1912 with thirty races, his best distance being 1 mile to $1\frac{1}{4}$ miles, covering the latter distance in 2 mins. 23 secs. He improved with age and his best races were at twelve years old, when he was a stone better than any other Arab. He was brilliant, generous and consistent, and extremely beautiful, and his performances recall Eleppoo in 1844, who won *twenty races straight off the reel*, in spite of a permanent penalty of one stone put on him against all comers. Clem was another well-known winner.

English jockeys and trainers came out in increasing numbers—F. Wootton won the Trials on Tangaroa, a fast Waler, in the record time of 1 min. 40 secs. Under 10 st. 7 lb. he ran five furlongs in 1 min. 1 sec.; six furlongs in 1 min. $13\frac{2}{5}$ secs. and won with the Arab Grand Duke.

In Bombay Arab races were still run in 1925, but the bulk of racing is now for Thoroughbreds, which on account of their sprinting speed hold the practical monopoly of racing everywhere. Egypt and Syria are also being overrun by English racehorses, and the unique traditions of Egypt's astounding racing records by Arabians for five hundred years under the Sultans will soon be forgotten. The Crabbet bred Mishwal "The Flying Arab" is one of the latest Arabians to make a sensation.

NEW ZEALAND

There were no quadrupeds in New Zealand except those left by Captain Cook, including very small rats. The early settlers imported horses for some time before the New Zealand Stud Book was started in 1862. The preface to this book states that the Thoroughbred horse of Australia and New Zealand owes its origin to imported English blood and to an admixture of Arab from India. We have, therefore, the usual history of racing blood. At first no pedigrees were kept in Australia or New Zealand, and New Zealand stock was founded on Australian and English stallions and Arabs. The first Thoroughbred horse landed was Figaro, and he was followed in 1843 by Aether and Riddlesworth.

The provinces of Wellington and Nelson held their meetings under somewhat trying conditions. The duties of the Clerk of the Course included extracting stones and glass from the sandy track—getting the dogs tied up and the pigs collected, and removing native picnic parties from the middle of the course. Nelson's first meeting consisted of one hurdle race with two entries over the most dangerous ground on record.

Things began to improve by 1855, and by 1928 the Canterbury Jockey Club was distributing £40,000 a year in stakes.

The first permanent Derby Stakes was run at its first meeting in 1860 and was won by Ada, which fitly stands at the head of the list of winners of the New Zealand Derby.

Trotting races were also run and among the highly bred sires imported at the end of the last century were Traducer and Musket. Musket had narrowly missed being destroyed as a two-year-old as he was not promising, but his trainer intervened and he won the Ascot stakes and was exported later to New Zealand. From him was bred the mighty Carbine (out of Mersey) who was sold for 620 gns. and went to Australia and eventually to England. He won five races in New Zealand and twenty-eight races in Australia, his total winnings being £22,526.

Other progeny of Musket figure prominently over twenty years. From 1930 we find Nightmarch, winner of the Melbourne Cup, by Night Raid by Radium and sire of the marvellous horse Pharlap, one of the fastest horses ever bred, for he beat the best Derby $1\frac{1}{2}$ mile record by no less than four seconds, though not over the Epsom course. He won £70,140 in stakes, and died mysteriously in America, shortly before he was to run for the richest money prize in that country.

Steeplechasing is most popular and the first three Grand Nationals at Riccarton were won by horses teeming with Arab blood. The course was laid out in imitation of Aintree. Only two out of six entries, a half Arab and a quarter-bred, saw the journey through. A stiff 4 ft. rail fence with 16 ft. of deep water on the landing side were included in the replica and the Quarter, a typical Arab in appearance, cleared 39 ft. from take off to landing.[1] The obstacles were modified in the second year, and Canard, son of Anteros, won it, the distance being four miles.

Trotters were firmly established by American trainers at the beginning of this century, Canterbury being the headquarters of the sport. The trotter Oakleigh also won the New Zealand Grand National in 1922 and 1923.

The champion mountain mare Prancio and an Arab stallion were exported from Crabbet in 1950.

---

[1] This must be close on a record.

Hunting scene with Francis Blunt, centre horseman, by Ferneley

CHAPTER XV

HUNTERS AND IRISH-BRED HORSES

FOX-HUNTING is the traditional British sport which has been the glory of our hard-riding squires of England and the pride of every man, woman and child of Ireland, from the earliest days of which we have records. Songs of the chase, the cry of hounds and the thrilling call of the horn and the galloping of horses have made hearts leap from the cradle to the grave.

And now in spite of anti-blood sport agitations and the dwindling area of ground under the encroachments of town planning and food growing, we still hold on to our hounds and hunters.

Perhaps now we have as good a type of hunter as can be seen in the world, both handsome and powerful, and the show rings provide a fine spectacle. Coursing has gone out as a sport for horsemen and the electric hare has taken its place. One hopes that electric foxes will not follow suit, but barbed wire is doing its nightmare best to ruin the joys of the English chase.

Meanwhile I admire the perfection of the modern hunting horses and show jumpers. Dublin Horse Show is a world-famous centre of assembly for the world's best riding horses.

The original stock of Ireland was much the same as in England. Oriental traders seem to have influenced both, and there are traces of survivorship in Britain mentioned by Strabo.

The *Brehon Laws* (the code which dated from the introduction of Christianity until the seventeenth century) laid down regulations about horses and races. Fines were imposed for "injuries done to or by Chariots in a fair or assembly or by furious driving." A chariot had six to eight spokes to its wheels and a good chariot was worth about twelve cows representing about £150 to £160 of our money. Royal chariots were worth as much as eighty or ninety cows.

The *Brehon Laws* also laid down conditions of warranty with a wealth of adjectives and super qualifications which few vets would now be prepared to endorse.

"A big horse, sound, young, noble, high-headed, load carrying, lively hearted, broad breasted, haughty, easy bearing, sleek, slender legged, well descended, free from spear thrusts, free from sword cuts; his form well set, tractable to the land, without lumps or

The famous jumper Tosca with Pat Smythe, the supreme winning pair in International Competitions

flags on his back, not broken backed, not rough stepping, not too low, not too high, not shy, not starting, not big mouthed, not ill stepping, not lazy, not lame, not kicking, not dusty haired, not blowing, not droop eared, not shaky, perfectly sound, easy ridden, obedient. *If he be not such he is rejected.*"

With these thirty-seven indispensable adjectives to fulfil the rejections must have been legion, in fact, the compiler might have been choosing a candidate for the Throne of Ireland instead of a mere quadruped! It recalls, indeed, the story of a French Countess who asked a friend to find her a footman. He must be well bred with perfect manners, a Greek profile, young, gentle, thoughtful, unselfish, loyal, handsome as Apollo, strong as Hercules, quick as Mercury, tall, slender, intelligent, good tempered, tactful; in fact, he must be endowed with every virtue and free from every vice. The friend listened in quizzical silence and then said: "Sapristi, ma chère, je ferai mon possible mais si je trouve ton homme je l'epouse!" ("Dash it, dear, I will do my best, but *if* I find your man I *marry him*.")

The *Book of Aicill* (one of the earliest law tracts) gives the relative value of horses as a tripartite division, "one-third for its body, one-third for its expectation (a somewhat cryptic word), one-third for its work, one-twelfth of its dam for the foal when foaled. The mare has a tripartite division—one-third in consideration of her body, one-third for her promise, and one-third for her foal and her work. If she be without foal she is to be returned and another given instead of her. If the foal be destroyed in the womb of its dam a ninth part of the value of the dam shall be paid for it, but if it be destroyed in the field the twelfth part of the value of the dam"—the reason is that it is thought greater injury will result to the mare by destroying it in the womb than in the field. It is not at all clear if the pre-natal destruction is deliberate or accidental.

In the *Rennes Dindsenchas*, the origin of the name Lagore in the Co. Meath is given (by Whitley Stokes) as follows:

"Glascu had on his mountain a grey British stallion named Serrach (a colt). This stallion followed the stud of Enna Aignech and they fled before him into the lake and were drowned; their names were 'Wind' and 'Sun' (Gaeth and Grian). Hence Lagore is derived meaning Loch Gobur, Lake of Horses." The words the Irish used for a horse were Ech, a steed; Capal, a beast of burden; Marc, a riding horse; Lair, a mare; Groigh (Grex) or Graifne, a stud; and Gobur, a Welsh or British horse, a white horse, or any horse having a white marking.

The first introduction of horses into Ireland is ascribed to a Nemedian (Scythian) tribe, and it is considered that their love of horses and style of riding long continued common characteristics of both peoples. The first horses of note mentioned by name by Irish writers were those in the Saga of Cuchulain, the great Irish hero. One of these horses harnessed to his car was coal black, more elegant than powerful with waving mane, rapid foot, arching neck, foaming mouth, and large speaking lustrous eyes. This noble creature, swift and shy, usually moved at the right side of the pole of polished yew. His name was Dubhfhoilean (the black seagull). At the other side snorted Liath Macha, a dappled grey

[Photo : *Sport and General Press Agency*

Supreme Champion Saddle Horse, White City, 1952
Mr. W. H. Cooper's Mighty Atom, one of the leading hunter champions

Mount Royal, in the author's opinion an ideal hunter type

charger with massive chest, light limbs, flowing mane and eyes of fire, neighing so loudly as he reared impatiently at times that the sound was audible afar off. The Arad (Charioteer) who guided these steeds with a bright gilded wand, was draped in a long Fallaing mantle of brilliant colour which covered him to his heels when he stood.

In the *Book of Rights*, continual mention is made of horses and their trappings having been paid as tribute . . . one chieftain is said to be entitled to "a horse and trappings from across the high sea." From *Tribes and Customs of Hymany* we find that the King of Connaught paid a subsidy to the King of Hymany as follows: "The King of Hymany, the Hero, is entitled to ten horses which came across the boisterous brine; to ten foreigners ready at deeds of anger, to ten standards and ten mantles."

Subsequent to the Norse invasions, A.D. 1014 to 1030, a famous white horse is constantly referred to. He was the gift of O'Hanley, who had fought at the battle of Clontarf (A.D. 1014), to Teig O'Connor, King of Connaught, known as Teig of the white horse— a most Arabian title like "Robia of the horses."

From the time of the Anglo-Norman invasion, A.D. 1172, Ireland had large draught horses, and the old type greatly resembled the Percheron. It is from these, crossed with thoroughbreds sent over from England and bred in Ireland, that the famous Irish hunters are descended.

It is interesting to note that at the time of the Norman invasion of Ireland, A.D. 1172, their riders carried a stick with a crook at the upper end, the same as the Bedouin camel stick, which they used to guide their horses. This seems to be a direct importation of an Arab custom, as also was their practice of riding with a single rein halter only and no bit or saddle.

Spanish and North African blood, as well as Arab blood, had been imported to Ireland by traders and Spanish settlers from the earliest days. The Irish Hobby horse was not a racehorse at any time, but an ambler bred mainly from ambling Spanish Jennets, the Astureonas. "Hobby" was not the name of a breed, but was used, as "galloway" was used, to denote a pony under fourteen hands, and as we use the word "cob" for a particular build of horse. It was applied to English bred' as well as Irish bred stock. "Haubin" or Hobby was a hawk and hobbies were used for hawking and (says Carve) chiefly ridden by effeminate persons and exported to France in 1666 as ladies' palfreys.

The Irish hobby of the sixteenth century was described by Blundeville as having a good head but indifferent body, slender and pin buttocked, tender mouthed, nimble, light, pleasant and easy to teach—mostly amblers, and "very meete" for the saddle and travelling, and he adds that the Irish use them for skirmishing with darts and light spears. He criticizes the horse for being rather delicate and nervous, apt to shy. John Major in 1520 describes them as of very gentle pace. White ones were also led in the Pope's procession adorned in purple and silver. In 1537 the Duke of Mantua wrote to his Ambassador in England to buy him an English bred hobby.

That they were not galloping racehorses is proved by Camden's reference to their ambling gait. Pliny says "the best horses which we call hobbies do not travel like others but have a soft ambling pace by alternate unfolding of the legs." There is a description of a race between pacers, A.D. 1170, outside London. The races of *these noble horses were not run at a gallop but by the fore and hind feet moving in pairs together.*

The running pacers of Peru could pace much faster than they could gallop. Stainhurst describing Irish horses says they are "of pace easie. In running wonderful swift; but in gallop both false and full indifferent" which is almost always the case with fast pacers. There were various kinds of ambling, pacing, and racking (rocking), some swaying more than others. Barnaby Fitzpatrick, elder son of an Irish chieftain, had a fine stud of hobbies in 1577. The old hackneys were described as rocking their riders to sleep.

The black hobby "running horse" which beat some imported Barbs was an ambler, and the horse Valentine, which afterwards "over-ran" him and was boastfully described by Gervase Markham in the seventeenth century as "plain English" and not to be equalled as a hunter, was probably of the all-round crossbred type described by contemporary writers as "a mixture of all the horses of all the Nations," and his performance left no trace. No such horses as Valentine or "the peerless" Puppie, claimed by G. Markham as also English, appear in any stud book either printed or private, nor are either of them recorded elsewhere.

Irish horses were in demand in Italy in the sixteenth century, but the Italian agents complained that the Irish were so busy fighting each other that business was thrown to the four winds. At one time the Italian hunters of the Roman Campagna used to be considered the world's best hunters.

In the sixteenth century E. Spencer refers to women riding in Ireland on the "wrong" side of the horse, i.e. "with their faces towards the right side," which is an old Spanish and African custom.

In Elizabeth's reign so many Irish horses were exported to Scotland and France that further export was forbidden in 1566-77, 1584 and 1602, and also in the reign of James I, and when Deputy Lord Chichester made a present of a fine horse of Irish breed to His Majesty, this monarch swore aloud that it must then certainly be a Papist for that he believed all things produced in Ireland, even the very animals, were Papists.

Sir W. Temple, 1673, deplored that during the long-continued wars in Ireland up to the awful wars in Cromwell's time, poor Ireland was reduced in the matter of horses and men to "carcasses and ashes," and later he made plans for reviving horse breeding.

The racehorses obtained from the dispersal sale of the English Royal Tutbury stud by the Duke of Ormonde in 1651 were wasted in miscellaneous crossbreeding. In despair at "the crooked ways of horse dealers" and the failure of his stud, the Duke eventually gave away the remaining crossbreeds to his son, Lord Arran, who shipped forty of them, including twelve Flemish horses, to England and up to the end of the seventeenth century racing was not prominent. In 1800 there were only eight courses in the whole of Ireland, but 1,500 saddle horses celebrated for their jumping powers were exported to England yearly as hunters, hunting being the chief Irish sport for centuries.

Large numbers of oriental horses were imported from time to time, but racing was neglected for half a century from 1690. It was not till 1731 that an Irish paper spoke of horse racing as becoming a great diversion. Ass breeding was a serious business and a prize of £25 was offered to anyone who would import from Spain a jackass of at least fourteen hands. These jackasses commanded a stud fee of £3 to £5.

Bred horses began to be raced about the time that the Byerley Turk was at stud there. He was an Arab charger ridden by Captain Byerley at the Battle of the Boyne. In 1673 Sir W. Temple advocated the encouragement of horse breeding, and in 1746 Sir Marmaduke Wyvill imported two Arab mares worth fifty guineas and thirty guineas, winning a premium of £20 because they were such beauties. M. Cox printed very long lists of stallions and of race meeting places from 1750, but no pedigrees. Sir Marmaduke also in 1752 imported four horses of his own breed, viz., two fine four-year-old geldings and a fine bay six-year-old stallion got by the Godolphin Arabian, and a brood mare by Belgrade.

Oliver Goldsmith wrote peevishly in 1757 about a mare called Irish Lass: "There has been more money spent in the encouragement of the Podareen mare there in one season than in rewards given to learned men since the times of Ussher!" Even to-day we fear our learned professors are lamentably behind our Derby winners in financial value! The little Podareen (Rosary) mare won a race against Othello after winning the Royal plates at the Curragh in 1745 and 1747. She was called Podareen, instead of her real name of Irish Lass, because she raced with a rosary round her neck, which might have confirmed James I in his contention that all Irish horses were Papists! It must have been rather an outsize rosary to go over her head; in fact, one may assume she carried the whole fifteen decades!

Othello had been bought by Sir Ralph Gore for 500 gns. and imported to Ireland. He ran several races, the best of which were the matches against Podareen and Bajazet, the latter one being for 10,000 gns. at the Curragh. Sir Ralph took the precaution of engaging six or seven jockeys to ride, but letting nobody know beforehand which would do so. Bajazet's jockey being unable to ride the weight was encumbered with a shotted belt. This he managed to discard and a spectator picked it up and cleverly slipped it back into the jockey's pocket before weighing in. Gore, however, saw the trick, and he seized the jockey and shook him so fiercely that he confessed, and the result was a duel. Gore arrived on the ground with seconds, surgeons and pistols, plus a coffin engraved with Lord March's name. This seems to have unnerved the Earl, who apologized and called off the contest. No crossing or jostling was allowed *except* by the two leading horses in the last half mile of each heat!

Enormous stakes were gambled on the Turf and at cards. One man lost his whole estate at cards and staked his wife on a conqueror and lost again. The incensed wife, however, took the opportunity of insisting on the stakes being paid over and, ignoring her husband's explanation that it was all a joke, went off with the winner.

Buck Whaley, a celebrated dare-devil, always squandering money on silly bets, crippled himself at last by jumping from the window of Daly's Club in College Green, Dublin, on to the roof of a passing cab.

CHAPTER XVI

MIXED IMPROVED PONY BREEDS

IT is becoming increasingly customary to speak of various equine breeds for which a standard of type has been laid down as "pure bred." As, however, many people speak of a *pure* breed when they merely mean a *specialized* breed, it may be interesting to recall the history of our British-bred and other ponies, of which we are justly proud, though speaking strictly scientifically, they are not of *pure* origin, by which I mean a pure species with a definitely fixed original type and no alloy whatever of any other blend. There are indeed very few breeds which can claim such a descent.

There were no "aboriginal" British equine breeds. Historical evidence shows that there was a general wild primitive type of pony termed "Celtic" distributed over South-West Europe, Iceland, the Hebrides, Norway and Sweden, France and Spain, and later over the British Isles. This is depicted on the rocks and cave drawings of Southern France and Spain, dating back some fifty thousand years. They all bear a family resemblance, and are quite distinct from the hideous Mongolian donkey-horse and its Prjevalski and Tarpan brethren of Russia and China native to the Steppes and which Professor Ewart, after many years of experimental breeding of Mongolian and Exmoors, describes as *"saturated with what for want of a better word we must call cart blood,"* and distinguished for an enormous, disproportionately long, narrow, coarse, convex head and mandible, and an asinine neck, erect mane, tail, hoofs, nineteen ribs and no forelock. The Celtic type has eighteen ribs, a very short, broad head, and was bushy tailed with rather crested neck and decided distinction and a dished profile, but pictorial evidence does not enable us to do more than say that it was probably the ancestral stock of all our mountain, moorland, and forest pony breeds, but there is no evidence of special varieties. The only ones which can be identified by their markings are the leopard speckled pony now being specialized as the Appaloosa and the parti-coloured ponies which survive as Pintos, and in the Shetland breed. All of these are connected by other evidence with India, Arabia and the Himalayas, and there is one prehistoric painting of a red pony with the Scandinavian tan muzzle and what looks like a red list down the back. This has a very dished face and arched neck.

The others all belong to the general, still existing, type of hill, dale, forest, and other semi-wild ponies, varying in size and coarseness according to the amount of cold or hot blood in their composition. The pre-Roman stock of Britain shown by the remains of very small chariots, harness and bits was evidently not over twelve hands, but we know that the ponies were conspicuously active. On the pre-Roman coins minted in England we see two types, a brilliantly dashing Arab and a stocky pony of no special breed. These coins were not copies of the Roman "Stater" model, as thought by some to whom all coinage leads back to Rome, as they predated the invasion, but show evidence of Oriental influence of some earlier colonization. No sign of the scythed chariots airily referred to by some writers has been discovered.

Champion Mignon, by Naseel. Farm pony, bred by Mrs. Nicholson

In the Middle Ages our indigenous semi-wild ponies were described as a heterogeneous collection without owners or boundaries in the vast forests and marshes of the south. Exmoor and Dartmoor were part of the same unfenced moorland open to any stray stallion in days when castration was rare. There was no supervision or control. No distinction was drawn between them and bitter were the complaints of contemporary writers of depredations by cart colts, asses, and scrub stallions all over the country.

Things got to such a pass that Henry VIII ordered the "killing and burying of all stock under fifteen hands unlikely to provide horses for military service and agriculture," and only the difficulty of catching and executing the Welsh mountain ponies prevented their total extinction. The ponies on Crown lands and moorlands which included Exmoor and Dartmoor, were, however, abolished forthwith regardless of breed. The only animals allowed on these lands by law were the heavy breeds. It is unlikely, therefore, that any

203

moorland pony breeds can date back further than Henry VIII, and there were still no ponies on Crown lands a hundred years later when a census was taken of all the animals on them. There is no question whatever of the survival of any prehistoric breed there.

With James I, a revulsion of feeling set in and Arabian blood was the rage, and though his Arabian stud was broken up and dispersed in 1649-53, Cromwell imported Arabs and Charles II imported the famous Royal Mares registered in 1727 in Chenys calendar, and whose pictures descend to us through the Milbankes. Racing was taken up in earnest to the vast indignation of Army men who regarded racehorses as despicable toys, unworthy of the British nation.

THE EXMOORS AND ARABS ON EXMOOR

Some time ago I ventured to classify Exmoors among our mixed improved pony breeds, congratulating breeders on the improvement made since the days when all early contemporary writers condemned them wholesale as "arrant jades one worse than the other running the moors at the mercy of any cart stallion or ass." One might have thought that when contrasted with the best modern selected specimens, pretty headed and stylish, breeders would have appreciated the compliment to their skill, but I was immediately set upon with more zeal than discretion and challenged to mortal combat. The grievance being that in defiance of all evidence to the contrary they should be described as a "pure native indigenous *English Celtic aboriginal* feral" breed in all its pristine purity dating back at least a hundred years (!) to the *Mongolian of Thibet!* As no breed can be both pure native and foreign the chain of logic seems more original than aboriginal and it may be useful to review the facts.

The history of the ponies begins in 1818. At this time they were a mongrel collection.

It is only in the last century that British breeders have begun reclaiming and specializing the "wild" ponies of certain districts and naming them after their localities, the usual Arab and Barb stallions being called in to improve them. Dartmoor and the New Forest never made any pretence of pure blood. The ponies have been crossed and re-crossed with every sort of suitable and unsuitable breed and the Exmoor certainly was no exception; in fact, Professor Axe says "no breed has been the subject of more fantastic crosses." The chief difference between Exmoors and Dartmoors was said to be a greater tendency to cow hocks in the latter, and a propensity to "mealy" (i.e. tan) noses in the former which would be a sign of Scandinavian blood, and certainly not confined to Exmoor.

As forests disappeared and civilization progressed certain holders of Crown lands made enclosures to keep out wandering stallions, notably in 1850 when a forty-mile fence was erected on Exmoor, but in the main the moors are always liable to trespassers, and anyone knowing the miraculous powers of these ponies to get out of, over, or even *under* all obstacles will realize that it is a case of "Neither bolts nor bars shall keep my own true love from me!"

With regard to the main crossings, midway in the eighteenth century a pony called

Katerfelto appeared on Exmoor. He was wild, elusive and mysterious and his performances have become legendary romance, but he actually did exist, for after ranging the moor for some years he was eventually caught by an ancestor of the Froude family and kept at East Anstey, but not before he had made such a prodigious leap that the place is still called Katerfelto's Leap. He was a cream stallion of striking appearance, standing about fourteen hands, with a black list down the back. No one knew where he came from, but he had been with the mongrel herds long enough to leave a lasting stamp, as testified by Mr. Froude Bellew. Traditions all agreed that he must have been part Arab, and some said lost by a circus, but no one ever really knew. Later, in 1794, a dark brown stallion, 14.1, called Katerfelto, was sold by Sir Thomas Acland, but this could not have been the original Katerfelto, for Katerfelto the Great had no pedigree, and this other Katerfelto's very mixed pedigree is given in the sale list as by Sportsman (Thoroughbred) out of a black Galloway mare, and advertised as Sir Thomas Acland's famous sire extensively used by him. There is no question of his having been of pure descent.

Sir Thomas Acland had rented part of Exmoor from the Crown, and when it was disforested in 1818, Mr. John Knight bought the Manor of Simonsbath with ten thousand acres, adding six thousand more later, and left Sir Thomas the moors on the Winsford Hill side of sufficient area to locate a few of the Katerfelto crossed ponies, the others numbering about three hundred and eighty were sold off, and only twenty were kept by Sir Thomas. Though not, of course, of "pure" origin, he inbred to a recognizable stamp.

Mr. Knight frankly crossed his herds with pack horses and even cab horses, and especially with two long-legged black Dongolese stallions; an unfortunate choice, as the breed is most unsuitable, being high on the leg, flat-sided, and lacking the Arab stamina, not being real Arabs but of "Berberi" (Upper Egyptian) type with white stockings and blazes and a sheep's head, and were tried in Egypt but discarded as inferior to the pure Arabian. However, the second cross back to the pony produced some good hunters and became the groundwork of the Knight ponies. Sir Frederick Knight carried on, and by 1860 his ponies were the talk of the countryside. He followed up with thoroughbreds Gohanna, Pandarus, Quicksilver, and Old Port, and a fine Arab called Cairo, which also appears in Welsh Mountain pedigrees. Champion Tan y Bwlch Berwyn was sired by an Arab Barb, Sahara, whose photographs give an Arab head and quarters quite unlike a Barb. At one time the Knight ponies numbered four hundred, about 13.1, with fine heads and good conformation. Dr. Watney crossed his Acland herd with the bay Crabbet Arab Nejran, and found them as hardy as the uncrossed pony stock and very handsome. Another Arab also called Nejran was running on Exmoor about the same time. He was an imported chestnut. Crabbet Nejran was out on the moors from 1893 to 1902 for nine successive winters. His photograph is on p. 213.

Sir Walter Gilbey wrote "Organized efforts have been made to *improve* the ponies, and in Devonshire and Somerset the original strains have been intermingled and alien blood introduced and these sires have produced *new and improved breeds*." It is to the skill and selection of later times that we owe our present types, though the war has nearly extinguished the Acland type, and the New Forest ponies are in a deplorable state and Exmoor no better.

It must be remembered, however, that it is easier to deteriorate than to continue improving unless material is at hand for improvement, and it is to be hoped that the Exmoor Society's recent ruling out of all ponies showing: "a *taint* of Arab or cart horse blood" (the juxtaposition is really comic) will not prove an "excess of zeal" resulting in a reversion to the days when they and the sister breed of Dartmoors were condemned as "arrant jades, ill-made, large-headed, short-necked, and ragged hipped, one more ugly than another." Things had not much improved when Rusper described them in the *Sporting Magazine*, 1831 and 1834, as "shaggy coat, immense pot belly, short ewe neck, big head, ragged manes and tail, 12 to 14 hands, and the Dartmoor larger and even uglier than the Exmoors." Note that this description was given fifteen years after the Acland type had been enclosed, and the rest of Exmoor cleared of ponies, and in 1903 Sir Thomas himself said the quarters were as bad as ever. The taint of cart horse (which really *is* a taint) cannot rid the breed of what is already there without recourse to a "taint" of quality! for improved as some of them undoubtedly were by partial segregation these ponies still show less of the original Celtic type and more alloy of cart horse than any ponies except Fell and Dale, which are frankly cart bred.

As late as 1903 Sir Thomas Acland wrote "for the last thirty years we have been in the habit of taking about twenty of the best mares and foals down to the better climate and grass of Killerton. As a result the shoulder is more sloping and the action improved, but the quarters are entirely another matter, and I am afraid many of the tails come down as low in 1900 as they did in 1870." The great improvement effected elsewhere was demonstrated in 1900, when a pony called Lodestar, bred by Mr. Turner West of Molland, North Devon, from improved Arab-Exmoor stock, won the Polo Society's first medal, beating the Acland ponies. An objection lodged by the Acland agent was overruled, and the Turner herd was inspected and passed by a specially appointed commission of chosen expert judges and Lodestar retained his medal as a superior pony.

The *Livestock Journal* of 1889 records the genuine Exmoor bred by Sir T. Acland as having a "remarkably neat *oriental* head," very different from that recommended by Miss Etherington.

In 1903 an Arab stallion had recently been borrowed from the Duke of Connaught and left two sons for stud on Exmoor.

There are still unenclosed herds living at altitudes of 1,200 feet to 1,700 feet, which are crossed with any sort of coarse, underbred small cart horse because the farmers have that fatal idea that they want weight, but the result is unfortunately the same as in the sixteenth century, i.e. degenerate weeds with coarse hairy heels and lumbering limbs. The breed is stunted from exposure and privation and has the disproportionately large heads and uneven growth that always follow arrested development.

Very few ponies remain of the Acland strain, and according to a writer in *The Field* of December, 1948, the old type was nearly extinct, there being only two stallions left. All fences having been destroyed in the war and large numbers of the ponies slaughtered for food, what remains of the breed, if not extinguished, will be completely mongrelized.

Some people, including Welsh pony breeders, seem obsessed by the idea that a pony cannot be strong and hardy unless it has a coarse head, and heavy bone, yet in the awful winter of 1946–47, the cross-bred Exmoors and Dartmoors suffered far more than the Arab-bred Welsh, and died like flies. Some Exmoors were found like snow statues standing frozen to the ground dead.

The type accepted by the Exmoor Society is: Height 11 hands to 12.3, black, bay and dun with tan noses, no chestnuts. [Dun and the tan nose point to a Norwegian cross.] Clean cut and neat head, wide forehead, short thick pointed ears, short shoulders, short back, wide low withers, large nostrils and eyes, quarters wide but drooping. They are active and good jumpers and are quick and alert. As to identity with Tibet the neat head, wide forehead, large nostrils and eyes are the extreme opposite of the Prjevalski Mongolian. The Prjevalski described by Salensky were all distinguished by characters entirely absent in the Exmoor, namely, complete absence of forelock, donkey tail bare on the dock, ending in a donkey tuft, and a stiffly erect bristly mane. They had white, not "mealy," noses, enormous clumsy heads, long and narrow to the point of deformity, pig-slitted eyes, contracted nostrils and blunt ears and enormous teeth nearly equalling in size those of a Shire horse, nineteen pairs of ribs and donkey hoofs. They were violent tempered and intractable and Professor Ewart said of them that for want of a better word they must be described as "Saturated with cart blood!"

This wild Mongolian asinine species belonged to the Gobi desert near China and when first discovered was classed among the asses. It was uncapturable and unapproachable and quite unknown to science and was never heard of at all till 1881, when Poliakof gave it a name after examining a skull presented to the St. Petersburg Museum by a hunter called Prjevalski who shot one on the borders of China. It remained unknown to Europe as a living specimen until 1902, when the first specimen was captured and brought to the Duke of Bedford's private Zoo and a few more to Russia even later. This disposes effectually of the myth that it has been bred pure in England for 2,000 years. The longest period in which any introduction could have been made is about forty years, and I have it on the authority of Professor Ewart's daughter that none of the ponies were bred from outside the zoo, and only one cross was attempted with a Highland pony which was proved sterile. In fact she tells me that Professor Ewart returned the stallion lent to him for breeding experiments in disgust and with much vexation and disappointment at its uncouth appearance and savage temper. It also proved sterile. There were two hybrids among the imported ones showing that the wild herd must have had domestic horses running with them, but these hybrids were infertile.

That anyone should wish to preserve this outrageous donkey-horse type in any breed at all seems to me completely crazy, when we have such lovely improved breeds at our command, but there is no accounting for taste.

Nicholson's wonderful pony, Gipsy Gold. Chestnut, 13 hands, dam of

Pretty Polly

The Widge Beast

It seems that Miss Etherington is allergic to all attempts to get her away from the donkey type. She first challenged me to disprove its identity with the Prjevalski and at the same time extending the period to two thousand years she claimed *pure* descent from what she calls the Old English Widge Beast, saying "we are proud of our Widge Beasts."

Unfortunately for the purity claim, the old English meaning of a Widge was "any beast of burden or low-class *mongrel* animal or ass" which was further described as "Neither steed nor palfrey, nor fair mule, but the *unworthiest beasts of burden*"! Perhaps the less said about Widge Beasts the better. Personally, I prefer the improved variety.

The latest fantasy eclipses all the rest for, still in pursuit of the phantom aboriginal, she announced in the Press that by reason of the stubbornness of a few West Country farmers and with the help of the exhumed skull of a pony called Janie she has traced the Exmoor of to-day in pure descent unchanged for over seventy million years. If reported correctly we can only congratulate her on not only sweeping away all historical records but also the whole prehistoric company of evolutionary multi-digitorials, and incidentally also ante-dating the usually accepted creation of the habitable world by some million years. We commend this enthusiasm but must suggest that Janie's little skull which has unearthed this prodigy of arithmetic had better be reinterred with the contents of the whole salt cellar.

The comment of an eminent professor of the Royal London Veterinary College is that "the elastic seemed to have been unduly stretched," and another professor from the Edinburgh Veterinary College suggests that the south country folk are doubtless anxious to claim the oldest horse in the world as their private possession.

Anyhow, whatever ponies may be called Exmoors to-day there were no ponies at all in the forests of that district for at least a hundred years in historic times, let alone seventy million years ago.

Dartmoor

Another crossbred, 12.2, small good head and ears, rising shoulders, tail well set, good bone and action. All colours. A mixture of all sorts and an attractive harness and saddle pony.

The breed has existed "Tant bien que mal" for centuries, picking up a precarious living as best it could. It was indistinguishable from Exmoors in the eighteenth century, being located in the same unfenced district and only about thirty miles apart, but Arab blood has transformed it. While in the last ten years Exmoors have degenerated.

Pre-war, I saw some beautiful ones, many of which show Arab-like heads and a type far removed from the uncouth breed described by early writers. The best Dartmoors and Exmoors have some resemblance but the Dartmoors show most quality.

Exmoor pony stallion of improved Acland stock now practically extinct

Mongolian pony, whose alleged identity with the Exmoor is physically and historically impossible. It has no forelock, a semi-donkey tail and erect mane

New Forest

The type now aimed at is a 12.2 to 13-hand pony, as well-shaped as can be found. They vary very much according to the thoroughbred blood in them, but the best are nice looking, with small heads and free action. Some are very nice looking, with an air of breeding which their sponsors are successfully trying to fix, but at present they cannot be called a type recognizable at sight among Dartmoor ponies similarly improved. The Great War has destroyed the "wild" herds.

Iceland

Iceland ponies are much like large Shetlands, and may be the origin of some of our pony types. The good ones are most attractive and well bred in appearance and exceedingly strong and useful; they have small heads and ears, large eyes and profuse manes and tails well carried, their backs are strong and level, and they move well.

Norwegians

These are good-looking ponies which are both large and small. They are noted for their dun colour with black dorsal stripe, and wherever this colour appears in other pony breeds it is a sign of Scandinavian blood as is also the tan muzzle.

Norwegian ponies have been also used for crossing, and their typical dun colour and black dorsal and shoulder stripes sometimes appear in the Welsh and Highland stock. They are handsome and very sturdy, some of them are, I believe, of true aboriginal stock, others are believed to have had a cross of Arab like most of the Celtic types. There are small and large ones, the small ones showing the best type being very handsome with arched crests, small ears and heads, large eyes, level back, and well set, well carried tails. Some small ponies might have come straight from the rock drawing (Fig. p. 24).

Highland

These are very pretty ponies round about twelve to thirteen hands. There is a larger, coarser type, called "Garron," which ranges about 14.2, but it is not looked on with favour by the Highland Society as it has been crossed with cart horse. This mainland type is descended from the Western Isles pony, a sharp, alert, thick-set, strong animal for carrying loads, riding, driving and light farm work.

The superior Highland ponies have been standardized to the following type: Head well carried and attractive, and broad between eyes; prominent bright and kindly eyes; short between eyes and muzzle, with wide nostrils. Ears short and well set. Viewed in profile, the breadth rather than the length of the head and jawbone should be pronounced. Neck strong but not short, crest arched with flowing mane, throat clean not fleshy,

Dartmoor pony mare (note the tan muzzle)

New Forest pony

Mrs. de Beaumont's Palomino Welsh, Jason of the Golden Fleece

212

shoulders well set back, withers not too pronounced, body compact, back short with slight natural curve, chest deep, ribs deep, well sprung and carried well back, quarters and loins powerful and thighs short and strong. Tail strong and well set on and carried gaily with a plentiful covering of hair almost reaching the ground. Legs flat in bone, flinty to touch, with a slight fringe of silken feathers in winter, but this must not amount to hairiness. Action free and straight. Colour: Black, brown, fox colour with silver mane and tail, various shades of dun or grey with no white markings. The eel stripe along back is a typical though not invariable feature, denoting affinity with the Norwegian. They are hardy, sound, very useful and surefooted. Eel-backed ponies used to belong to parts of Wales.

RHUM

The ponies of Rhum are another handsome, useful breed of the same general utility, and very like a sturdy Welsh of good quality.

CONNEMARA

This is a race long famous for hardiness, sureness of foot, and general utility. Once again we find the ever-recurring history of blood from Spain, Arabia, North-West Africa, and probably the same "native" pre-Roman foundation imported by the Oriental

Crabbet Arab stallion Nejran, turned out on Exmoor for eight years

colonists and later Norwegian sources. Until late years it retained the typical Spanish amble. The outlying districts have, unfortunately, been disastrously contaminated with Clydesdale, Hackney half-bred Thoroughbred, and stallions without pedigrees. These violently conflicting types always tend to heterogeneous conformation. A Welsh stallion called Cannon Ball, grandson of Prince Llewellyn, was, however, successfully used twenty years back, and Arab blood infused quality during the present century.

[*Airborne Pictures, Aldershot*

Miss Susan Barthrop's Heather's Own, Connemara pony of outstanding type, winner of many 1st prizes (owner up)

214

The present type, fostered by the fifteen-year-old Society, is from thirteen to fourteen hands, with good action and rather excessive bone for their size.

There were yellow and dun ponies in Siberia and golden yellow horses in North Africa, and each spread to other countries, the colours reappearing periodically in many pony breeds.

Fifteen years ago a Society was formed to preserve what was considered the best type, i.e. a compact, deep bodied pony, short back, well ribbed, standing on short legs with good bone, sloping shoulders and well balanced head and neck. Height ranging from

Miss M. de Beaumont's Highland pony mare, champion Charmian of Skene. Winner Lord Arthur Cecil Memorial Challenge Cup for best M. and M. Pony Brood Mare, Cheltenham, 1949

13 to 14 hands, and the best selected ponies about 13.2, with good action; bone seven to eight inches. (The old Spanish amble should in my opinion be encouraged in ponies of the Andalusian type as it is a hall-mark of their ancestry.) Colour: Grey, black, bay, brown, and dun, with sometimes roan and chestnut. Grey is the predominant colour. Dun can be taken as a sign of Scandinavian-Norwegian blood, and as it was very prevalent before the indiscriminate crossing took place we may assume that there was much of the hardy Norseman's pony blood in the old stock. The prevalence of yellow

ponies in the West of Ireland probably originates from the Palominos of North Africa, but where there are black points the Norwegian predominates.

A lovely grey Connemara mare won at Banstead Show in 1949.

DALES

Belong to Yorkshire and other northern counties. They are small, active cart horses, 14.2 or sometimes more. Black, brown, bay, a few greys, but variegated colours and chestnuts are never found in what is now called the pure breed. They have hair on the heels, quarters sloping, eight-and-a-half inch bone, are good trotters and pack ponies.

FELL

The heaviest pony breed, fourteen hands. Belongs to the high moorland and hill districts of the northern counties, probably descends from the Scotch Galloways, and is still called Galloway. Thick and strong, well set up tails; pony heads with large bright eyes, eight-inch bone; very powerful in harness and can carry heavy weights. Black or brown with few white markings, also grey. Coarse hair on heels.

TARTARY

A tiny breed of parti-coloured ponies under ten hands.

SPAIN

A small "wild" type often *striped* about the neck. There also used to be a type something between a Shetland and Welsh which can be seen in Velasquez pictures of royal Princes. Fat, very pretty ponies with masses of mane and tail.

Various types of small ponies were found all over the Continent, those of the Camargue (all greys) living in marshes became famous and originated from Arab blood left after the Saracen wars.

SHETLANDS

These should be classified as *Equus caballus microscopicus*. (See p. 33.)

Shetlands are a breed apart and are, I believe, truly aboriginal primitive stock, especially the parti-colours which should be encouraged as much as possible as once they die out they will never be replaced. The type, colour, and size can be traced back to the Himalayas, where tiny ponies under 10 hands seemed indigenous, and they can be seen in the early cave drawings. It is the smallest and most fascinating of all ponies, and being under forty inches in height it has been extensively used in coal mines. The Stud Book was started in 1889. Specimens of twenty-six inches are sometimes seen. They are of all colours. In my opinion the skewbald and piebald Shetlands are directly descended from

Champion Welsh Mountain Pony
COED COCH SIARADUS

Arab-Percheron Cob

Bernard Mills's Arab Liberty horses and Shetland ponies

[By kind permission of Mr. Bernard Mills

the old primeval stock, and this marking is a valuable hall mark of pedigree and is in danger of being lost as it is rarer than it used to be.

They are ideal children's ponies and can do lots of work, being fast trotters in harness and very sweet tempered, sound and sure-footed. They are long-lived and a pony of Mr. W. L. Polson died at the age of 58.

Points.—Head *small* and fine, of Arab character; eyes very large and set low in the head—nostrils wide and mobile; ears short and pricked; mane, forelock and tail very profuse, tail set high and well carried; back level and short; quarters never drooping, but wide and strong; shoulders deep and well laid back; body compact with well sprung ribs; legs short and muscular, flat cannon bones, clean long pasterns. Hind legs straight and strong, not cow hocked, feet round and solid. Action true and springy, forefeet well thrown out from shoulders and hocks well flexed. A pony of perfect symmetry and beauty, very smart and fast for its size and full of fire. The present fault is a head much too big for its body.

A Shetland pony, eleven hands, was matched in 1784 to go from Norwich to Yarmouth and back again, forty-four miles in three hours forty-five minutes, carrying five stone with ease. Shetlands are described, 1831, as exceedingly beautiful, with *very small head.* A nine-hand pony carried a twelve-stone man forty miles in one day.

Hackney Ponies

The piebald Hackney pony, Maggie, foaled in 1878, was the most popular winner that ever went into the show ring. She won over four hundred first prizes and was pre-eminent in saddle as well as harness, but this colour is now very rare. Extravagant artificial action is the outstanding aim of this breed, based on good natural action and suggestive of Andalusian ancestry.

Type and Points.—Head small, convex, tapering to the muzzle, eyes large, ears small, neck rather long and thick set, shoulders good, but usually low in withers. The formlessness of the withers, which show no dip where the top line of the neck joins them, is characteristic, but does not interfere with their action; girth and middle-piece inclined to be shallow and tightly modelled; tail set on and carried high, a carriage which is often faked; legs short and hocks strong; feet good; colour mostly dark brown and black, and four white feet are common in the best strains—this again is a link with Spain; height from 14.3 to 15.3, sometimes reaching 16.2. Coat silky.

Action.—The shoulder action is exceedingly free, the knee action high, but must not consist of an up-and-down, perpendicular stamping. The foreleg must be thrown right forward, the foot dwelling a moment in the air before it reaches the ground with that peculiar grace which makes a horse seem to float and fly over the ground. The hock action must be free, the stifle joint being well brought forward. There should be no dishing or side to side throwing. Freedom of movement and stride are essential. Head and

219

Champion Greylight, Welsh Mountain Pony (Starlight strain)

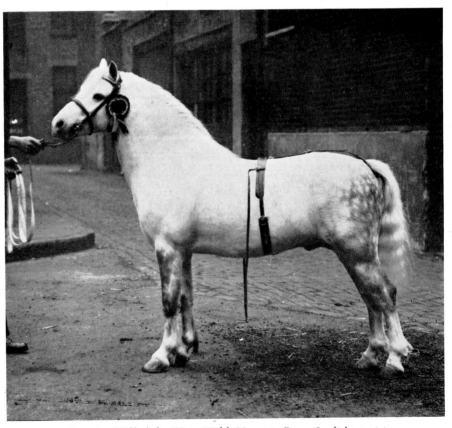

Champion Will o' the Wisp, Welsh Mountain Pony (Starlight strain)
The true type of "Arab in Miniature"

tail carried well. This breed nicks very well with the Arab and is closely similar to the spectacular American saddle horse, which shows much eastern blood and has a better head.

CHILDREN'S PONIES

Children's ponies may be found among any of the small breeds beginning with Shetlands. For young children between five and nine a steady *old* pony is much the best—young ponies cannot always be trusted, and ponies of sixteen and eighteen, and even twenty are not too old for the purpose; they are not as eager to prance and play up as the young ones. The chief points required are a good mouth, not too light but not hard, and a placid, good-tempered disposition. Choose a pony with large kindly eyes and intelligent expression, a wither which by either height or breadth will keep the saddle in the middle of the back, good shoulder action and easy paces. Surefootedness is most important so avoid marked knees. An old pony with clean knees is likely to be pretty certain on its legs or the knees would betray its past. Age does not appear to weaken the legs. Look out for turned-in toes, or toes turned out, the pony should stand with its feet straight and should move straight.

A great asset is a pony trained to stand still if the rider accidentally falls off, and wait about if the rider gets off on purpose.

A child's pony should not be too broad in the back so as not to stretch the rider's legs unduly, but now that stirrups are worn so short this is not as important as it used to be and the most ideal child's pony of my acquaintance, Tan y Bwlch Gwyno, is by no means narrow; on the contrary, she is like a miniature (elegant) cart horse, but her manners are so perfect that no undue strain is put on the rider to keep in the saddle on her broad back.

WELSH MOUNTAIN PONIES

These are the best bred and most beautiful of all pony breeds, and may be rightly considered the world's most attractive and fascinating pony. It has the same Celtic origin, but differs from the others in having belonged to districts which bear evidence of early oriental influence. Like all the others it has been evolved by an age-long history of crossing and re-crossing with thoroughbred, Arab, and Barb, and less good elements, but has a much larger percentage of Arab and later of Hackney pony blood than the others. Welshmen knew the value of Arab blood, and fresh infusions were constantly reinforcing the stock which has been universally praised in all historical records.

But Wales was destined to produce a special type of outstanding excellence by the same sort of accidental providence by which someone suddenly breaks the Bank at Monte Carlo. At the end of the nineteenth century there appeared one of those outstanding miracles of merit and prepotency which revolutionizes a breed just as the Darley Arabian was the spark which has since set the racing world in a blaze of fame, and Napoleon's white Arab chargers stamped the Percheron breed. The pure white, 11.2 pony champion,

The Right Hon. Lady Wentworth's Welsh Mountain pony foal, cream coloured

[Photo: *Sport and General*

E. D. Richard's stallion Mathrafal, Supreme Champion, Welsh Cob

Dyoll Starlight, shot into sudden fame and became a star of the first magnitude, and this famous grey (white) strain has held an incredibly brilliant show record for nearly half a century. Instead of being proud of their celebrity there are, strangely enough, people who object to them and to their spectacular colour as "miniature Arabs," and with the absurd idea that Arab blood would spoil the "true old pure Welsh type" and make it "narrow, useless and wishy washy" the Stud Book was not long ago closed to further

Mrs. Inge's Welsh cob, Marble

Arab crosses; the ringleader of this attack was apparently the Secretary of the Welsh Pony Society, whose warning against Arab blood appears in the *Book of the Pony*. Of all the criticisms of the Arab breed by its worst enemies, I never before heard it accused of being "wishy washy"! and what is meant by *pure* Welsh is difficult to follow. Here again we have the fallacy of an original imaginary native breed entirely contradicted by history and experience. If Arab blood was going to spoil the breed it would have done so long ago, as the Welsh Stud Book pedigrees are saturated with Arab blood.

Having pointed this out I was immediately challenged to prove that any cross of Arab has been registered for the last twenty-five years. Nothing daunted by a list of sixteen, including crosses to the famous Arabs Champion Skowronek, Champion Crosbie, and Cairo, it was almost incredible that Captain Howson promptly extended the period to a hundred years, queried the facts and accused me of "rash and sweeping statements." The rashness was surely on his side and the facts on mine, for the records of Arab blood are legion. Leaving out the numberless crosses of Darley Arabian and other early Arabians when the ponies were called Merlins from that famous pony stallion which ranged the hills and which pre-date the hundred year limit, the records are too voluminous to quote

223

in detail. Just to go on with, there are a hundred and twenty-six ponies by five Arab sires alone, registered within half that time, not to speak of outside contemporary records of the famous Arab-Welsh Studs of Lord Oxford, Sir R. Vaughan, and Mr. Hill, described as the best of their time.

The Welsh Stud Book contains far more "sweeping statements" than any I have ever made. The tables and genealogies of Vols. II and IV are conclusive, and are, moreover, accompanied by the following commentary on leading strains. "There is no need to apologize for owning up to the fact that Arab blood *seethes* in their veins . . . one might as well apologize for the Bible . . . it needs none."

Referring to the proverb "Cherchez la femme" it goes on: "Seek for the Arabian and apply it whenever anything a little out of the way good in any breed of nags is brought to our notice. Some sand-born influence generally turns out to be a clue to their superiority."

Vol. IV.—"It cannot be too strongly pointed out that we as a Stud Book Society have never tried to filch names and label them Welsh in the hope that future generations in the days when no remembrance of the former things is forthcoming may cherish a belief that everything good entirely owes any superiority it may possess to an exclusive indigenous stock. We have never tried to hush up any origin if so it is, be it Thoroughbred, Arabian, Yorkshire Coach Horse or Norfolk Hackney."

A truly prophetic warning of exactly what is happening now, and Welshmen should take it to heart. The present narrow-minded attempt to falsify history is almost identical with a similar attempt to foist an imaginary native English breed of racing mares into Thoroughbred history. In both cases we are now up against an heretical departure from the Stud Book records apparently due to an attitude of mind described by a Welsh writer: "They were born in Wales, had their being in Wales, and dwelt in Wales. What more is wanted *in spite of alien blood* to consider them Welsh and call them Welsh?" By all means let us call the Welsh ponies Welsh and the racehorse English, but why resort to a camouflage of facts rightly despised by the compilers of the Stud Book and against which in the case of Wales they warned future generations as unworthy of serious records, justly priding themselves recording facts as they are and not as some people would like them to be.

In Vol. I the true type is laid down. There is no ambiguity in the matter. This is the standard.

"The Welsh Mountain pony in its purest state is under twelve hands, and can best be described by stating that it is *an Arab in miniature*, and any judge of horses upon seeing these ponies must at once perceive the great similarity they bear to the Arab. The pony has the perfect Arab type of head and also Arab setting on of tail and carriage of tail the instant it moves. In some parts a thick-set pony is found, but those best able to speak on the subject state that *the pure type is the miniature Arab*."

This finally brands as heterodox the recent slashing attacks on "the miniature Arab" type which utterly revolutionizes the principles of the Society.

Referring to the genealogies, we find that the main strains are Arab from Cymro Llwyd, son of the Cythartha Arabian and Alonzo the Brave, a registered Hackney, and of these

224

The Right Hon. Lady Wentworth's Welsh mountain stallion Coed Coch Glyndwr, several times champion sire at the National Pony Show now the property of Miss de Beaumont

Vol. IV says: "To omit mention of this family of Welsh Flyers and Comets would be like attempting to produce Hamlet without the Prince of Denmark. This constellation has irradiated Wales with their constant presence and has extended itself far and wide . . . all lineage returns to them."

A brief summary of origins is necessary, the stud books being out of reach of the general public. From Sir Richard Crawshay's Arabian are descended the innumerable progeny of Cymro Llwyd, True Briton, Welsh Jack, Caradoc, Eidwen Flyer (grandsire Arab), Trotting Comet, Old Welsh Flyer (great grandsire Arab), Cream of Eppynt, and countless others. There are a hundred and twenty-six ponies descended immediately from

WELSH PONY STALLION APRICOT.
Formerly the property of the late Colonel Vaughan, Nannau.

Sire Arab, dam Welsh

five sires alone—in Vol. IV we find that Cymro Llwyd was also known as Trotting Lion and Merthyr Tydfil. Irish Whisky was by Trumpeter—Arab mare; Shooting Star's dam descends from Caradoc. The grand-dam of White Flight was Polly, an Arab mare.

Vol. II says: "The Comets and the Welsh Flyers may have arable ancestors" and advice is given (p. XXXI) as to how Arab blood can be introduced with benefit to counteract them.

Vol. III: "It is owing to the *likeness* and *identity of characteristics* which they bear to their elders and betters the Arab and T.B., that the Welsh pony shows when this reversion to the small is contemplated. *It cannot be produced from a better source.*"

Colonel Sir Robert Vaughan owned a remarkable strain from Arabs and "Barb Arabs." The celebrated Apricot was out of a Welsh dam by one of these; he was thirteen hands and a winning racer, and his picture shows almost pure Arab type. Sir Robert's stud was at one time the best in existence. In 1893 Mr. Mainwaring said Apricot was the greatest sire in North Wales, and everything had Apricot blood.

The Eppynt hills bred the eel-backed pony. In 1891 the Allbrightlee Stud farm at

226

Shrewsbury had Welsh mares and two Arab stallions: "Desert Born," bay, fourteen hands, and "Ali Baba," grey, fourteen hands.

John Hills was breeding from an Arab stallion at Church Stretton.

We find Arabs registered in 1892: Stallion by an Arab ex Peggy (half Arab).

No. 16, Grey Friars by Ackbar (Arab). No. 921, Raxane, pure Arab, and two imported Arabs. No. 1700, Gwyndy First Flight, half-Arab sire; Eastern Fashion, by Akbar. No. 1891, Ora, bay, an imported Arab; three Arabs and a half-Arab mare; and No. 2394, a mare by an imported Arab.

The Earl of Oxford's celebrated strain of Welsh ponies were all closely inbred to Lord Clive's Arabian and famous for extreme speed, one of them being backed to beat any bigger horse at a feather weight.

The results are reflected in the early records:

1819 *Sporting Magazine*.—"The small Welsh Merlins are a spirited pigmy race still occupying some hilly walks in the interior of the Principality."

1831 *The Horse*.—"The Welsh pony is one of the most beautiful little animals that can be imagined. He has a small head, high withers, deep yet wide barrel, short joints, flat legs and good round feet. He will live on any fare, and can never be tired out."

In view of the fact that Starlight's dam Moonlight was described as a "Glamorganshire pony of the best blood," the history of their origin and what is meant by the best blood is interesting. The *Sporting Magazine* of 1838, Hippius writes: "Mr. Williams of Aberpergwm in Glamorgan selected pony mares of a small breed and of the best shape. They were put to an Arabian; the produce (half-Arab) were carefully chosen as dams and covered by other steeds of the desert, so that ere long the stock will become nearly perfect Arabians with the advantage of being inured to the climate and adapted to the size which the pasture of that locality will form. The sires resorted to have been the Arabians Buckfoot (a celebrated 14.2 Arab racehorse from India), Fair Play, Orelio, and the two Muscat horses lately sold at Hampton Court.

"I was struck with the beauty of the form of some of these little animals as they galloped over the turf, their active wiry make, and their handsome eastern heads." He adds that the bigger ones if graded to fourteen hands may be highly valued as summer hacks and distinguished for speed in galloping races.

Mrs. Dargan, writing the history of the Welsh pony in 1913 to Mr. Stone, who purchased some for America says:

"The Welsh pony stock was improved with Arab blood over and over again.

"Apricot became an unperishable tradition in Merionethshire. In 1850 Mr. Morgan Williams put Arab sires with his droves on the hills behind Aberpergwm, and it was in this region that in recent years Moonlight was discovered roving and unshod by Mr. Meuric Lloyd, and this dam of *certain Arabian descent* gave Wales her Dyoll Starlight."

Notwithstanding this reinforcement of his aristocracy there were too many doors left open. The larger pony of the lowlands becoming mixed with the Cardiganshire Cob, and some owners were guilty of letting half-bred Shire colts have the run of the hills. In time the only safe spot for the mountain pony would have been the topmost hillcrests, but for the founding of the Welsh Stud Book, but unfortunately there is a section of clumsy, sluggish cart-horse Shire blood which has spoilt the larger cobs.

As a Radnorshire breeder said: "there is a touch too little of the Arab and a touch too much of the Flanders," and the writer continues: "I must admit that the mountain pony has also been affected by these later introductions, but in a far less degree, and the coarser strain is fortunately not of Eastern potency." Thus about forty-five years ago all the herds were uncontrolled till, alarmed by the contamination with cart-horse blood, breeders got together to separate the wheat from the chaff and the Stud Book was started in 1902 to exclude base blood, and to point out that the true type was the "Arab in miniature." It will therefore be evident that the recent idea that it is a modern departure from the good old Welsh stock is pure nonsense. That Starlight and his son Greylight were the ideal "Arab in miniature" is beyond all argument.

It is incontestable that the Hackney strain has imparted a free action not seen in other pony breeds, and in point of fact, Hackney and Arab blend particularly happily, as the Arab head counteracts the Hackney, and the Hackney action raises the Arab knee action.

THE STARLIGHT STRAIN

This spectacular combination of hereditary and trained action has been the pride of Wales as a super harness pony ever since Starlight made it famous as an outstanding example of the success of the Arabian cross. As to Dyoll Starlight's reputed pedigree by Glasalt out of Moonlight, if he had only the grudgingly admitted "remote cross" of Arab, how can anyone explain his having the Arab number of ribs and the lumbar vertebrae, and the extravagantly prepotent type and colour persisting crescendo over nearly half a century? Type is type, and practical breeders like myself do not easily believe in miracles and the further mystery of how a particularly common black or brown pony so inferior that he was gelded on purchase for farm work in 1893 could possibly in 1894 have sired a superlative line of exquisite white ponies exceeds the limits of reasonable credibility. Remembering also that at that time hill mares were at the mercy of accidental matings of which the owner would be the last to hear (however freely discussed elsewhere), I frankly confess to complete scepticism. My scepticism is reinforced by information received from leading Welsh breeders who knew both ponies well. Glasalt was a dark brown (see N.P.S.B.) out of a dark bay mare, and his sire, though grey, was also by a dark brown from dark brown ancestry on the male side, and most unlikely, even had he not been a gelding, to have produced a white breed. The leading breeder Tom Jones Evans writes:

"He was 'a very ugly coarse pony' of no class, and Moonlight was served by an Arab which was being ridden in the district where the farm hand bringing in Moonlight from the hills had stopped for a drink."

I have hitherto refrained from pressing the matter as Mr. Lloyd's daughter naturally

228

enough does not like the idea lest it should reflect on her late father's integrity, but there is no reflection, except perhaps on his credulity. If the extreme merit of the foal and the fact that Moonlight never again produced anything good roused any suspicion in his mind we do not know, but the registration having been made, stood uncontradicted. I confess that if my tortoiseshell pussy cat suddenly produced a white Persian I should want to know where she had been and should not accept the Manx Neuter cat over the way as the perpetrator of the deed without strong misgiving, but I might think the less said the better.

Whatever may be the exact facts his career as a sire is unrivalled. Practically all his stock was white like himself. His best son was the magnificent Champion Greylight, a toy Arabian with spectacular action and carriage of the tail, a lovely little head and proud crested neck. It was no wonder he was snapped up immediately by an Australian for 1,000 guineas. Walter Winans secured Starlight's next best son, Champion Bleddfa Shooting Star, foaled 1901, afterwards bought by Mrs. Green for the Grove stud. He won seventeen firsts and championships, the last being at the age of twenty. He was a magnificent mover, full of fire and bounce, and maintained supremacy till his grandson, Champion Grove King Cole II, foaled 1911, gradually overhauled him. This marvellous little stallion, beginning with two firsts as a yearling, won no less than thirty firsts and nineteen championships and medals. When Mrs. Green's stud was broken up in 1927, he and all the best mares went to the White Mountain Starlight Pony stud at Crabbet Park, including Champion Ness Thistle, winner of over a hundred first prizes and specials. She was eventually sold to Mr. W. Hay of Winestead Hall, Hull, and was killed by lightning.

Other descendants of Starlight were Champion Fairy Queen (five championships), Ch. Nantyrharn Starlight (twenty-three firsts and seven championships), Ch. Grove Moonstone, by Shooting Star (sent abroad), Ch. Grove Lightheart (six championships), Ch. Wentworth Lady Starlight, an exquisite mare (thirteen firsts and five championships) (both by Starlight); Ch. Lady Greylight (eight firsts and four championships), Ch. Wentworth Windfall, a first-class deep red-brown stallion of extraordinary beauty, both by Ch. Greylight, and Ch. Grove Sprightly, a grey with remarkable action and winner of numerous championships, which I sold to Tom Evans, where he died at the age of thirty-two. He was in my opinion too coarse in bone and head.

Champion Wentworth Springlight was the best pony of Crabbet breeding, which died of yew poisoning before he had established himself as a sire. Champion Wentworth Windfall sired Wentworth Grey Princess, purchased by Mrs. Inge and dam of the outstanding champion pony Tan y Bwlch Prancio, the leading pony mare before the Hitler war and sent by Crabbet to New Zealand. These Starlight ponies are unrivalled for good looks and action and make the most perfect fairy-like harness ponies envied by all beholders. The leading pony stallions now are Coed Coch Glyndwr, a super perfect type, and Wentworth Golden Star, presented to Miss de Beaumont, grand champion of all pony breeds in 1949 and 1951, a magnificent type of superb carriage and action, but not super highly trained to spectacular harness action like the best of his ancestors and chief present rivals.

Hall-marks of these ponies are small, very pretty head, broad forehead, small sharp ears, very big dark blazing eyes and tapering face, with large mobile nostrils and curved throttle. Nicely curved neck with sloped shoulders, but not usually very high withers, short, stout wide-ribbed body, wide level quarters, with a *tail set level* with the back, and good and often high tail carriage, lots of hair on mane and tail which must on no account be hogged or docked. Astonishingly free shoulder and hock action and enormous vitality and generosity of temperament. Ewe necks, goose rumps, and ugly heads and big ears are a sure sign that Starlight is no longer predominant. Their speed of foot is surprising, and they have a natural aptitude for jumping, which is their one drawback as they will jump out of most enclosures unless extra securely fenced in as they can jump their own height, even lie down and squeeze *underneath* anything they can't jump! They are very hardy and thrive even on poor pasture. Longevity is common to all Welsh strains. There is a recorded case of a white Welsh mare having thirty-three foals, her last foal a bay colt born at thirty-nine, and she lived to be forty-three. These ponies require no attention and can be left to foal in the open, and the foals gallop after their dams within a few hours of birth.

Their tempers are good and most generous, always willing to work—jibbing is unknown.

Grey (as I have said in my chapter on colour) is a foundation pure colour, for it cannot be produced sporadically from any other colour, or by reversion, or by any artificial means, and once gone it is for ever lost. It must, therefore, be as ancient as anything in the world's history and generally shows great signs of good blood.

In view of the recent claim that the pure old hardy Welsh breed has been *proved over and over again* to be alone capable of surviving winter on the Welsh hills, it is interesting to note that the Hackney cross runs riot in the old genealogies and combines with the "*seething*" Arab blood in forming precisely the old hardy strains which survive to this day. *Neither* the seven hundred and twenty-nine registered Hackney crosses nor the hundreds of repeat crosses of Arab have prevented this survival—dare I suggest that the Arab stamina has been an asset? We find indeed that in the record winter of 1946–7 the breed survived where coarser bred Exmoor and Dartmoor ponies perished by the hundred and an S.O.S. had to be broadcast to save what remained with special supplies of fodder. At that very time we find Miss Broderick testifying that the almost pure Arab ponies Penwen and Berwyn were out in the worst of the blizzards of 1946–7 without damage, and this confirms Mr. Fred Unwin's experience of Arab crosses forty years ago on the top of the Cotswolds.

This bogey of Arab "wishy washiness" can therefore be returned to the bogey hole from which it has been unearthed.

I owned almost all the leading champions (thirty of them), beginning with Champion Dyoll Starlight himself, and found them unbeatable in beauty and stamina. Miss Broderick's Tan y Bwlch Berwyn is an outstanding type in the 13.2 class, and is by an oriental sire. Nobody in his senses could call him narrow or useless.

Moreover a hot controversy as to action now threatens to split the harmony of the Welsh breeders, forgetting that their ponies are the only ones which by reason of geographical inaccessibility escaped the Henry VIII massacre, and also the contamination of alien breeds and can reasonably claim to descend from the tiny pre-Roman chariot ponies as traditionally super-harness ponies. The pony of to-day threatens that survival.

Trained and untrained ponies are all shown together, though they cannot justly compete together. The limelight inevitably centres on the spectacular trained trotter. There is no doubt which the public rightly prefers, and the cut diamond eclipses the uncut diamond. Very few judges are competent to assess the merit of the diamond in the rough and it finds itself discarded.

Unless separate classes are provided the glory of Wales will go to America, where they are being trained for racing in harness.

We find the following Arab-bred ponies registered since 1934:

Craven Cyrus (1441) by King Cyrus (Arab), King Cyrus (Arab), Craven Electric Light (1543), Craven Moonlight (8909), Craven Radiant, Craven Toss (8877), Craven Newlight (1599), Craven Kibla (8719), Craven Araby (8718), Craven Titbit, now a leading winner, Tan y Bwlch Berwyn, Tan y Bwlch Penwen, Tan y Bwlch Penllyn, and in their pedigrees Cairo, Champion Skowronek, Crosbie (Champion Arab London), and Jordania, an imported mare dam of Cairo. Sahara, sire of Berwyn, was called a Barb but had an Arab head.

There are other Stud Books which would welcome Arab Welsh ponies, but it is a scandal they should be excluded by the Society which ought to value them most.

The leading breeder of Welsh ponies for many years was Mrs. Green; Tom Jones Evans of Craven Arms, Salop, was one of the leading judges, and Miss Broderick owns what is at present the finest collection of mares in Wales.

Tom Jones Evans and Grove Sprightly were celebrated as an outstanding winning pair, and the best pony he has bred is Craven Titbit, with the Arab cross showing itself conspicuously in his make-up.

The Welsh Pony and Cob Society has divided the ponies into three classes: Welsh Mountain pony up to twelve hands; riding type ponies up to 13.2; the still larger cobs show strong Hackney type, are good-looking harness type; but high-actioned cobs are generally rough rides and the higher the action the rougher the ride, especially on a broad "cart horsy" animal. The Hackney cross has been of great benefit in several ways but should not be overdone.

There is a very interesting variety of Welsh pony surviving in the possession of Sir G. Tyrwhitt-Drake. The ponies are about twelve hands and cream-milk coloured with pink skins and pale turquoise blue eyes, and though akin to Albinos they never go white. They are of the real Welsh stamp with pretty heads.

The pigment of the eyes is so slight that when the sun is on them they appear pink showing blood vessels through the lens, but in ordinary light they are blue.

231

Let no one accuse me of advocating lavish and indiscriminate returns to Arab blood. What I have said is that the blood is already there. To deny it is childish and to ban it altogether not only unwise but might well prove suicidal should type degenerate and need revivifying.

OTHER BREEDS

Sir R. D. Green Price—November 1891 *Livestock Journal*—reported a breed of ponies in Breconshire near Llanstyd that was spotted and piebald, and a breed round Knighton which was mouse-coloured with wall eyes and a black stripe down the back, and cream-coloured with black stripe down the back; and greys.

Spotted, skewbald, and piebald are original Welsh colours, it is only fashion which has put them out of favour.

It will be seen that all small ponies, except Shetlands and Hackneys, are built up from the same primitive Celtic Continental foundation improved by Eastern blood as pointed out by Ridgeway.

Hackney, Thoroughbred, Spanish, Barb and the coarser northern breeds all have had their share in the modern breeds. Barb and Spanish shows itself in convex heads and goose rumps—Arab blood in large eyes and high tail carriage. Cart blood in heavy heads, small eyes, and hairy heels. Scandinavian blood shows in the dun colour and black list while direct reversion to prehistoric type is seen in parti-colours. Black is not a pure bred colour and denotes inferior blood, except in all black breeds such as the Drenthe funeral horses. The best tend to resemble each other as do all horses bred with an ideal shape in mind because good points tend to be the same in all breeds, for instance, it is difficult to differentiate at a glance between the Highland "Skerryvore" and some Welsh types.

In view of these facts, I see no reason to modify my classification of our Mixed Improved pony breeds. The mixture has of late years been so well chosen that they have improved into really attractive high-class types of which any nation may be proud.

COBS

Cobs are not a breed but a type, and controversy rages as to how they can be bred.

They are stocky, short legged and general utility animals, usually pony sized, i.e. fifteen hands or under. A fine type can be bred from a good Arab sire and a small Percheron mare (see p. 217).

Hackney sires might produce good results on very heavy ponies, but high action is not desirable in a cob as the higher the trotting action the less comfortable it is to the rider. Thoroughbred sires such as are available to ordinary breeders are too uncertain in their results, but an Anglo-Arab would in my opinion be a good mixture for producing cobs with the right mares. High action, however, is now being encouraged.

Hunter and the Hack: A typical Cob. Oil painting by John Ferneley, 1782–1860

Anglo-Arabs

This modern re-cross of Arab to Thoroughbred is a very fine riding horse and hunter and, indeed, no mean racehorse. He has a natural aptitude as a hurdler and steeplechaser and show jumper. Less hot than the pure Arab and with more rein and stride and more stamina than the Thoroughbred he is, perhaps, very nearly the ideal hunter.

The Arab-Hackney cross is remarkably good looking. It has a better head than the Hackney and better action than the Arab, so each improves the other.

Ferneley painted an excellent picture of the hunter and cob of his day which clearly demonstrates the two types we still try to breed. Cobs differ from other horses chiefly in their stocky broad build, suitable for hacking at moderate speed, and their confidential temperament. They should not be highly strung or fidgety. They are or should be the ideal mount for elderly riders whose ambitions do not include racing the wind or jumping Becher's Brook. They should therefore be of moderate size, easy to mount and willing to potter about a farm and be tied to a gatepost without trying to uproot it. Some can jump moderate obstacles if required or do a little harness work.

Naturally they vary in capacity according to their conformation, but they should not depart from their province in the direction of the light hack. "Cobby" has become a

233

Foxhunter with Lt.-Col. Llewellyn up

Fine type of heavy-weight hunter, John Peel, winner at Dublin, 1949

term descriptive of a closely knit broad animal just as "ponyish" is descriptive of a certain conformation departing from the horse type.

Cobs are intermediary between ponies and horses, just as Galloways used to indicate a 14.2 general utility semi-racing type. There is now a distinction drawn between riding horses and hacks which is so nebulous as to be negligible in practice. I believe that a riding-horse owner has a certain contempt for a hack. Heaven only knows why as both serve the same purpose.

POLO PONIES

Polo originated in Persia and was the great game in India in the days when a height limit of 14.2 made it a most popular game in the British Army, as it was within the financial scope of the young officers who could pick up Arab ponies at a reasonable cost. Arabs were pre-eminent at the game owing to their quickness at turning and sprinting. For the general public most of the fun went out of the game when in 1919 the height limit of 14.2 was abandoned. The limit now is up to 15.2 and the game is for the wealthy few, not for the many amateurs who play for recreation. One cannot help regretting that there is not still a game for the 14.2 ponies. The rules for registration in the polo and riding pony stud book are:

(*a*) By an entered sire out of an entered or registered dam.

(*b*) By a registered sire out of an entered dam.

(*c*) By a Thoroughbred Arab or Anglo-Arab sire out of an entered dam.

(*d*) Entered or eligible by pedigree for entry in the G.S.B. and passed as suitable by an inspector duly appointed by the society.

In the approved register a pony of riding pony type can be passed by a council inspector.

It might be useful to point out that pony is a misnomer for horses of 15.2, as the Jockey Club definition of a pony is only up to fifteen hands.

CHAPTER XVII

THE OLD ARABIAN RACING FOUNDATION BREED

THE ORIGIN OF SPEED

Equus Arabicus or Kehilan Ajuz (ancient thoroughbred) the root stock from which the Southern and Western varieties are derived and from which the English thoroughbred racehorse takes its name and origin.

FROM time immemorial the Arabian was recognized by all writers as the oldest and fastest breed in the world, the old "Kehilan Ajuz," the world's original "hot" blood from which all quality, fire and speed is derived.

All old writers, both Eastern and Western, were unanimous as to his antiquity, purity, and superiority over all breeds both as a sire and a racehorse—it is only during the last few decades that some irresponsible writers have tried to deprive him successively of his country, and his pedigree and his antiquity of origin.

The idea started by a French scientist that the Arabian was a mixed breed appearing apparently from nowhere in particular six centuries after Christ was based on the misconception that Arabia was always a barren desert where no horses could live. The author of the Libyan mirage theory took it up, adding some embellishments of his own, but illogically substituting the Sahara, a still worse desert, as the birthplace of an ancestral "bay Libyan with star and bracelets." It is astonishing how such an idea could possibly have been credited even by the most ignorant student of history as it is flatly contradicted by geological, historical, physiological, and chronological evidence. To begin with, Arabia is geologically proved to have been originally fertile—a land of trees and water, the evidence of which can be seen in ancient riverbeds, of forests long vanished, of water-scarred rocks bearing marks of torrential rains but now arid and sun-cursed, and everywhere a progressive drying up still proceeding with alarming rapidity.

In the old Arabian poems we find comparisons of wild horses darting like fish in the water, a simile which could not occur to the poets of a waterless land.

Arabia had, we are told, a mild climate. Even as late as 648 B.C. the Jebel Shammar range of barren rocks was covered with shady woods, and Isaiah, chapter xxi, verse 13, says: "In the forest in Arabia shall ye lodge." There are still traces of the fossil forests of Egypt where there is now neither vegetation nor water. We read in Isaiah also of the doom of that fertile land, by which Arabia should become a desert and a desolation and a curse for ever with a sword upon its horses and a curse of blood and war and fire which should parch the earth with brimstone and the land be turned into boiling pitch so that no man should pass through it, and the Arabian should not pitch his tents there any more, and it should be inhabited by dragons and ostriches. Jeremiah repeats the prophecies 595 B.C., chapter l, verse 37, "A sword is upon their horses (Chaldeans)," verse 38, and "a drought is upon her waters; and they shall be dried up . . . the wild beasts of the desert . . . shall dwell there, and owls shall dwell therein: and it (the land) shall be no more inhabited for ever." Chapter xlix, "Arise ye! go up to Kedar (Arabia), and spoil the men of the east." Calamity and loss of camels were among the disasters of those grim prophecies, "Hazor shall be a dwelling for dragons and a desolation for ever. There shall no man abide nor son of man dwell in it." (In the Arabic version "dragons" are jackals.)

These curses have been fulfilled only too well. Arabia was devastated by volcanic eruptions of vast magnitude which left desolate the enormous tract of the terrible Harra (or hot land), now a chaos of black lava rocks where nothing can live. That twice repeated curse of blood still goes on in the blood feuds, while the fire of blazing skies reflected in the glare of flaming sands is completing the work of destruction. The highlands of Central Arabia which once supported wild asses and horses are becoming more and more waterless. The Hebrew word translated "ass" merely means "fast runner" and might apply to either or both.

Again Jeremiah says: "And the wild asses (the word in Arabic is equally horses) stand in the high places. They snuffed up the wind like dragons and their eyes did fail because there was no grass." The tribes are being forced north or else squeezed into ever-narrowing limits as pasture dwindles and wells vanish. Southern Arabia, where vineyards once flourished, is already a vast area of forgotten dried-up lakes and mysterious "singing sands" of inconceivable dreariness. Sands where the incautious traveller is engulfed for ever. And now everywhere modern weapons and modern transport are penetrating and threaten to obliterate altogether the horse which the sword has spared and the camel on which the foals depend for their sustenance. Even the Meccan pilgrims may now go by motor car and the speed of a mare in war is no longer the first and only consideration of the tribes.

Going back to the Biblical records, the Israelites were forbidden to keep horses as connected with idolatry and sun worship. The old Arabian horse idols were Ya'uk and Ya'bub (swift horse). Solomon's tribute of horses from Coa, the translation of which word has been variously argued, was identified by Lady Anne Blunt as a place in Nejd, not far from Dereyeh, almost in a line between it and Mecca, and it was at once recognized by the Nomads as being in the most famous horse breeding district of Arabia. It was not till King Solomon took matters into his own hands and became a royal horse dealer on a grand scale that the war chariot came into general use in Israel. He took tribute of horses from all the Kings of Arabia, including the Queen of Sheba, and Egypt, where a chariot cost 600 silver shekels and a horse 150 shekels, and he had forty thousand chariot horses and twelve thousand saddle horses for his own use and acted as intermediary between

Egypt and the Hittite and Canaanite kings. It must be remembered that Egypt had captured thousands of Arabian horses in the wars of Seti and Rameses, 1500 years previous to Solomon.

One of the earliest Biblical references to the glory of the equine race is Job's celebrated passage which has been somewhat confused in translation. Reference to the Arabic original version makes it clear that the horse was ridden with a spear; the word for horse is "faras," always used for a ridden horse, not a chariot horse, which would be "Rakib." The difference between the horse and his rider and the chariot and its rider is also shown in Jeremiah, chapter li, verse 21, in the curse against Babylon and Chaldea. "I will break in pieces the horse and his rider; and with thee I will break in pieces the chariot and its rider." The old term *to ride in a carriage* used still to be a Victorian one. The word usually translated "neck" is the Arabic technical word for a bounding gallop quoted by El Naseri. Also the translation "*afraid" as the grasshopper* makes no sense at all; the word is "bounding." This is a stumbling block over which many translators of Arabic MS. poetry have tripped, translating it "lifted up" or "afraid," neither of which are correct and even verge on absurdity. The galloping is invested with thunder, not the neck.

As to the trumpet, there is a confusion caused by there being no neuter tense in Arabic. "*He* says Ha" is really "*it* says Ha" and refers obviously to the trumpet, not the horse. Bedouin riders also cry "Ha" in a charge, but on consideration I am sure that the sound referred to the trumpet warning given by the camp attacked, and not to the rider or the horse.

At first the modern absence of trumpets in the desert seemed puzzling, but reference to Numbers shows that Moses was ordered to make silver trumpets for the children of Israel to be blown as an alarm in the journeys of the caravans in the desert, chapter x, verses 5, 6, 9, 11. Reference to this is again made in Exodus, chapter xix, verses 13, 19. At that time travellers evidently did blow trumpets as a warning, which explains the phrase that the horse was not afraid of them but rushed eagerly to join in the fray.

The value of this fine passage is in the extreme antiquity of the desert horse of the Arab raiders, whose forays were greatly dreaded by Job, who was a herdsman not a nomad warrior, and deeply impressed by the nobly bred horses of his enemies of the desert. I may add here some other inaccuracies in translation. The dragons of the wilderness are as I have said, merely jackals in the original Arabic; the rhinoceros is the antelope and the ericius is the jerboa. This passage was very much earlier than the Assyrian Kings or even the Chaldean raiders, that "bitter and swift nation" whose horses were "dreadful and terrible, light as leopards and swift as evening wolves" who were the terror of their enemies. It would seem therefore to be certainly a reference to the horse of the tribal raiders of whose attacks he had good reason to fear. Wolves start on their forays at sunset. They were also described as swift as eagles in search of prey and as doves bound for the water springs. The Chaldeans were an Arabian dynasty from Bahrein dating from before 1000 B.C. and lasted 500 years.

In later times Ezekiel, chapter xxiii, 12, speaks of the captains and rulers of Assyria clothed most gorgeously, horsemen riding upon horses, all of them desirable young men. Verse 23, "All the Chaldeans, Pekod, and Shoa, and Koa, and all the Assyrians . . . all of them riding upon horses." Sargon 722 B.C. captured "herds of horses without number from East Arabia driving them before him into Syria, and in North-East Arabia captured 2,000 horses." The rock inscriptions B.C. of Central Arabia and Syria testify to the antiquity of horses and horsemen with lances—camels and antelopes, gazelles and ostriches. There is one horse with a central horn which looks uncommonly like a unicorn and there are actual records of unicorns in a compound at Mecca.

There are nomad traditions of giraffes and there were certainly elephants in Syria and Iraq. There were wild horses in Syria and North Arabia, the capture of which is recorded in Assyrian history. The Nabatean Arabs, 84 B.C., brought tens of thousands of horsemen against Antiochus XII. The word translated "wild ass" in the Bible is equally wild horse and the finding of mules by Anak among his father's asses would be a natural thing. Translators obsessed by the idea that no wild horse could exist in the desert, as it is now, have tried every possible way of getting a different explanation of the word horse or mule, just as they have tried to explain away the eating of locusts by St. John the Baptist, whereas locusts were, of course, and still are, a common diet in Arabia and considered a heaven-sent delicacy, roasted over the fire and tasting, as Lady Anne Blunt says, like chicken.

Apart from Nomad tradition of the original wild horse we have the historian El Kelbi's records (A.D. 786) of Arabian horse pedigrees which date back nearly five thousand years to the original wild horses of Yemen Hoshaba and Baz, a mare owned by Baz, son of Omain, of Lud, son of Shem, son of Noah, c. 3200 B.C. Zad er Rakib, a stallion reputed to have been given to the Beni Azd by King Solomon, c. 1000 B.C., was a foundation sire of different blood and from his line, combined with that of the Baz mare, descend a succession of celebrated horses to a mare called Sabal, dam of Awaj (Ajuz), the old Kehilan Ajuz strain of which this seems to be the first written record, and which belonged to the Beni Helal before their migration to Egypt. From Upton we find that there has been historical confusion between King Solomon (1000 B.C.) and Solomon (Suleiman 1635 B.C.) great-great-grandson of Ishmael, from whom sixth in descent was Rabia el Faras, who had an ancestral breed of horses.

All the eminent writers seem to have unaccountably overlooked the startling pictorial evidence of the ancient origin of the Arabian in the rock carvings of Arabia and of the horse idols worshipped by the ancient Arabs under the name of "Swift Horse" and above all in the wonderful temple inscriptions in Egypt 1800–2000 B.C., and with the contemporary detailed lists of countless horses and two thousand mares captured in the wars of Seti and Rameses against the tribes of Syria and Northern Arabia long before Libya had any horses, which only reached North Africa with the invasions of the Beni Helal.

The Egyptian wall inscriptions show that the type captured in Syria and North Arabia was pure Arabian with the typical very high carriage of tail, arched neck and small head. It was these horses that were the racehorses of the world and they are depicted in brilliant galloping action both ridden and driven in light chariots.

The immense booty of thousands of mares and records of stud masters indicates breeding on a large scale. No horse of this type or of any type is seen on earlier Egyptian monuments where they are completely absent, but a similar one is on the rocks of Arabia and somewhat

Scene from Battle of Kadesh at Abu Simbel, 2000 B.C.

Arabian rock inscription *c.* 2000 B.C.

modified on the Greek vases. The Assyrians are allied but a little heavier, and lacking the airy grace of the Egyptian horses. Long previous to the Christian era there was extensive racing in the regions of North Arabia.

Ashgar Merwan was a celebrated horse never beaten and was descended from a horse called Ziad, whose name is recorded on an Arabian rock inscription 500 B.C. Many generations previously an ancestor of his called Harun was purchased for 1,000 gold dinars at Basra by a trainer called Mouslim and was unbeaten at racing for *twenty years*. At one of the big race meetings Mouslim ran the first twenty winners. Other famous racehorses were Bitan and Buteyn. The daughters of Awaj (Ajuz) of Beni Helal are referred to in pre-Islamic verse as of noble descent, "Kehilan."

The ancient tradition of wild horses in Yemen is quite independent of Islam's romantic legends, and Charles Doughty mentions how the nomad children "fled away to play at wild horses" a game which must have dated from Baz, great-great-grandson of Noah, whose mare Baz was the first recorded wild horse captured.

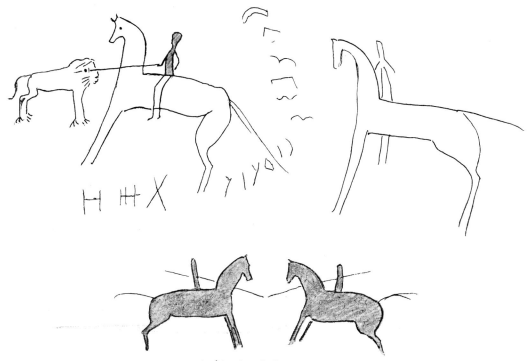

Arabian inscription 2000 B.C.

There are endless other proofs of antiquity, but these should be sufficient to convince us that the idea of the Arabian as a late derivation from the Barb is an absurdity.

Passing to the equally wrong idea that the Arab was a war horse only and never a race-horse, the evidence is just as strong as that concerning his antiquity. He was the first and for centuries the only racing breed. Racing was carried on by the Hittite tribes 1300 B.C., and there is a treatise of that date with detailed instructions for training. There are Arabian *race* horses on the Greek vases and an archaic Greek statuette. There are lists of four hundred and thirty famous pre-Islamic racehorses, some of which will be given at the end of this chapter. The great race of Dahes and el Ghabra was run over fourteen miles for a stake of a hundred camels, and owing to the machinations of rival race gangs, ended in the winners being assaulted and the stakes forcibly taken by the losers, supported by the judges, and the outraged tribe became the "Riders of Death," carrying on war for a

241

hundred years. The Prophet was an enthusiastic racehorse owner and carried on racing in Syria not with the legendary "five mares," but with more like fifty than five.

Arab racing was a craze in Egypt at least as early as A.D. 600, and went on till the Napoleonic conquest. It was at its height under Sultan el Naseri, who had a stud of seven thousand horses of the best Arabia could supply at fantastic prices, giving £30,000 for a single stallion, and spending as much as £80,000 a day on purchases; the top price of £67,200, which remains a world's record, given by one man for a horse of any breed was paid by him for the Karta racing filly.

It must be insisted on that, as Lady Anne Blunt explained, all later traditions founded on Islam must be treated in a totally different class to the primeval unwritten tribal traditions unknown to townsmen and scribes. As a Muteyr bedouin said to her, "these things are written in books but *we* took them with our hands," meaning that books were unreliable, but the firm traditions which were passed word for word from generation to generation and sung to the "rebab" over the camp fires are those which remain unaltered. This may seem strange to our ideas in which stories passed from one to another are proverbially incorrect as "Russian scandal," but in Arabia the poet-singer to the rebab (lute with one string and a bow) is a recognized authority who dare not for his life deviate by a word from the known facts. Should he err, he is for ever disgraced. No one reads or writes, therefore their memories are acute to a degree practically unknown in Europe. I have been more than amazed at the Egyptian native servant's capacity for detail. Unintelligent, obtuse and stolid he may appear, but give him any odd sum of money, make a long list for yourself, and send him out shopping for a myriad of small articles worth fractions of piastres. On his return he will recite his purchases sing-song, item by item, add them all up in his head and say "and here is your change." He has kept everything in his head correctly and forgotten nothing. You have not had to repeat your instructions, once is enough.

Just as "thoroughbred" now denotes the whole racing breed, so "Kehilan" (the Arabic word of which thoroughbred is the literal translation) denotes and has always denoted the whole Arabian breed, Kehilan Ajuz means the Old Arabian thoroughbred; strain names are mere adjuncts used for identification, and when we speak of Kehilan of some body or something or somewhere it is as if we said a Thoroughbred from Sledmere or Mentmore or the Aga Khan or of the St. Simon or Pocahontas strain. Very valuable and indeed essential as hall marks, but possessing no special characteristics other than the ones common to all pure Arabians.

Ajuz is not a strain at all; it merely means ancient. All sorts of travellers' tales have been invented concerning an old woman or a crooked stallion, but the former is a post-Islamic myth and the latter a misprint! The simple straightforward meaning is the pre-Islamic nomad use of the word "old." It is to Lady Anne Blunt, who combined the knowledge of a scholar with the advantage of having lived among the horse breeding tribes of Arabia, that we owe this information which is the key to understanding the confusion caused by the semi-religious romances which grew up with Islam and were distorted by the Algerian myths and superstitions embodied in Abd el Kader's book and Dumas' *Horses of the Sahara*, which are far removed in their fantasies from the simple Nomad traditions of Nejd. These were unadorned by romantic fable and therefore too dull for the flowery writers of Islamic days, who were townsmen and had an almost journalistic love of sensation and liked to lend a religious flavour to everything—as typified in the supposed El Khamsa, the five foundation mares of the Prophet, which are quoted as the five main strains and universally accepted as fact by Islamic writers and repeated by moderns, yet have in reality no historical foundation; they do not appear in the lists of the Prophet's horses, and no authority ever quotes the same five. Mohammed Abdu, the Grand Mufti of Egypt, rejected it as a pious fairy tale. There are, in fact, far more than five strains, and the substrains are legion and changing every day under new owners and the localities after which horses are known in Arabia. These sometimes become so numerous that the main strain is dropped and the Kehilan of something becomes the Kehilan of something else, and eventually the something else without the Kehilan, which being generic, is taken for granted. Dahman, for instance, is now known only as Dahman of somebody and not as Kehilan Dahman.

All Kehilans are fundamentally equally good, just as Thoroughbreds entered in Weatherby's are equally registered stock, but just as some strains of Thoroughbreds have achieved fame through their performances, and some studs have achieved prominence through the skill of their owners or by a lucky chance have become possessed of celebrated mares, so certain Arabian strains have become celebrated and have a hall mark of extra excellence, and this is the only value of a special strain. The theory advanced by some writers as to exclusive "strain breeding" has no foundation and to segregate any strain would indeed be utterly impossible. All pure strains can therefore be bred together with equal success so long as type is preserved. All have the same points at which to aim, any departure from which is a fault; and those who pretend that they can pick out a strain at sight are either charlatans or very ignorant. The idea of a coarse bony racing type is a fallacy. If a horse departs from the right type it is not a good Arab. Native dealers often hoodwink Europeans with stories of this sort to cover the defects of the animals they wish to sell by making them believe an "off-type" is characteristic of a strain and the Managhi strain has been the chief scapegoat. The impossibility of attaching any particular type to any strain is obvious if one considers that *name* of the strain goes with the dam who may, however, have very little of that blood.

For instance a mare called a Seglawieh may descend as follows:

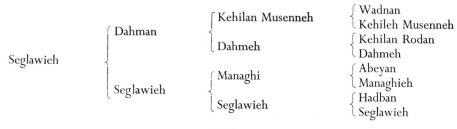

243

She may therefore have only three repeats of Seglawi blood to eleven of other strains—
or she may be an almost pure Seglawieh yet be called a Managhieh. Let those who claim
to know strains by sight consider how foolish this is. Take for instance a Managhieh mare:

```
                                            ⎧ Seglawi
                            ⎧ Seglawi      ⎨
                           ⎪               ⎩ Seglawieh
              ⎧ Seglawi   ⎨
             ⎪            ⎪                 ⎧ Seglawi
             ⎪             ⎩ Seglawieh     ⎨
             ⎪                              ⎩ Seglawieh
Managhieh   ⎨
             ⎪                              ⎧ Seglawi
             ⎪             ⎧ Seglawi       ⎨
             ⎪            ⎪                 ⎩ Seglawieh
              ⎩ Managhieh ⎨
                          ⎪                 ⎧ Seglawi
                           ⎩ Managhieh     ⎨
                                            ⎩ Managhieh
```

with eleven crosses of Seglawi to three of Managhi she is still technically a Managhieh.

Strains are dealt with fully in my book *Thoroughbred Racing Stock*. The terminal "h"
denotes the feminine, such as Seglawi .. Seglawieh; Hadban .. Hadbeh, the usual
feminine being the "h." But before a vowel it takes a "t." In Kehilan Ajuz you do not say
Kehileh Ajuz for a mare, but Kehilet Ajuz.

Racing in England was started by the Romans, whose best cavalry was the Thamudene
Arabian contingent. They built hippodromes in the north as the Egyptians did under the
Mameluke Sultans. As I have pointed out the first Arabian racehorses we know by name
were Arundel and Truncefice (see p. 57), which raced for £1,000 at the Court of
King Edgar, and it was the world-wide racing celebrity of the Arabian which caused our
ancestors four hundred years ago to import Arabians for racing, and Arabians were beating
all comers as early as 1588, making "the best of the English runners look like worn-out
jades."

The advent of the great Arabian sires marked the beginning of what has since become
the world's greatest miracle of speed and it is from the Arabian originally the sole and only
source of speed that he gets his name and origin, for Thoroughbred is a direct translation
from the Arabic Kehilan Ajuz (Kehilan for short) which is the generic name for the
whole Arabian breed—Kehilan meaning thoroughbred and Ajuz ancient, the distinguishing strain names being a later addition identifying owners and districts.

The Thoroughbred, specialized over three hundred years, has now completely outstripped his progenitor on the turf. Our two-year-olds move like rocket bombs, and so
do their prices, and no other breed can live with him on the course. The Arab has been
eclipsed as the fire is eclipsed by the sun—but without fire there would have been no
sun and the fire is still a force to be reckoned with. He is still the fastest unspecialized
natural breed, as far superior to all other breeds as the Thoroughbred is to him.

In stamina and at long distance racing beyond a hundred miles, the Arabian still retains
absolute supremacy over all breeds, including Thoroughbreds, and an Arab several
generations bred in England, and 15.2, holds the world's championship against all breeds
for record distance, record time, record weight, and record soundness. Under heavy
weights up to eighteen stone, the pure Arab still holds the world's record (even for

speed) over these abnormal distances. Arabs bred in England at Crabbet Park stud hold the following world's champion open records:

1. Three hundred and ten miles under a weight of 17 st. 7 lb. competing against all breeds, including Thoroughbreds, won by the horse called Crabbet in U.S.A., 1921. This includes the records for speed over a distance, weight carried, soundness and small amount of feed consumed and condition after the race, and is not likely to be beaten for many a long day. The horse had won other races of 100 miles and 84 miles and 154 miles in his spare time.

2. The record for 306 miles under 14½ st. held by Ramla, bay mare bred at Crabbet, run in U.S.A., 1919—followed by a mile race the next day. Competing against all breeds. Other Crabbet stock have won other long distance races, including the 250-mile English test, won by Belka, 1921. She carried 13½ st., but the race was confined to Arabs, and though a remarkable performance, is of nothing like the same importance as the American races. Shahzada, a horse with a cross of Azrek in his pedigree, won two 300-mile races in England and was second to Belka in 1921, and an Arab horse originating from the Blunt's stock in Egypt won the 1,800-mile race round Portugal.

Astraled, sire of Ramla, at the age of twenty-two, went from Oregon to New Hampshire in twenty-one days. This is shown on the map to be approximately about 2,500 miles, an almost unbelievable average of 119 miles daily, if the points of arrival and departure have been given me correctly.

The reason the Arabian exercises such a permanent influence on his descendants is that he is a separate species, differing in some fundamental particulars from all other horses. Apart from the obvious formation of the gazelle head he has a different count of ribs, lumbar and tail vertebrae, which by the way are never found in the prehistoric genus *Equus*. The common horse has six lumbar vertebrae (i.e. the ribless vertebrae) and nineteen pairs of ribs or sometimes eighteen, and eighteen tail vertebrae. The Arab has *five lumbar* vertebrae and in many cases *seventeen pairs of ribs* (sometimes eighteen and occasionally six lumbars) and sixteen tail vertebrae. The old type of very convex-headed Barb had nineteen ribs and six lumbars and the Thoroughbred has eighteen ribs and six lumbars, and occasionally varies towards the Arab count. Fickle, a mare by Solario out of the Derby and Oaks winner Fifinella, not only had an exaggeratedly pronounced concave Arab profile which she transmitted to her foals, but a post mortem showed that she had seventeen ribs and six lumbars. It is probable that many more Thoroughbreds have this count of ribs. I have just had a post mortem on Rissla, a very beautiful Arab mare three generations bred in England. Her count of ribs and lumbar vertebrae was again 17–5. This count is, as I have said, unique in horse breeds. Her dam Risala had seventeen ribs and six lumbar vertebrae.

The Arab also has the shaft of the ulna complete and the individual vertebrae are shorter than those of other horses and the bars of his mouth much longer and his cheek teeth shorter. The larger the teeth and the shorter the bars the more cold blood there is in a horse. The little Mongolian actually has teeth as big as a shire cart horse. Like everything else in the Arab breed the teeth are more finely chiselled and the edges of the bones sharper and the texture like ivory. This ivory bone is dense and smooth and very strong, the bone of a common horse is coarse and porous in texture and more apt to break. It must also be remarked that the underjaw of an Arabian is widely different to an ordinary horse skull. Not only is it much more widely spaced at the join of the throat than other jaws, but the circle of the jowl is much larger and more circular, its edges are sharp to

The Author

the touch and the space between the jaws much hollowed out, and the shaft from jowl to chin is perfectly straight and sharp edged, whereas the cold-blooded horse skull is thick and *convex* as may be seen in the Tarpan to an extraordinary degree. Seen from the underside the "V" of the two sides of the jaw is much wider than in ordinary horses. There should be room to put your fist between them under the throat. The eye sockets are very much lower in the skull and shaped as a blunted rounded oval with sharp edges. An underbred skull has an angular and smaller socket higher up and nearer the edge of the skull and it is often irregular and rough-edged. The Arab tail is set level with the back and naturally carried high. Its muscles are strong at the root and it should spring up directly the horse is in motion. There are cases when a horse has carried his rider's cloak aloft when it fell off galloping. He also uses it in a minor degree as a rudder in turning sharply. This argues great strength of back and muscles, and owing to the short spine the horse is able to carry more weight, being much closer ribbed up than most horses. The ribs, too, arch outwards, giving more lung power.

These racial peculiarities which persist in a marked degree in cross-breeding stamp the breed as a foundation not as a derivation. It is the dominating factor to which other breeds assimilate themselves and the species can be classified as *Equus Arabicus*.

I have not had much opportunity of verifying the rib count of the common Eastern horse, but from what I hear he seems to have eighteen ribs and five lumbar vertebrae. Anglo-Arabs vary between the two.

Judging.—When asked to give an opinion about an Arab, a man who knows horses well will often say "Oh, I know nothing about Arabs," just as if one had asked him his opinion of some strange insect! A man who knows good Thoroughbred breeding stock, or indeed a good light horse of any breed should have no difficulty in picking out a good Arab. He has only to judge it as good Thoroughbred breeding stock with the difference that the head must be small and profile not convex, the eyes large and set low in the head, and that the tail should be set high and carried high when in motion, and the neck and throat arched. There is no mysterious secret about an Arab as a horse. A good Arab is a good horse plus the distinctive head, neck and tail. Heavy bone is not necessary in blood-stock and is not allied with speed. Quality makes up for quantity, but the tendons must be straight.

Faults that are faults in all bloodstock are faults in an Arab just the same. The vertebrae of the Arab withers are usually shorter than in a Thoroughbred, so that the withers appear lower, but the angle of the shoulder must be just as sloping, and the action just as free, but breeders should aim at well developed withers.

The worst judges of Arabs are: (1) The men who have travelled in the East and think they know all about them, but whose eye is spoilt by inferior "Kadishes." (2) Hunting men who are accustomed to heavy big-boned types and cannot recognize the fact that "the battle is not always to the strong," as represented by thick legs and heavy heads. These men belong to the school of General Fairfax, who classed bloodstock as "over-valued pigmy baubles!" Those who wish for details can study the following rules. No one should expect heavy bone in a blood horse or an Arab. (3) The Military type of old dogmatic Indian Colonel who tells you that when he was at Poona he was in charge of the best ponies in the country.

POINTS OF THE ARAB HORSE

The head small and profile concave, tapering to a very small muzzle; eyes very large and brilliant and circular, and placed much lower in the skull than those of other horses; forehead extremely broad; nostrils very flexible and set on in line with the profile (not at the end of the nose) and capable of enormous expansion; jowl very deep and wide,

247

and the bars of the mouth much longer than in ordinary horses; ears small and very sharply cut, quick and pricked; neck arched and set in to the jaws in an arched curve, the windpipe being extra detached and loose; the withers are not so high as to be "ox-shouldered" but slope into a strong level back; they may be broader than those of other horses; the actual height of the withers has no bearing on the position of the shoulder-blade but only on the position for keeping back the saddle; chest broad and deep; body well ribbed up; quarter broad and level; tail set on a level with the back and carried high; legs with iron tendons, large strong hocks; big flat knees, springy pasterns and well developed thighs; feet hard and round, action free and fast, both trotting and walking.

A true Arab should be full of vitality and fire. A ewe-necked weedy lifeless stallion is not worth his keep and stallions which look like mares should be avoided. A sire should have a strong arched crest and a flashing eye and be of a bold though good tempered disposition. Mares are quieter, but should also be showy and striking to look at. The Arab is essentially a horse, not a pony. He is stunted in his own country by semi-starvation, hard work and privation and therefore seldom now exceeds 14.3 to 15 hands though the ancient records of Bahrein speak of horses reaching 16 hands. Transported to England he rapidly developed in height and scope without any loss of type or stamina owing to good feeding and favourable conditions and this natural increase is much to his benefit and will probably exceed 16 hands in time. All else being equal in type and quality the bigger the horse the better. If he is pure bred the type will remain. Lady Anne Blunt in her diary, 1878, said the tallest and most beautiful horse they had seen in the desert was a Samhan el Gomea, only three years old but already standing fully 15.1, with enough bone to satisfy even a Yorkshireman but showing no lack of quality.

The continued breeding of Arabs as a revitalizing force is not only a national duty but an international one as it is the only breed which could never be replaced, and in the present increasingly severe conditions of life in Arabia there is danger that he might disappear from the world as the Quagga and some Zebras have done. This would be disastrous for horse breeders everywhere, for the Arabian stallion alone possesses the prepotency, soundness and super-abundance of vitalizing quality which blends with other breeds successfully. Good as the Thoroughbred is he cannot do this. However, the best classic types are never available, being far too commercially valuable to be within reach of ordinary breeders. The world must therefore depend on Arabian blood for improvement and pure Arabian studs should be kept as reserves on which to draw for the future; we must never forget that the Arabian has an absolutely unique record for speed and beauty and as an improver for other breeds for the last five thousand years, and men of every nationality and profession have united in testifying to its value. The pure Arabian is still the same as he has always been and where he is well fed and specialized his size increases and his good points accentuate themselves. Feed him and groom him well and he will astonish you. Keep the blood pure and as foundation stock and as an improver he has no equal.

ANGLO-ARABS

Anglo-Arabs are next to the Thoroughbred for racing, and crosses from the same stock, though not of classic class, can and do win races even on the British Turf. The Crabbet bred half-Arab Chip alone won twenty-two races against Thoroughbreds often carrying top weight. Alfragan out of a half-Arab mare by Bend Or ex Basilisk (Crabbet Arab) won the Dee stakes and High Weight Handicap at Goodwood by six lengths.

Many years ago, in consequence of Mr. James Weatherby's great admiration for, and confidence in, the potentialities of the Arabian breed, he restored the original Oriental section by instituting a new section for Arabs in the General Stud Book with the following introduction (see Vol. XIV, General Stud Book):

"A recent importation from the believed best Desert strains will, it is hoped when the *increase of size* has been gained by *training, feeding and acclimatization*, give a valuable new line of blood from the original source of the English Thoroughbred."

This was an unprecedented tribute to the breed and it was on this support and encouragement that the Crabbet stud was founded starting an Arab revival, and it is on these principles that it has been carried on ever since—and I may add successfully carried on, for, as he rightly prophesied, there has been (when kept under favourable conditions) an all-round increase of size, excellence and beauty, regretfully admitted now unattainable in Arabia owing to ever degenerating adverse conditions yearly growing worse. The improvement here will probably be still further developed by selection as time goes on, and it has already stood the world's hardest endurance tests beating all breeds, showing that it has lost none of its stamina under English methods. It has not been bred for speed alone and I have repeatedly said that no pure Arab can live with modern sprinting speed, but the improved stock, even mated to inferior Thoroughbreds, has produced horses that could and did win a lot of races on the English Turf against the specialized speed of three hundred years, which is more than any other breed can do or ever has done.[1] One first cross alone won twenty-two races, even when heavily handicapped. I do not wish this to degenerate into a stud advertisement, but I must point out that, unspecialized as they are, they hold the world's open championship record against all breeds for long-distance racing, weight carried, soundness, and even speed over one hundred to three hundred miles, and that over a less severe course not one of seventeen Thoroughbreds finished or got much more than half way. Crabbet stock also holds sixteen world's records against other Arabs, demonstrating that improvement has been marked.

With regard to general merit, the Crabbet Stud has established itself as the world's leading Arabian breeding stud. In addition to winners of hundreds of races and four world's race records against all breeds, it has bred over 250 show ring champions, three world's champions and a number of grand champions, and innumerable champions have been bred from stock sold. The progeny of Champion Mesaoud alone includes 200 champions, and out of the 8,159 horses registered in the *American Arabian Stud Book*, 7,445 are pure

[1] Refer p. 244.

or partly pure Crabbet. Crabbet bred horses and mares hold eighteen world's racing records. Out of the 400 horses registered in the *Egyptian Stud Book* all the foundation mares and twenty-five of the foundation stallions are pure Blunt-Wentworth stock, and 385 out of the 444 registrations are also pure or partly pure. South Africa is following suit and the same proportion exists in Australia where all the champions for years have been Crabbet bred; and the Argentine imported a number of Crabbet stallions. The Stud has exported to fifty-five countries.

I believe that it is safe to say that no other Stud can show anything approaching this consistent record.

Fuller records of Anglo-Arabs will be found in *The Swift Runner*.[1]

Minor crosses of Thoroughbred sire and Arab dam have been the only cross which has ever held its own with modern Thoroughbred speed. Chip by the Thoroughbred Chippendale out of a Crabbet Arab mare won twenty-two races (twelve flat races and the rest steeplechases) competing against Thoroughbreds, often by large margins carrying top weight. French Leave won seven races, one by a distance; Chip also won a 2½-mile race by a distance and one of 2 miles by 40 lengths and lost five others by a head or neck only, yet the materials used were only moderate.

Two-thirds Thoroughbred and one-third Arab seems a particularly good mixture. Altogether Anglo-Arabs from Crabbet stock have won over fifty races on the modern British turf and been second or placed 136 times. Further back there are records of 200 races in England and Lounger was second for the Ascot Gold Cup and Dandizette and Translation were both second in the Oaks. Lilias won the Oaks. The Exquisite was second in the Derby and Defence third in the Oaks and Metropolitan and the Ranwick Plate, dead heating with the best Thoroughbred of the day. In France number-less races have been won by Anglo-Arabs. Tutican won twenty-six races (£4,435 in stakes) and Nana Sahib, a magnificent grey half-Arab, won over £2,000 in stakes.

They have also a special gift for jumping and have won highest honours in Olympic international high jumping competitions where their reputation grows daily as cup after cup is carried off.

They are first-rate hunters and hacks.

To sum up.

I think I have said enough to prove that there should be no future doubt on these points:

(1) The extreme antiquity of the Arabian breed as a pure root stock.
(2) The absolute prepotency of inherited type.
(3) That the Arabian was the sole *original* source of speed and beauty.
(4) The importance of developing the pure stock to its utmost capacity for future generations when it will be extinct in its own country, lest it be numbered like the quagga and some zebras among the things of beauty that are gone for ever.

[1] George Allen & Unwin Ltd.

Supreme Champion Grand Royal

Champion Serafix, Sire Raktha, Dam Serafina

251

Indian Magic